The International Library of Sociology

ENGLISH PRIMARY EDUCATION

ARBOR SCIENTIA

ARBOR VITA

Founded by KARL MANNHEIM

The International Library of Sociology

THE SOCIOLOGY OF EDUCATION
In 28 Volumes

ENGLISH PRIMARY EDUCATION

A Sociological Description

Part I
Schools

by

W. A. L. BLYTH

Routledge
Taylor & Francis Group

LONDON AND NEW YORK

First published in 1965 by
Routledge

Reprinted 1998, 2000, 2002
by Routledge
2 Park Square, Milton Park, Abingdon, Oxon, OX14 4RN
Simultaneously published in the USA and Canada by Routledge
711 Third Avenue, New York, NY 10017
Transferred to Digital Printing 2007

Routledge is an imprint of the Taylor & Francis Group

First issued in paperback 2013

The publishers have made every effort to contact authors/copyright holders
of the works reprinted in *The International Library of Sociology.*
This has not been possible in every case, however, and we would
welcome correspondence from those individuals/companies
we have been unable to trace.

British Library Cataloguing in Publication Data
A CIP catalogue record for this book
is available from the British Library

English Primary Education - Part I: Schools

ISBN 978-0-415-17762-7 (hbk)
ISBN 978-0-415-86402-2 (pbk)

Publisher's Note
The publisher has gone to great lengths to ensure the quality of this
reprint but points out that some imperfections in the original
may be apparent

To teachers in primary schools

Contents

Contents of Vol. I

Contents of Vol. II

Contents of Vol. II

Tables

xi

Preface

I N 1963 the Central Advisory Council for Education (England), under the chairmanship of Lady Plowden, was required 'to consider primary education in all its aspects and the transition to secondary education'. Thus, for the first time since the publication of the two reports of the Consultative Committee of the Board of Education on *The Primary School* (1931) and *Infant and Nursery Schools* (1933), primary education has been singled out for specific official scrutiny. This should stimulate the English educational world in general to 'consider' primary education more closely and to examine its various 'aspects' more carefully.

One of these aspects may be legitimately termed the sociology of primary education. Since 1945, British sociologists have paid increasing attention to education, so that the sociology of education is now an established and expanding field of study and research. Its impact has already been felt on our general habits of thinking about education, and more specifically on the Central Advisory Council's recent reports *15 to 18* (Crowther Report, 1959) and *Half our Future* (Newsom Report, 1963). Yet it is noticeable that most of the research, and most of the general writing, in the sociology of English education has been confined to secondary and further education, almost as though sociologists thought that life began at eleven-plus. Even Ottaway's pioneering textbook (1953) displayed this emphasis. Ironically perhaps, it was through examination of the problems of secondary education, and particularly those of selection for secondary education, that the attention of sociologists has been increasingly drawn towards primary education too.

Meanwhile, there has been a growing tendency for writers about primary education itself to pay attention to sociological factors, both those associated with the organisation of primary schools as communities, and those more directly related to the home and community background of primary-school pupils. This sociological awareness is particularly evident in books such as those by Atkinson (1949), Mellor (1950) and Ross (1960), and is also apparent in the official handbook on *Primary Education* (1959). Yet there is still no single, systematic, comprehensive work which combines a general sociological description of English primary education with a survey of the results of sociological investigations in this field. The present volumes have been written in the belief that there is a need for a study of this kind, and that it is required now, as an introduction to the sociological 'aspect' of primary education, while the Plowden spotlight is focused on primary schools.

The result is something of a compromise. This is perhaps inevitable, if it is to be of service to the various types of reader who may be interested in the subject: students preparing to teach in primary schools; experienced teachers who appreciate the importance of sociological considerations; teachers and others who themselves wish to pursue some further study or research; and the general public who as parents and citizens recognise the importance of primary education as a social process in English society. But because it is a compromise it concentrates neither on research, nor on a purely theoretical interpretation, nor on practical prescription and advice. Therefore it cannot be appropriately entitled an investigation, nor an analysis, nor a do-it-yourself manual for teachers, though it embodies elements of all three. It is simply a sociological *description* of English primary education; an account of the whole social process and its institutional framework, including much of the data familiar to the historian or the psychologist or the expert in teaching-method, but seen from the standpoint of a sociologist and presented, I hope, in such a way that its various readers may find in it something of value to them.

It is slightly subjective in presentation. This I admit freely and without apology, for I believe that in writing of this kind, objectivity is very difficult, perhaps impossible, to attain. It may even be in a sense undesirable, for it could convey the impression that a writer has no great feeling for his material and little sense of commitment to his society. For the same reason, where a personal experience or a personal opinion is involved, I have made no attempt to camouflage the first person. On the other hand, I have tried to make my judgments and formulate my opinions with due regard for the evidence, especially evidence derived from research, and I have endeavoured to prevent personal interpretation from degenerating into bias.

It has been found preferable to present the material in two volumes, each of which is self-contained, though carrying references to the other. In Volume I, the emphasis is laid on primary schools themselves as social institutions. In Volume II, attention is focused on some historical, demographic and social aspects of the background of English primary education. Where necessary, in each volume, research results are considered, but space does not permit a discussion of techniques of investigation. That would require yet another volume.

The subject-matter is confined to England, not through any narrow patriotism but through recognition that this in itself constitutes a very extensive subject, one which is of immediate interest to a wide circle of readers, while the circumstances in Wales, and more so elsewhere in the British Isles, are such as to demand separate consideration. However it has frequently been necessary to quote official statistics for England and Wales, because that is the only form in which they are available. This must be taken into account when absolute numbers are considered, but it makes little material difference to relative proportions especially since over 94 per cent of the joint population live in England.

For the sake of simplicity, all footnotes are placed at the ends of volumes and, within each volume, all references are made by name and date to the comprehensive bibliography at the end.

In the final preparation of the manuscript, I have been greatly assisted by colleagues and friends who read it in draft form and have made trenchant but helpful suggestions. For help of this kind, I should like to thank Mr. K. A. Lloyd, Headmaster of Old Hall Drive County Primary School, Gorton, Manchester; Miss E. Wyneken, formerly Principal Lecturer in Education, Mather College of Education, Manchester; Mr. M. J. Storm, Principal Lecturer in Geography, Bulmershe College of Education, near Reading; and three of my former colleagues in the Department of Education at Manchester University: Mr. A. Cashdan, Dr. H. Entwistle, and especially Dr. J. B. Coltham, whose great knowledge and experience of primary education, combined with her remarkably painstaking scrutiny, saved me from a wealth of mistakes and misjudgments. I hope that the book's remaining deficiencies will not distract its readers from its main purpose, that of stimulating all those who are concerned about English primary education to think sociologically, to see its function in relation to the past and present of English society, and perhaps to play some part in extending our knowledge in this fascinating, important, and still largely unknown field. In that way they will perhaps facilitate the writing of a more adequate book, when this has served its turn.

W. A. L. BLYTH

Manchester, 1964

Preface to 1967 Reprint

THE text of this book was originally published in 1965. Since then the publication of the Plowden Report, early in 1967, has somewhat altered our perspectives. Consequently the present re-issue has been amended by a complete revision of the Conclusion to Volume I, which now takes the form of a comment on the Report itself and in particular on its sociological aspects and significance. The opportunity has also been taken to correct a few errors and to include some recent additions to the relevant bibliography, including specific references to material from the Report. However, this reprint is not a re-edition. The statistical and other information presented in the rest of the book remains unaltered, for the substitution of more recent data for the existing material would have entailed nothing less than a complete revision of large sections of the work. So *Statistics of Education in 1962, Part I* remains the source of much that follows, while the numerical data kindly supplied by various organisations also date from the same year or thereabouts. Even the archaism 'Ministry of Education' still appears; not because I regret its demise, though as it happens, I do, but in order to minimise the re-setting of type.

It has not escaped my notice that children born when my statistical data were current are themselves about to enter primary education. However, eager readers may find it stimulating to discover recent figures for themselves, including those reproduced in the Plowden Report, and to judge for themselves whether they afford grounds for modifying the conclusions which I drew from the earlier figures. I hope, too, that they will realise that some of the researches, mentioned in the text as 'current', have now been triumphantly completed.

W. A. L. BLYTH

School of Education, University of Liverpool, 1967

Introduction

THE term 'primary' applied to education implies the first and basic stage of the educative process. This could take place at any time of life, from the cradle, where it almost literally begins for the genius, to old age, at which it is sometimes and heroically undertaken by members of hitherto illiterate communities. It might also be regarded, as Ross (1960, Ch. I) neatly suggests, as the most important stage, the stage of 'primary' importance. But in industrial societies the term 'primary education' has also come to be associated with a particular age range. It is generally found in all societies that the years between five or six and eleven or twelve are those in which children are psychologically and socially ready to leave the immediate family circle and to begin the processes of intellectual and social learning among their peers. This period of life is thus divided on its early side from the years of true infancy, before the age of five or six, and also from the later phase in which formal education and societal tutelage overlap psychological and physical adolescence. These middle years between infancy and adolescence, or in the current jargon, between the toddler and the teenager, have in fact become so closely identified with the incidence of primary education that they are sometimes described as the 'primary years'. The legal definition of pupils at this stage in the Education Act, 1944 (Sec. 8.1) and the Education (Miscellaneous Provisions) Act, 1948 (Sec. 3), embodies this assumption, but for a sociological appraisal of English primary education it appears preferable first to consider the cultural features of the middle years of childhood and then to look subsequently at their educational needs and institutions. For this purpose I propose to describe the period of life between five and twelve by a characteristically English term: the 'Midlands' of childhood.

A consideration of children in different present and past cultures makes it possible to sort out the characteristics of Midlands children which are relatively independent of place and time. It is possible here to give only a very brief outline of these, but fortunately there is no lack of accessible literature which can be used to elaborate it.[1]

First, these children are recognisable by the stage of their skeletal, muscular and glandular development and by the degree and nature

1

of their sensory discrimination. If there is a sense in which 'children are children the world over' it is this. It is as easy to pick out the Midlands children in a group of Patagonians as in a group of Paddingtonians. The proportion of head to trunk, the slender rounded contours and the lack of secondary sex characteristics are generally familiar. There is, too, the same gradual refinement of muscular balance and hand-eye co-ordination. A comparison of different patterns of growth curve (Tanner, 1961, p. 23) shows that except in the case of lymphoid development associated with the thymus gland, there is a period of relative quiescence between five and twelve, and especially between eight and twelve, a general absence of sharp contours which makes the term 'Midlands' all the more appropriate. There are, of course, individual differences in rates of growth and a slow but steady development throughout the period, so that beside a well-developed eleven-year-old a child of five looks and feels a baby. At about seven or eight, too, there is often a minor but significant spurt of development which may be regarded as a low escarpment dividing the earlier Midlands from what Rudolf Steiner (Harwood, 1958, Ch. 8) calls 'the heart of childhood'. Nevertheless, when compared with the periods before and after, the Midlands years display a marked degree of homogeneity.

It was even at one time suggested that their termination in the grace and balance of the ten- and eleven-year-olds represented a survival of proto-adulthood from some golden age before adolescence was invented. Far-fetched though this may be, it is certainly true that this pre-adolescent piedmont, followed sooner or later by a rapid increase in stature and psychological development, is a widely known phenomenon in all societies. Not only is this so, but in most societies the movement of individuals through the Midlands is itself watched with interest. The occasional landmarks such as second dentition, a birthday, a minor growth spurt, or the attainment of particular feats of skill, are regarded by parents and children alike as noteworthy. Even resistance to disease tends to be greater during the later part of this phase rather than before or after, though accident-proneness is fairly high. In general, then, there is little to upset the even tenor of physical development, but since children in this period of life become relatively self-sufficient in their everyday physical needs, the Midlands acquire a comparative timelessness which is absent from most other phases of the life-cycle.

Cognitive development also displays relatively universal characteristics. It is only in very recent times that reliable data have been made available about the growth of the brain, and there is still much controversy about its interpretation; but it seems fairly clear that there is a process of progressive elaboration of the cortical structure which is open to considerable variation according to the nature and

2

extent of environmental stimulus (Hebb, 1949). By the time a child reaches the Midlands years it is probable that the decisive influences on cerebral development have already been felt, and thereafter the children appear to travel along similar paths though at different rates. Although it is not yet possible at the Midlands stage to measure the activity of the brain itself, it is certainly practicable to trace its effect in intelligent behaviour, and this has been systematically done over the years by investigators such as Gesell and his collaborators in the U.S.A. and by Piaget and his team at the Institut Jean-Jacques Rousseau in Geneva. The degree of correspondence between their findings itself indicates something of their inter-cultural validity.

According to Piaget, most children pass during these years (Peel, 1960, Ch. 3) through two main phases of development, that of *intuitive thought* which shows the first decisive stage towards the effective use of concepts and that of *concrete operations*, in which some thinking becomes 'reversible' and the child is able to bring into play a considerable part, but not all, of the logical apparatus used by mature adults. The principal element still lacking even at the end of the Midlands is that of abstract thought and the use of hypothetical propositions and more complex *schemata* and strategies of reasoning. In general, the transition from mainly intuitive to mainly concrete-operational processes takes place at about seven or eight, though it must be emphasised that these stages are found in average children performing average mental tasks. All children are quicker to complete the sequence in some types of tasks, slower in others. Some children are also quicker in all tasks and some slower.

It is important to remember that these phases of cognitive development also condition the formation of concepts related to emotional, social and moral development as well as to formal education. Given the general pattern of social pressures within a society, the facility with which children's socialisation takes place must depend in part on the growth of their cognitive capacity for communication within society and for the internalisation of its values.

Social and emotional development are in themselves much more difficult to establish as processes common to the Midlands of childhood in all societies. Indeed, it is difficult to postulate any common features other than those associated with physical and cognitive development. The gradual growth of skills is bound to be related, in any society, to the maintenance of prestige, but a fat boy is likely to have a different level of social acceptance according to whether he lives in a society in which everybody must swim, or in one where everybody must run. Similarly the attainment of verbal skills will be differently evaluated among herders than among traders. The emotional equipment of the developing Midlander, once confidently assigned to a constellation of identifiable instincts, is now scarcely more definable than as a state of aliveness whose actual direction and drive is socially determined: and nobody denies that the Midlands are an age in which children are very much alive.

These, briefly and inadequately defined, are the only general characteristics of middle childhood. Even these, it must be emphasised, are only relatively stable. Not only are there many individual differences, but the whole process of maturation is undergoing steady acceleration in accordance with what Tanner (1961, Ch. 7) calls the *secular* trend. This expresses the world-wide tendency for the height and weight of children at any one age-level to increase, and for the incidence of puberty, that recognisable boundary-stone of the Midlands, to be advanced by some four months per decade over the past century. If the Midlands are to be defined in developmental rather than in chronological terms, their upward limit is thus liable to a regular downward adjustment, and in view of the height/ weight acceleration, a corresponding adjustment at the lower end is also arguable. Although according to Tanner (ibid., pp. 115–16) there is no one clear explanation for this secular trend, it must be regarded as a qualification of any claims for stability even in physical or cognitive development, even in this relatively stable age. It follows that children in primary schools, especially girls, are now sometimes already leaving the Midlands and beginning to encounter the bewilderments and problems associated with the differential onset of puberty (Douglas, 1964, p. 76).

Many other features of the middle years of childhood were formerly claimed with some confidence as general characteristics. They included the ways in which children develop a web of social roles inside and then outside the family, the patterns of interest which they evince at different ages, and the nature of their aesthetic development. The Report of the Consultative Committee of the Board of Education on *The Primary School* (1931)[2] is itself an example of this type of writing. It is quite true that, within a particular culture and within a particular period of time, generally accurate descriptions of attitudes, interests, and social development can be made. For example, children aged five to seven in England have a recognised pattern of phantasy life related to stories and art. Seven to eleven are years for more objective interests such as collecting and construction, while children at this age are also enthralled by animal life, though in different ways in the two sexes. Again, children below the age of seven show unstable social relationships; then the so-called 'gang' stage supervenes. Girls are more restrained and co-operative; boys more adventurous and competitive (Watson, 1952) and so forth. But this is not the same as claiming that these are innate or universal characteristics. Their innate components are unlikely to be different from those which have already been mentioned. While it would be unjustifiably dogmatic or wishful to claim that the innate equipment of all children was either limitless or equal to that of all other children, it is probably true that its plasticity and malleability is very high, much higher than was formerly believed either by psychologists or administrators. If this is true, it increases the importance of the role played by education and renders more essential a sociological approach to the study of education.

Such, then, are the children who experience primary education in England. Before that education can be considered sociologically, however, it is also necessary to comment briefly on its legal basis.

B. THE LEGAL BASIS OF
ENGLISH PRIMARY EDUCATION

This in turn is grounded in history. As will be more fully indicated in Volume II, Chapter II, the contemporary pattern of English primary education stems from three traditions: *elementary, preparatory,* and *developmental.* The first of these is associated with the limited, utilitarian atmosphere of the Board School; the second, with the upward-looking, socially exclusive orientation of the private or preparatory school; and the third, with the emergence of what is usually described as a child-centred conception of education. From the confluence of these three traditions there has emerged a series of adjustments and compromises. The present legal basis of English primary education represents the formal expression of the most recent phase of adjustment.

In common with most aspects of contemporary education in England, primary education derives its legal justification from the Education Act, 1944 (7 & 8 Geo. 6, Ch. 31). In that Act there was legally recognised, for the first time, a distinct category of education termed Primary. Section 7 of the Act states firmly:

> The statutory system of public education shall be organised in three progressive stages to be known as primary education, secondary education, and further education; and it shall be the duty of the local education authority for every area, so far as their powers extend, to contribute towards the spiritual, moral, mental and physical development of the community by securing that efficient education throughout those stages shall be available to meet the needs of the population of their area.

Section 8 continues thus:

> (1) It shall be the duty of every local education authority to secure that there shall be available for their area sufficient schools—
> (a) for providing primary education, that is to say, full-time education suitable to the requirements of junior pupils; . . .

The term 'junior pupil' was defined in Section 114 as 'a child who has not attained the age of twelve years'. The position was slightly

5

amended by the Education (Miscellaneous Provisions) Act, 1948, Section 3 of which re-defined primary education as:

> full-time education suitable to the requirements of junior pupils who have not attained the age of ten years and six months, and full-time education suitable to the requirements of junior pupils who have attained that age and whom it is expedient to educate together with junior pupils who have not attained that age.

This somewhat clumsily-worded change was effected in order that the remaining pupils between ten-and-a-half and twelve years of age, that is those '. . . who have attained the age of ten years and six months and whom it is expedient to educate together with senior pupils', could be legally educated in secondary schools. The meaning of 'expedient' in this context was not defined.

From the standpoint of the three traditions of primary education already mentioned, this constitutes a curious overlap between the preparatory and developmental traditions. Such premature transfer to secondary education could be regarded as 'expedient' either because the children were successful academic performers who might romp into a Sixth Form early enough to benefit from a prolonged stay there, or because they were biologically and psychologically pubescent. Both characteristics may well occur in the same individuals (Tanner, 1961, p. 44) but in practice Sec. 3 of the 1948 Act has probably been invoked more frequently and ostensibly on account of cerebral than of glandular precocity. How often it has been deemed 'expedient' to move pupils into secondary schools because of the 'bulge', or for some other reason of sheer administrative necessity, is of course a different issue.

All these requirements apply to full-time compulsory attendance. But in addition, Section 8, sub-section (2) of the 1944 Act lays down that:

> In fulfilling their duties . . . , a local education authority shall, in particular, have regard . . .

> (b) to the need for securing that provision is made for pupils who have not attained the age of five years by the provision of nursery schools or, where the authority consider the provision of such schools to be inexpedient, by the provision of nursery classes in other schools.

By Regulation, the age of entry may not be lower than two in the case of nursery schools, or three in the case of nursery classes. (Schools Regulations, 1959, S.I. 1959, No. 364, Sec. 7(2)) This, however, is not one of the sections of the 1944 Act which has been given priority, and indeed a series of Circulars, notably Circular 8/60, have forbidden local education authorities from expanding their provision of facilities for children below the age of compulsory full-time attendance. This question will be more fully discussed in Chapter II.

For the most part, the remaining legal provisions governing primary education are similar to those which lay down the pattern for secondary education, though Sec. 8, sub-sec. (2)(a) makes it clear that primary and secondary education should be conducted in separate schools. Prominent among these remaining provisions is the establishment of differences between county schools and the three types of voluntary schools (Secs. 9; 15) through which the issues at stake in the Dual System since 1870 were amended and re-defined in 1944. The religious aspect of primary-school provision will be considered specifically in Volume II, Chapter V, but at this stage it is relevant to observe that the actual distribution of voluntary schools is not uniform over the country, so that some children live too far from a particular type of school to be able to attend. For these, there is a proviso (Sec. 25, sub-sec. (4)) whereby they may be withdrawn from religious instruction of a type to which their parents object. In the case of a voluntary school (Sec. 28, sub-sec. (1)) the parents can require the school to provide the same agreed-syllabus instruction as would be given in a county school, but there is no means whereby a more dogmatic pattern of religious instruction can be demanded in a county primary school on the grounds that the nearest suitable voluntary school is too far away. Oddly enough (Sec. 26) this facility *is* guaranteed by law in the case of a county secondary school. Perhaps this was originally decided because the number and range of voluntary primary schools was greater than that of voluntary secondary schools; but it remains a quaint anomaly.

While it is the local education authority's duty to guarantee the adequacy of school provision, it is the parents' obligation (Sec. 36) towards a child to

> ... cause him to receive efficient full-time education suitable to his age, ability, and aptitude, either by regular attendance at school or otherwise

and Section 39 spells out the legal penalties for a parent who defaults on this obligation. Court proceedings (Baker, 1964) have indicated how difficult it is for any parent to prove that education given 'otherwise' than at school can be deemed to satisfy Section 36, so in practice this means that primary education is virtually confined to schools.

The motive behind this piece of social control is twofold, deriving in both respects from the developmental tradition. On the one hand there is a deep suspicion that what the Americans would call 'non-school education' is either of doubtful efficiency, or else would give its recipient an unfair advantage. But alongside this there is a belief held with equal conviction that education is essentially a social process and that it must be conducted in a communal institution and not just at home. None the less, the law does provide officially for the rare exception: the child with an unusual disease, for example, or whose domestic circumstances make normal school attendance virtually impossible.

For purposes of school attendance, all county and voluntary schools are deemed efficient. The legal position with regard to particular schools is left largely to the discretion of local education authorities, though the Minister of Education (Sec. 37, sub-sec. (3)) has some powers in this respect too. Some authorities allow parents a considerable range of choice in addition to the statutory option between county and voluntary schools, while others endorse a quite rigid zoning so that, within the voluntary and especially the county category, school attendance implies in some areas attendance at a particular school. This, which may appear quite an innocuous administrative device, has in fact considerable social implications which will be further examined in Volume II, Chapter IV.

Parents' obligations under Section 36 may also be discharged by placing children at a registered independent school as defined in Section 114 of the 1944 Act:

> 'Independent school' means any school at which full-time education is provided for five or more pupils of compulsory school age (whether or not such education is also provided for pupils under or over that age), not being a school maintained by a local education authority or a school in respect of which grants are made by the Minister to the proprietor of the school.

In practice this also includes those departments of direct-grant secondary schools which cater for children who are 'junior pupils', for no 'grants are made by the Minister' to primary schools, or in respect of junior pupils attending secondary schools.[3] At present, attendance at any registered school is accepted for this purpose, although under Section 71, as will shortly be pointed out, there are statutory powers which could be used to restrict attendance to schools recognised as efficient.

The actual conduct of a maintained school is also given a legal basis by the 1944 Act. Not only are its establishment, premises and conduct provided for (Secs. 8, 10, 23–30) but there is a requirement, embodied especially in Secs. 17–18, that each county or voluntary primary school should have an instrument of management setting up 'rules of management', and a body of managers; with special provisions in the case of voluntary schools and also for schools in the areas of minor Local Government authorities—non-county boroughs, urban districts etc. Dent (1955, pp. 29–30) points out that the restricted status of managers, when contrasted with that of secondary-school governors under the same Act, reflects the greater tradition of independence accorded to secondary schools in England, which is perhaps another way of saying that in primary education, especially in its administrative aspects, the elementary tradition dies hard. However, in practice the significance of managers in primary schools is not very great. Except where questions of status or denominational needs are involved, they tend to be quiescent. Some, to be sure, are genuinely and specifically interested in the schools which they 'manage'; others are scarcely known in the schools, and even view their appointment in terms of its political rather than its educational significance (see Vol. II, Ch. V). Most fall between these extremes, but find it very difficult to set aside time to fulfil their obligations as they ideally should. Some observers might remark that the work of existing managers constitutes a poor argument for improving their status, while others might retort that the insignificance of their status is itself a primary cause of their lack of constructive interest.

It is, however, not on the overt but sometimes effete control by Boards of Managers, but on the administrative apparatus established by local education authorities and on the intangible but effective sanctions of custom and usage that the detailed legal and administrative control of primary schools depends. The essential link between individual schools and 'the Office' is in practice maintained by local advisers and inspectors, just as the relation with the Ministry of Education is sustained through Her Majesty's Inspectors. Though there is frequent minor frustration and occasionally a deeper conflict between schools and their administrative partners, there is also a great deal of understanding which not only ensures that day-to-day problems are dealt with, but also confers on the schools an assured status within the functional apparatus of society and avoids the disharmony which can result when an institution feels itself to be nobody's business. At the same time, the widespread acceptance of primary education throughout the national community, and the generally benevolent attitude shown towards its independence, ensures that it operates in a comparatively favourable atmosphere, provided that a minimum of instructional efficiency is guaranteed. Some primary schools, in additional to their formal relations with local government, form an intimate part of neighbourhood and parochial organisation, as will be further discussed in Volume II, Chapters IV and V; but of course this lies outside their legal obligations.

Staffing and finance of primary education are also governed by statute. Section 24 of the 1944 Act determines the appointment and dismissal of Staff, except for appointments for religious education which are covered by Sections 27–8. All appointments are made through the usual machinery of advertisement, application and interview, though in primary schools they are sometimes made to the establishment of the local education authority rather than to a particular school. (Instances have been known when the location of a candidate's appointment was not divulged until the last minute, as though premature disclosure might have endangered national security.) The factors that are, or are widely assumed to be, relevant in the making of appointments and promotions is a whole subject unto itself, and will be discussed in Chapter VII. As for dismissal, this is in practice a rarity except for immorality, when even a suspicion of improper behaviour towards young girls or boys is enough to set the local press ablaze, after which a clear proof of innocence is often insufficient to enable a teacher to remain in practice at his post. (In such cases, obviously, it is almost always a man who is involved.) Gross inefficiency, on the other hand, is almost too readily condoned. I sometimes suspect that, in their fight to ensure stable employment, the teachers' unions have erected such safeguards against dismissal for incompetence that it is quite possible for the relatively easy-going, ineffective, or inefficient teacher to be carried along for years by a team of long-suffering colleagues without actually doing anything blatant enough to attract the attention of officialdom.

The financial provisions for primary education are part of the complicated structure of educational finance in general. Sec. 100 of the 1944 Education Act provides the basis for the financial partnership between central and local government in education, but the detailed implementation of this partnership has been defined and modified in several ways, particularly in 1959 when, by the Local Government Act, 1958, financial assistance, which had previously been allocated as a variable grant earmarked for education, was merged in the general Exchequer grant or 'block grant' as it has come to be known. In addition, Section 100 by its opening words:

The Minister shall by regulations make provision . . .

leaves the approval of the distribution of educational expenditure largely in the hands of particular Ministers. In practice, their Regulations have often appeared weighted against primary schools in respect of salaries, class size, capitation allowances, and permitted minor improvements, so that sometimes the impression has gained ground that primary education receives its due only when sheer pressure of numbers renders it essential—and not always then. There may be a conclusive reason for the ostensible priority given to secondary education when it is necessary in order to complete the reorganisation recommended by the Hadow Report in 1926, or when it involves the provision of essential facilities for scientific or practical studies, but it is not surprising that primary-school teachers tend, as will be discussed in Chapter VII, to think that their schools are the Cinderella of the national system.

There are other schools too which cater for children of Midlands age, and these will be discussed in Chapter V. They include special schools, independent schools, and a very small number of approved schools. The provision of special schools is a statutory obligation laid upon local education authorities by the 1944 Act. Section 8, sub-section (2)(c) requires them to have regard:

> to the need for securing that provision is made for pupils who suffer from any disability of mind or body by providing, either in special schools or otherwise, special educational treatment, that is to say, education by special methods appropriate for persons suffering from that disability . . .

and Section 9, sub-section (5) adds that:

> Schools which are especially organised for the purpose of providing special educational treatment and are approved by the Minister for that purpose shall be known as special schools.

Sec. 33 empowers the Minister to define categories of pupils requiring special educational treatment, and Sec. 34 specifies the duties of the local education authorities in respect of the ascertainment of handicaps.

Independent schools are in a different position. Their definition in the 1944 Act has already been cited (p. 8 above). Their registration is required by Part III of the same Act, which did not come into force until 1957 (Dent, 1961, p. 152). Section 71, sub-section (1) governs the conditions which must be observed if a school is to remain on the register:

> If at any time the Minister is satisfied that any registered or provisionally registered school is objectionable upon all or any of the following grounds—
>
> (a) that the school premises or any parts thereof are unsuitable for a school;
>
> (b) that the accommodation provided at the school premises is inadequate or unsuitable having regard to the number, ages and sex of the pupils attending the school;
>
> (c) that efficient and suitable instruction is not being provided at the school having regard to the ages and sex of the pupils attending thereat;
>
> (d) that the proprietor of the school or any teacher employed therein is not a proper person to be the proprietor of an independent school or to be a teacher in any school, as the case may be;
>
> the Minister shall serve upon the proprietor of the school a notice of complaint . . .

Grounds (a), (b) and (d) are enforced, and disputes arising from their enforcement are referred to the Independent Schools Tribunal (Education Act, 1944, Sec. 72). But condition (c) raises a difficulty, for it implies official inspection, and for one reason or another it has not yet proved possible to recognise all independent schools. At present therefore there are two categories of independent schools, those 'recognised as efficient' and those simply classified as 'other independent schools', the latter catering on the whole for younger children and being smaller in size than the 'recognised' schools, a point on which more detail will be given in Chapter V. How long this 'other' category will survive depends on a number of factors, including the speed with which inspection can be carried out, but recognition is becoming more and more valued, and the Incorporated Association of Preparatory Schools, the nearest equivalent in primary education of the Headmasters' Conference, makes recognition obligatory upon its members. (Dent, loc. cit., p. 160).

The few approved schools which accommodate children under the age of twelve do not owe their status to the Education Acts at all but to the Children and Young Persons Act, 1933, Section 79, and come under the jurisdiction not of the Ministry of Education but of the Home Office, though in practice the two departments maintain a fairly close liaison. Their age-structure, which will be discussed in Chapter V, allows of some flexibility. As regards administration:

> Every Approved School has its own board of Managers and it is their job, subject to the approval of the Home Office, to decide the lines on which their school shall run. (Gittins, 1952, p. 34.)

It is worth mentioning also that a very few nursery schools and special schools catering in part for children in the Midlands years are in receipt of direct grant from the Ministry of Education, under Section 100 (1)(b) of the Education Act, 1944, and under the Direct-Grant Schools Regulations, 1959 (S.I. 1959, No. 1832) which that section empowers the Minister to make. These schools are usually long-established institutions and the conditions of grant are somewhat similar to those for direct-grant grammar schools, except of course that there are no academic criteria which schools or children have to satisfy.

Outside the provision of schools there falls the whole range of ancillary services which were extended and placed on a more regular footing by the Education Act, 1944, and subsequent Regulations. Sections 48–57 govern medical inspection and treatment, milk, meals, board and lodging where necessary, clothing, transport and minimal cleanliness, all of which are provided free or at a limited charge. In all these respects it is the school itself which figures as the centre for welfare provisions, a point which will be discussed in Chapter I and subsequently in relation to the schools' social roles. Some of these welfare provisions, namely medical inspection and treatment, milk, meals and even clothing may under certain conditions also be extended to independent schools (Sec. 78).

Such are the principal legislative provisions on which contemporary English primary education rests. In themselves, they exemplify a series of compromises between different religious, social and political pressure groups and demands, which constitute the most recent phases of the social influences outlined in Volume II, Chapters II and V. But collectively they embody certain assumptions which are sociologically important. First, they do guarantee at least a nominal adherence to the principle that primary education should be something separate, at least within the great majority of maintained schools. (The same requirement is not laid upon independent schools, though many of them follow suit.) Then again, the community at large takes responsibility for the wellbeing of these schools not only in the narrower sense but also in respect of the general welfare of the children. It is true that, wedged between the Ministry of Education, the local education authority, Her Majesty's Inspectorate and their own Managers, individual schools may appear to have only a circumscribed and precarious freedom of action, but in practice this freedom is far from negligible and is widely respected. Except for the historically contentious field of religious education, the prescription for actual teaching is left delightfully vague, though certain minima are expected under the Schools Regulations and more may be in fact required by social pressure especially under the shadow of secondary-school selection. Finally, however solicitous the community may be for the schools for which it is collectively responsible, it places few obstacles in the way of those who wish to contract out of it, or to set up schools by means of which others may contract out.

In fact, the whole statutory basis of primary education could be summarised by saying that it represents an attempt to fuse the elementary, preparatory and developmental traditions into one administrative pattern, with official primacy accorded to the last, but with the other two imperfectly absorbed. The elementary tradition obtrudes most noticeably in the relative inferiority of conditions prescribed for primary schools in comparison with secondary schools, while the preparatory tradition is most conspicuous in the comparative exemption of independent schools from the basic pattern laid down in the 1944 Act itself. But in one respect at least the developmental tradition is unchallenged. Primary education, as a stage in its own right, is incontrovertibly established.

I

An Analysis of Primary Schools as Social Institutions

IN order to make a specifically sociological appraisal of the various types of primary schools to be found in England today, it is necessary to formulate some schema of analysis. The choice of an appropriate schema depends largely on the approach which one adopts towards sociology in general. To discuss the merits of different types of theoretical approach would be impossible within the limits of the present volume, but I think that the following pattern would be reasonably acceptable to sociologists with different basic points of view. It is based on the main divisions of sociological studies suggested by Ginsberg (1944) in a paper read to a conference on Sociology and Education held in Oxford during the Second World War. He delineated three main areas of sociological enquiry: social structure; social function and control; and social change. The relevance of the first to a study of institutions is obvious. The connection of the second with the first has been emphasised by modern anthropologists, while the relation of both with social change gives due place to the historical dimension. Within this conceptual framework, a place can be found for particular institutions and their sub-systems, for the development of various social roles and their corresponding status-patterns, for the establishment of cultural and sub-cultural patterns, for mechanisms of social control, and for the internal and external processes of material and cultural change which are constantly at work eroding and modifying the nature of the institution itself. Since it is possible to use this type of analytic framework in the study of particular institutions within a society, it can be adapted to the specific consideration of primary schools.

Existing sociological analyses of schools have largely been conducted in the United States, with special reference to High Schools, whose social systems are more elaborate than those in schools for younger children. Probably the most important studies are Hollingshead's of 'Elmtown' (1949), Wayne Gordon's analysis of the high school whose principal he had been (1956), and Coleman's more ambitious survey of several high schools reported in *The Adolescent Society* (1961). One of the few comparable investigations in the elementary grades is discussed by Dahlke in his *Values in Culture and Classroom* (1958), though his book ranges far beyond the particular context of his research. One or two less ambitious investigations are mentioned in the general literature on elementary[1] schools, such as Blair and Burton's *Growth and Development of the Pre-Adolescent* (1951), or in individual studies such as Stendler's *Children of Brass-town* (1949), Barker and Wright's unusual investigation into the 'psychological ecology' of a mid-Western city (1954), and the social action researches on the modification of children's values reported by Kilpatrick and Van Til (1947), Foshay and Wann (1954), and Taba (1955). But none of these is a real institutional study.

In England, such writing is virtually limited to secondary schools, while discussions of primary schools as social institutions have figured mainly in official reports and elementary textbooks, or in sensitive but sociologically unsophisticated descriptions of individual schools which provide important source-material for a sociology of primary education but do not themselves qualify as sociological analysis. The application of the present schema in the field of English primary education is therefore something of an innovation.

The first of Ginsberg's major headings is *social structure*. In practice, this can be further divided, as Wayne Gordon (loc. cit.) shows, into three: formal, semi-formal, and informal. The *formal structure* comprises two aspects, physical and social. The importance of the former is stressed by Stewart:

> They sit in desks usually, often in rows, all facing one way, although contemporary furniture and classroom organisation is tending to change this. The basic grid of rows and aisles helps to define the area of attention somewhat and enables the teacher placed at the front of the class and usually with a somewhat higher desk, possibly a dais, to supervise the class and when necessary to become a focus of attention. The desk helps to indicate the sobriety of behaviour expected, the rows to show the neatness of planning and habits which teachers hope to see appearing in their pupils and the formation represents as a whole a 'unit' for class teaching and many teachers would feel uneasy if they had not these rows to deal with—they might consider that the classroom would then become slovenly and un-businesslike, at least in appearance.
>
> (Mannheim and Stewart, 1962, p. 136)

Here, Stewart is actually referring to twelve-year-old children, but many junior and a few infant schools present a very similar picture. Now, however, there is increasing recognition of newer and more flexible patterns of physical organisation within and between the teaching spaces in primary schools; indeed, the Ministry of Education has given official recognition to this by sponsoring experimental primary-school building, for example at Finmere in Oxfordshire and at Rolls Road in Camberwell, the school which was studied by the Plowden Committee. However, innovations of this type are the exception, and there exists a wide range from these to the older patterns, so that for any one school it is important to find out both the basic architectural layout and the use which is made of it, before the formal structure can be adequately appraised.

The other aspect of formal structure is concerned with the classification of the children into teaching units, and formal sub-division for other purposes such as houses in boarding schools. It also includes the distribution of official status-positions such as captains, prefects and monitors. In a primary school, this social sub-division is relatively simple and in nursery schools it dwindles away to almost nothing, but in the upper reaches of junior schools it is more clearly demarcated and in one respect at least, that of streaming, it has become a subject for close educational and political scrutiny, including now an official enquiry by the National Foundation for Educational Research.

Then again it is important to consider the composition of the various formal divisions and status-positions in the school and to discover what, if any, relation there may be between these and the social background of the children. If, for example, it were found that some children were more prone to be trusted or distrusted than others, this would be a social fact worth investigating further because of its implications for social policy. It is not, as a matter of fact, easy to measure the social background of children, but it still remains important to consider the possible relations between broad social categories such as 'urban', 'rural', 'lower working-class' or 'lower middle-class' and the formal structure of primary schools.

Teachers themselves constitute an essential part of the formal structure of schools: that scarcely needs saying. But they are abruptly and necessarily distinct from the children. There is greater age-discontinuity between teachers and pupils in primary than in secondary schools, especially since age is the prime basis for classification among the pupils but not among the teachers. Formal structure among teachers is in fact so distinct from formal structure among the children that it will be more convenient to discuss it separately in the last chapter. However, it is necessary to stress at this point that the formal structure among the staff can and does have repercussions on the formal structure among the pupils.

The *semi-formal structure* covers all those activities such as societies, teams, clubs, which are not an essential part of the main divisions of most schools but which operate to some extent under official aegis and with official emphasis and approval. In secondary schools they are more extensive than in primary schools, except in the case of primary boarding schools, but they figure sufficiently in day primary schools also to be worth including in a structural analysis. It is important to know how many pupils take part in semi-formal sporting or other activities, and also what *sort* of pupils do so, and what significance these activities have in the life of the school as a whole. For example, membership of a school team may be technically an aspect of the semi-formal structure, but it may also be closely bound up with the formal organisation and may be of equal or greater significance in the children's eyes and those of some of their teachers, and consequently perhaps for the children's development.

Informal structure is a subject which merits attention in any primary school. Almost from the start, children build up an increasingly complex system of inter-personal relations. Indeed, as has already been stressed, school becomes for many children in the Midland years the very focus of social life. To a large extent, these relationships are conducted within individual classes, though they may merge into networks spreading throughout the school and its district. It is important here to consider what patterns of social organisation are typical of children of each sex at each age-level, and also to examine the ways in which the social situation of a primary school can affect the particular informal structure which develops within it. Much can be discovered about informal relations among children by means of direct observation, but in addition the development of sociometric techniques (Evans, 1962; Evans, 1963–4; Blyth, 1960) has rendered possible the accumulation of empirical evidence about informal relations in junior schools, as will be seen in Chapter III.

Here again, as in the formal structure, the adults in schools require separate consideration, although their informal relations also react upon those among the children. In Chapter VII, some reference will be made both to these and to the ways in which a teacher's role requires him to participate marginally in the informal relations among the children and to take them into account when planning his own activities.

The next aspect of primary schools to be considered is their *social function*. There are five basic roles which primary schools may be said to discharge in contemporary English society: to instruct; to socialise; to classify; to promote social welfare; and to develop autonomy for themselves. Since this five-fold classification is fundamental to the approach which will be followed in subsequent chapters, each of these roles requires further definition.

First: *instruction*. Whether one judges from the volume of controversy or from the nature of the formal structure of primary schools, there is no doubt about the importance attached to instruction, especially in the basic skills. Despite the impact of the developmental tradition, there is still general support for the view that primary schools instruct, and that the expansion of children's cognitive horizons is among their principal objectives. However,

17

instruction is often broadly and generously defined, so that this role may at its best involve an exciting intellectual adventure and concurrently an extension of social learning.

The second role is that of *socialisation*. This is more directly associated with the developmental tradition, and implies that primary schools are places where children learn to live together in such a way that they will continue to live, in later years, in a manner appropriate to a civilised community. This may also involve some instruction; but socialisation is more than instruction, and it is doubtful whether social values can be acquired in any other way than through participation in collective living, even though the excellence of the social values may depend heavily on the quality of the social living and the influences with which it is surrounded, and the wisdom with which this environment is adjusted to the developing capacities and vision of the children. The actual patterns of socialisation in primary schools vary according to the fundamental beliefs of the teachers and others who influence policy, but there can be little room for dispute about the importance of the socialising role itself.

Next in the series comes *classification*. In England today, one aspect of classification—that of selection for secondary education—has been so prominent that the existence of others is masked. But in fact, classification is a continuous and ubiquitous process in primary schools. Children come to be classified informally according to the aspects of the curriculum in which they do well or badly, and also according to their physical and social abilities and attainments. From all of these they may derive a general reputation which adheres to them as a stereotype, as tends to happen also in their peer-life outside school. For some of these classificatory processes official records are kept—of physique, for example, and of general and specific abilities and attainments, and of personality ratings—but others are informally but decisively committed to the children's own minds and those of their associates.

The American social theorist Talcott Parsons has pointed out that in American elementary schools there is a simple relationship between the instructional, socialising and classificatory roles. In his stimulating paper on *The School Class as a Social System* (in Halsey, Floud and Anderson [eds.], 1961, Ch. 31) he indicates that instruction and socialisation (which he groups together as 'socialisation' in the sense of 'the development in individuals of the commitments and capacities which are essential pre-requisites of their future role-performance') are carried out in the same social context, namely the school class, in which classification takes place. In fact (p. 336 of the book quoted) the two processes largely coincide because

... the main process of differentiation ... that occurs during elementary school takes place on a single main axis of *achievement*.

18

In Parsons' writing, 'achievement' has a specific significance, being contrasted with 'ascription'. Ascribed characteristics are those which an individual derives from his initial status and attributes in society, while achieved characteristics are those which emerge later and largely as the result of education. In his article, he goes on to point out that the two aspects of socialisation in his sense, 'cognitive' and 'moral' or in my present terminology 'instructional' and 'socialising', are systematically confused, so that a 'good' pupil is both one who learns well and one who behaves well. Finally, Parsons indicates that in American society the differentiation which takes place in the elementary school is accepted as valid both by its beneficiaries and by those who are less fortunate and that the teacher, almost always a woman, is the focus of a specific kind of social solidarity which permits these social processes to take place. Although Parsons' theory may not be directly applicable to English primary schools, it is stimulating in its comments about the inter-relation of the first three roles, and will be mentioned again in subsequent chapters.

The fourth role, that of *welfare*, is less comparable to anything which would be found in the U.S.A., for American democracy is more associated with corporate living and equality of esteem than with public responsibility for social welfare. In England, however, the welfare role of primary schools has a statutory basis (p. 12 above) and indeed several observers (Mellor, 1950, p. 88; Gray, 1955) have pointed out that schools have become focal points of the Welfare State, just because almost the whole child population passes through them. This welfare function is derived in part from traditional religious and philanthropic concepts of social service, and in part from widely-accepted views about the functions and responsibilities of the modern State. In addition primary schools have a specific welfare role for, as Mays (1962) points out, they are nowadays the only true neighbourhood institutions. In the eyes of many citizens, a headmaster or headmistress who knows a district and its families in a uniquely comprehensive way, and who already exercises official responsibility in relation to medical inspection, milk, school meals and clothing, is a far more approachable person than would be found in the local offices of this Ministry or that. Since he or she already has some discretion in respect of 'free dinners' and clothing, and is consulted when children are before the courts or on probation, it appears also reasonable to assume that a Head has some general competence and even authority to give advice to local people about their pressing personal problems.

Needless to say, this welfare role makes considerable and often unrecognised inroads upon teachers' time and energy and emotional resources, especially when it is added to clerical work as well as to a full teaching programme. On the other hand, some teachers find their greatest satisfaction in discharging it, and in schools for the

19

handicapped, it can easily become the main consideration. Incidentally, a Head Teacher has somewhat different role-expectations from an Assistant, and can usually adjust the time-budget more flexibly, so that the welfare role may be more directly discharged by a Head than by the rest of the Staff.

Not that this welfare function has gone unchallenged. There are still quarters in which the proliferation of welfare services in primary schools is deplored, or at least regarded as a tiresome distraction from the instructional (and perhaps the classificatory) role on which they should concentrate. Objections on these lines, usually emanating from those who have never known what it is like to be entirely dependent on a public agency whose formal language and bureaucratic structure appear as something alien, are not likely to be taken seriously by teachers of any political or ideological persuasion who are in close touch with the less privileged sections of the national community. They are unlikely to set aside the pressing needs of some in order to maintain the advantages of others; neither, however, are they likely to overlook the existence of those ubiquitous though numerically insignificant families whose attitude towards social welfare falls little short of calculating exploitation.

Last in order of consideration comes the *autonomous* role, and it is the most difficult to define. It is closely associated with the developmental tradition; ultimately, it is the role which obliges each school to be itself. For this purpose it must draw on the collective experience and talents of its staff, and on the support of various elements in the community, but for the rest it grows spontaneously. Paradoxically, although this role is independent of society, it is imposed by society. Children in the Midlands years approximate most closely to parental ideals, as was long ago emphasised by Willard Waller in his classic textbook (1932, Ch. 3). Schools are, so he said, a repository of ideals, and children are expected to gain from them a chance of being better people than their parents are; for in this way parents can project on their children the ideals which in their younger days they set before themselves. This is often held to imply both economic and moral betterment, and hence relies on the two conjoint aspects of achievement referred to by Talcott Parsons (p. 18 above). For this reason, teachers are themselves expected to be above average in moral standards, ethical behaviour and public spirit, though they need not expect to be above average in economic rewards.

However, social ideals vary from one part of the community to another, even within the catchment area of one school. A school must do more than reflect the culture of part or even all of its pupils. It cannot even be content to reflect that culture in its idealised form. The only way in which it can realise its autonomous role is by cutting purposefully adrift from the culture-patterns associated with the various parts of its clientele and creating something new and worth-while in itself. Once this is achieved, it can lead to the establishment of a social climate in which the operation of the usual conventions and counter-conventions of society and of its subdivisions are minimised, so that individuality and initiative can develop within an accepted framework of stable and considerate behaviour. Feeling that theirs is a good and satisfying school, the children are then more favourably disposed towards it, more ready to go along with it in the implementation of its other roles, and incidentally thereby more tolerant towards others whose cultural background differs from their own. The effective implementation of the autonomous role involves the consummation of the other roles also.

To continue with Ginsberg's classification of the subject-matter of sociology, the next topic to be considered is *social cohesion and control*. Without this, an institution disintegrates. The legal basis of control was discussed in the Introduction, but to a sociologist or an anthropologist that is only one aspect of social control in general. It involves also the establishment, acceptance and maintenance of norms, some of which are explicit rules, but most of which constitute the unwritten mores and folkways of a society. It also implies some consideration of the ways in which social control is enforced or, as would normally be said of schools, the means by which discipline and good tone are maintained. This may depend in part on the sanction of explicit rewards and punishments, but is based at a more fundamental level on a web of role-expectations, or in other words on a series of coinciding assumptions on the part of teachers, pupils, parents, and society at large about what adults and children in a primary school should do, and about how they should behave. Within each of these aspects of social cohesion and control, there is scope for varying degrees of consensus or of disagreement, provided that a necessary minimum exists.

Norms are familiar to children in their peer-society, as will be shown in Volume II, Chapter III. Thus, when they are brought together within the formal context of a primary school and its subdivisions, they are already predisposed to establish norms of behaviour appropriate to their age-level and the process of norm-establishment continues and becomes more sophisticated inside and outside school, the two processes developing concurrently. But there is one important difference between them. The norms which are built up in school are at least partly influenced by the school, by its staff, and especially by the head teacher and the individual class teachers influencing their own charges. This is, in fact, one of the principal means by which a primary school discharges its socialising role. Usually, the establishment of norms is centred round an acceptable routine, especially in infant schools. Provided that this routine is simple and comprehensible, and sustained with sufficient competence

21

and agreement by the staff, then the legal status of primary schools and their widespread acceptance in society renders it likely that the routine will itself be followed and maintained with the minimum of stress and will in addition satisfy a basic need for security in the children, at least until the middle years of the junior school.

However, in the later junior years the children often begin to experiment with more independent patterns of social organisation, deliberately designed to assert, at least temporarily, their capacity to oppose and to dispense with adults. At this stage, the norms of behaviour may run counter to the school and its aims, thus rendering the norms of the children's society inadequate as a means of fostering social control in the school. In this situation, when the children may be'ranged opposite the teacher in an implicit trial of strength, it becomes necessary for the teacher to adopt some of the more active methods of social control which will shortly be discussed and to indicate, by a combination of skill, maturity of behaviour, good humour and explicit sanctions, who it is who is ultimately in command. This point will be further discussed in Chapter IV.

Formal *rules* have a limited part to play at any level in primary schools. Whereas the unwritten norms, which are much more significant, can be deliberately whimsical or obscure in order to encourage a feeling of solidarity among the initiated, and must in any case take account of the pre-existing texture and characteristics of the children's society, explicit rules are devised, and are known to be devised, by adults. They should therefore logically be few, clear and prescriptive. Their ancillary nature is thus made apparent, for their restriction to a few areas of communal activity makes it clear that the principal mechanism of social control must be something other than rules. Their intention is manifest. For example, anyone can see why there must be some regulation of movement in corridors; therefore, if rules are made about walking or running inside the school, they are likely to be respected and observed.

The next point to be considered is the *positive maintenance of social control* itself. This has two principal aspects: the official system of rewards and punishments, and the self-maintaining processes which most social institutions tend to develop. Rewards and punishments may themselves be further subdivided, for they involve both the administration of an explicit code of procedure and the discharge of a part of the teacher's role. For example, if there is a strict rule that the tormenting of animals is forbidden, and a clear understanding that its infringement carries with it a specific punishment—a hiding, perhaps—then if a boy breaks the rule, he gets his hiding, and knows why. (If a girl breaks it, the consequences are less predictable.) None the less, it makes a world of difference whether the hiding is administered in front of a tittering class by an exasperated beginner, or if it is conducted in secret, accompanied by a verbal tirade, in the fastnesses of a Head Teacher's room. Similarly, where there is a convention that a 'star' is given for good work, its effectiveness varies immensely according to whether it is perfunctorily stuck in by a class teacher in the midst of supervising the distribution of milk, or by a Head Teacher who makes a specific business of interrupting a conversation with a County Organiser to perform the little ceremony and to impress on the Organiser what an achievement that star represents.

The actual nature and range of rewards or incentives in use in a school, and the correlative series of punishments or disincentives, are closely related to the basic aims and values of the community. To some extent they are the signals by which the instructional, socialising and selective roles of the school are rendered explicit, and their use may be one means by which the three roles become interconnected. Some rewards and punishments are clear and explicit, like the rules with which they are coupled. Others rely on more subtle means, as happens when a particular child is selected for the privilege of running an errand, or when an unduly assertive boy is made to sit glowering among the girls. In some denominational schools, divine approval and supernatural sanctions may be quite freely deployed. Sometimes, on the other hand, the entire process of social control is divorced from explicit acts and is made to depend on the tacit giving and withholding of human approval. Jules Henry (1955) even suggests that in some teaching situations, especially among American middle-class children in the Midlands years, a warm emotional link can be established between teacher and pupils in which the commodity given and withheld is not just approval but downright affection, and that this can be manipulated in the place of explicit reward and punishment, though only at the expense of the healthy autonomous development of peer-life among the children.

Usually, however, there is some mechanism of official sanction, though it is often sparingly used. In practice, punishment excites more interest than reward, and among punishments it is corporal punishment which provokes the most intense reactions. Although there have been individual investigations into its consequences (e.g. Hopkins, 1939) and a full-scale study by the National Foundation for Educational Research (Highfield and Pinsent, 1952), teachers and others are still prone to speak about it from the fullness of their prejudice rather than in the light of objective research.

The aspect of explicit reward and punishment which directly involves the teacher and his role will be discussed in the final chapter. But in addition the maintenance of social cohesion and control depends in part on a self-regulating and self-maintaining system which emerges in almost every school and class. Social psychologists such as Klein (1956) have demonstrated that primary groups will persist as long as membership of the group is important to its adherents. Since, as has already been pointed out, membership of a school class is important to primary-school children, there is a built-in probability that any class will maintain itself as a going concern. It is true, as has already been indicated, that the older children may become more ready to exercise their group solidarity independently of the teacher rather than under her aegis, but that tendency does not develop very far within primary schools, while if anything it intensifies the need to belong. Even when there are marked cleavages within the informal structure (Blyth, 1958) it is unlikely that there will be an overt disruption. Thus most teachers can rely on this flywheel of social momentum, and are more likely to find difficulty in securing acceptance of unpopular children than in maintaining the cohesion of the class as a whole.

Sometimes the children themselves develop overt and notably unsubtle ways of enforcing conformity. Merei (1949) in his study of 'marginal children' indicated how group pressure is brought to bear upon those who are farthest from the centre of a social system. When that system is a school class, held together by legal sanctions, they can escape only by truanting, as some do, thereby exacerbating the situation, though social isolation is scarcely ever the prime cause of truancy (Tyerman, 1958, p. 224). But in addition to overt pressures, primary-school classes provide examples of what Merton (1957a, pp. 60 et seq.) terms 'latent function maintenance'. For example, when a class all take to marbles or to a particular type of sweet or ice-cream, this activity does not only have a meaning in itself but also serves to cement the feeling of group membership among the children.

Another social process which becomes increasingly important in the maintenance of cohesion as the children become older is the development of an articulated structure of roles within the informal social system. While they are practising this aspect of social development in their out-of-school peer groups, an analogous process is under way in school. However, the nature and extent of this process depends substantially on the social atmosphere within individual classes, for, especially in the junior school, the development of roles and their variety and significance depends in large measure on the degree of active participation in the social organisation of the class which a teacher permits. This point also will be further considered in Chapter IV.

In addition to these specific roles, children come to assume a generalised 'good-pupil role' which also contributes to the cohesion of a school. Girls are especially ready, it appears, to do this. They come, they learn, they paint, they do P.E., they sing, they pray, in an attempt to please and to do well even if they cannot excel: as Parsons suggests (p. 19 above) they accept this role almost irrespective of their performance in it, a trait which they do not necessarily maintain at the secondary stage. This good-pupil role itself presupposes that a primary school is a going concern, and acts as a further mechanism operating in favour of social control.

With all these social forces working in their favour, primary-school teachers have their own role-expectations fairly well-defined: more attention will be given to teachers' roles in Chapter VII. But this does not imply that teachers always discharge their roles with equal efficiency. Nor does it indicate that their task is easy. What it does suggest is that teachers have to deal with a social institution which has a momentum of its own, in which they cannot and should not participate as equals, but which they can guide and influence so that its group organisation and interests develop in such a way as to coincide with their basic aims for the children.

When the formal, semi-formal and informal structures of a school, its social roles, and its mechanisms of cohesion and control have been considered individually, there still remains a need to consider the *total culture-pattern* of the school as a whole, its 'separate culture' as Waller (1932, Ch. 9) calls it, and that of its component classes. For this purpose it is necessary to look with the eye of an anthropologist rather than that of an analytical sociologist; but it may well be true that this rounded, holistic way of looking at a school is particularly congenial to those who are practically engaged in primary education. They can train themselves to note the regularities which appear in the daily and weekly and termly programme, those which are officially intended and those which appear to arise spontaneously. Conversely, they can note the incidents and occasions which disrupt these regularities; the moments of excitement, disharmony and calamity, and their impact on the social climate of the school and the class. The practice of systematic observation of this kind can itself suggest hypotheses about the school's social life and about its culture in depth. Incidentally, in the course of improving its knowledge of a school community and of its ways, a staff can often noticeably increase its own effectiveness, particularly in relation to the school's autonomous role. 'Action research', as it is sometimes described (Foshay and Wann, 1954) includes systematic observation in addition to more specific testing, and can involve not merely the understanding of a school's culture, but also a means of transforming it.

This leads directly to a consideration of the final topic in Ginsberg's schema of analysis, that of *social change*. However true it may be that primary schools are self-regulating systems, it is also true that they are susceptible to long-term modification through the slow erosive processes of social development. This can happen in either of two ways. First, the external circumstances of a school may alter. The social composition of a district may change, the impact of a general or local bulge in the child population may be felt, or there may be reorientation of general parental attitudes towards primary education. Such developments are frequently mentioned in official publications and other general writings on education, especially those concerned with processes of social change (Dent, 1944; Dent, 1954; Simon, 1957), but there is a dearth of local studies, especially at the primary level.

Secondary education is a little better served, both locally through the work of Flann Campbell (1956) and Halsey (in Floud, Halsey and Martin, 1957) and on the wider plane in the writings of Olive Banks (1955) and Taylor (1963). The last of these is a particularly illuminating study of the impact of social change on secondary modern schools. But primary education still awaits its Taylor, and primary schools their Campbell. This is partly because less controversy has centered round primary education, but also because the actual information available from local records is often scanty.

The other aspect of social change is concerned with internal innovation and development. As has been noticed in studies in other fields such as industrial sociology, group situations do not remain static. As some members leave and others join, the balance of values and interests alters, and this process is accentuated when there is a change in several of the key personnel among teachers and children at the same time. Sometimes, of course, the internal innovations are intentional. A Head Teacher may decide that the children should take a more active part in the Assembly, or that the i.t.a. or oral French should be introduced. Or, a class teacher may try an experiment in active methods of learning. Here it is probable that some knowledge of sociological processes might help to ensure the success of deliberate innovations in primary education (Young, 1965).

Structure; process; change: these are the principal areas of study which will be considered in the following chapters, and it will be apparent that they overlap considerably. For example, when a teacher says:

Barry! I'm surprised at you! Boys in 3A never used to behave like *that*!

the incident could be said to illustrate simultaneously the formal organisation, the socialising and classificatory roles, the maintenance of social cohesion and control, and perhaps also the advent of social change. The actual categorisation of the event depends on the point of view from which it is viewed. It exemplifies structure and process and change. Nevertheless, it is legitimate to consider the three aspects separately for purposes of social analysis, and they will be used in this way in relation to the principal types of primary school in the order in which children encounter them.

Thus nursery, infant and junior schools will be analysed in turn, along the lines already indicated. However, since a great deal more is known about the sociological aspects of junior schools than about the other two, nursery and infant schools will be considered in a single chapter whereas two will be devoted to junior schools alone, the first concentrating on the structural aspects and the second on social processes. Some children, however, do not attend these main categories of school, and so in Chapter V the different types of 'minority school' are considered according to the same basic framework of analysis. Subsequently, in Chapter VI, special attention will be paid to the transfer from primary to secondary education, though here it will be necessary to use a rather different approach. Finally, after the whole institutional apparatus of English primary education has been considered in its relation to the development of children, a chapter is given over to adults in primary schools. For schools are adult-and-child institutions, and a collective review of the place of adults within them is essential if this sociological description is to be complete.

In order to give some quantitative basis for discussion of these institutions of primary education, extensive use will be made of data from the official *Statistics of Education in 1962*. Therefore, to some extent, the topics which figured in these statistics have received fuller treatment. This does not, however, imply that those topics are the only important ones, or the most important ones. It is simply that quantitative information on other aspects is less readily available.

II

Nursery and Infant Schools

A. NURSERY SCHOOLS AND NURSERY CLASSES

THE first phase in the main sequence, that of nursery schools and their equivalents, is something of a social anomaly. In numerical terms, they are themselves 'minority schools'. Yet they deserve to be treated as a part of the main stream of educational development, for they are statutorily an integral part of primary education, as Section 9(4) of the Education Act, 1944, makes clear:

> Primary schools which are used mainly for the purpose of providing education for children who have attained the age of two years but have not attained the age of five years shall be known as nursery schools.

This anomaly is brought out in the official statistics of maintained and independent schools, where the category 'primary' excludes 'nursery' in all types of school, in bland contradiction to the Act. Indeed, in general parlance the apparent intentions of the Act are flouted, for the term 'primary' tends to be confined to children over five; often, indeed, to those over seven.

This is linked with a second anomaly. Legally, as has just been pointed out, nursery education is a part of primary education. Yet if the Midlands years are a culture-phase determined in some measure by the incidence of full-time primary education, then the nursery years must lie outside. Indeed, if physical and psychological growth are taken into account, the separateness of the nursery years becomes more apparent. At this point the identity of the Midlands years and primary education cannot be fully maintained. It is perhaps appropriate to look upon this incomplete forecourt of primary education as an outpost or protectorate of the Midlands. If nursery education should become widespread or universal, the boundary of the Midlands would then be extended to include the nursery years. In that event, there would be some cultural homogeneity throughout the primary years; but the physical and emotional developments during the total age-range would be so great as to render the expanded Midlands less uniform than at present.

Expansion on this scale belongs, however, to a conjectural future.

Nursery and Infant Schools

The present position in nursery education can be seen from the following table, which embodies the extent of nursery-school and nursery-class provision in January 1962. It includes all types of nursery-age provision, including private-school and special-school places, both of which will be mentioned again in Chapter V but which are included here in order to set the maintained-school provision in its complete perspective.

CHILDREN UNDER FIVE IN ALL SCHOOLS: JANUARY, 1962

(ENGLAND AND WALES)

(Source: *Statistics of Education in 1962*, Part I, Table 7, pp. 30–1 and Table 8, pp. 32–5).

Type of School	Age and Sex						Number of Schools
	2		3		4		
	Boys	Girls	Boys	Girls	Boys	Girls	
Maintained nursery	1,101	1,000	4,561	4,244	5,127	4,531	455
Direct-grant nursery	45	37	172	152	160	127	20
Independent nursery recognised as efficient	25	25	81	70	80	59	10
Other independent nursery	35	28	399	405	1,166	983	205
Total in nursery schools	1,206	1,090	5,213	4,871	6,533	5,700	690
Classes in maintained primary schools	77	48	5,855	5,406	92,300	86,895	
Classes in direct-grant schools	0	0	0	0	71	270	
Classes in independent schools recognised as efficient	9	20	285	321	2,317	2,765	
Classes in other independent schools	87	86	1,478	1,245	6,319	5,638	
Total in classes under five, other than classes in nursery or special schools	173	154	7,618	6,972	101,007	95,568	
Total in special schools (see Chapter V)	118	152	247	202	405	304	
Overall total	1,497	1,396	13,078	12,045	107,945	101,572	
Estimated total in age-group	377,000	356,000	371,000	352,000	362,000	342,000	
Percentage in maintained nursery schools	0·30	0·28	1·23	1·21	1·42	1·33	
Percentage in all nursery schools	0·32	0·31	1·41	1·38	1·81	1·67	
Percentage in classes in maintained schools	0·02	0·01	1·58	1·53	25·50	25·41	
Percentage in classes in all schools	0·04	0·04	2·07	1·98	29·83	29·70	
Percentage in all maintained schools	0·32	0·29	2·81	2·74	26·92	26·74	
Percentage in all schools	0·36	0·35	3·48	3·36	31·64	31·37	

From this it can be seen that the provision of all types of school place is very low before the age of four, when it rises above 30 per cent in all. However, from another table (ibid., Table 14, p. 45) it appears that the total number of children in 'classes of pupils under five', the nearest available approximation to genuine nursery classes in January 1962, was 60,689, whereas the preceding table includes some 179,000 children aged four alone. The reason is that the four-year-old category includes not only nursery-class children and others in classes consisting mainly of under-fives, but also children admitted to infant classes before their fifth birthday. Genuine nursery provision, in all types of nursery school and nursery class, was presumably limited to about 10 per cent of the child population.

The reason for this low percentage is to be found in Ministerial policy. Faced with demands for expansion in all sectors of education simultaneously, successive Ministers of Education have concluded, however reluctantly, that nursery schools and classes cannot claim any substantial priority. A quite unequivocal statement of this point of view is to be found in Circular 8/60, 31st May 1960, which until recently[1] embodied current policy:

> No resources can at present be spared for the expansion of nursery education and in particular no teachers can be spared who might otherwise work with children of compulsory school age.
>
> At the same time the Minister values the excellent work being done in nursery schools and classes, and is anxious to ensure its continuance, both for its own sake and as a base for expansion in the future . . .
>
> (therefore one possible type of expansion without further demands on resources could be effected through part-time nursery attendance) . . .
>
> The advantages of such arrangements are easily seen. At best the effect is to provide, without any additional staffing, accommodation or expense, a better introduction to school life for twice the number of children.

This point of view embodies two social and educational assumptions. First, it expresses a belief that the efficiency of later education does depend on the first stage, and a realisation that part-time attendance may have positive value, though this is indicated in rather crudely quantitative terms. Then again, it suggests that teachers and other resources can be shuttled from nursery schools to other schools and back again, whereas nursery training tends, as will be mentioned in Chapter VII, to be a rather self-contained process. In addition to both these considerations, it is probably true that nursery schools are not widely accepted in English society and that a Ministerial pronouncement restricting their expansion, however hedged about it may be with provisos, will tend to command considerable support.

The official statistics do not indicate how far Ministerial encouragement of two-shift attendance has been implemented, but figures derived from recent N.U.T. survey of nursery education (N.U.T. 1964, Table 1, p. 6) indicate that 4 per cent of all nursery *schools* (not pupils) were organised on a part-time basis, while another 25 per cent took some part-time pupils. This information does not however, indicate whether these percentages are increasing year by year.

In respect of the actual provision of nursery places, Sec. 8(2)(b) of the Education Act, 1944, empowers a Local Education Authority to provide for children under five either in nursery schools or in nursery classes. By the Schools Regulations, 1959 (S.I. 1959, No. 364) and the Grant Regulations which they replaced, nursery schools may accept pupils at two, but nursery classes must wait until three. (Sec. 7(2)). Some Authorities concentrated on one type of development, some on the other, and a few on both. The origins of nursery education as a statutory concern go back to the Fisher Act of 1918 and, because expansion has been almost frozen since the end of the Second World War, the present distribution of nursery provision reflects in fossilised form the pattern of inter-war and wartime provision. Data made available by the Nursery School Association[2] show the actual distribution of nursery *schools*. They are surprisingly concentrated in a broad crescent stretching from Greater London through the northern and western Home Counties to Oxford and Birmingham, thence through the Potteries and the textile towns of East Lancashire across the Pennines to the Bradford area and northwards to County Durham. The highest number of nursery schools in a single Authority's area is to be found in Birmingham; London comes next.[3] Outside this 'nursery-school crescent' there are only a few minor concentrations, notably in Bristol, Nottingham, Liverpool and Hull. No similar data are available for nursery classes, so it is not possible without detailed enquiry from each L.E.A. to ascertain which areas with few nursery schools have, perhaps through deliberate policy, a substantial proportion of nursery classes, though this applies to some cities such as Manchester. Since in January, 1962, the total number of nursery-class places was 60,689 as against 20,564 places for children under five in nursery schools (*Statistics of Education in 1962*, Part I, Table 8, pp. 32–5, and Table 14, p. 45) it is evident that there is a considerable number of Local Education Authorities which emphasise nursery classes, though some make neither kind of nursery provision.

However, the data from the Nursery School Association do make it possible to point out where the full nursery-school provision exists. This, involving three years' span at the maximum, in a separate institution, has generally been regarded as superior to nursery-class education, and this opinion is embodied in the official policy

31

enunciated by the Coalition Government in the White Paper on *Educational Reconstruction* (1943):

> Though it is not proposed that Local Education Authorities should cease to have the power of providing for children from 3–5 by means of nursery classes in infants' schools, it is hoped that new provision for children under 5 will be mainly in nursery schools which, in addition to providing a more suitable environment for young children, are nearer to the homes than large infants' schools and give less opportunity for the spread of infectious diseases, (p. 8).

That, of course, was in the days when expansion was still expected. In present conditions, one can only emphasise the comparative felicity of the under-fives who live in the nursery-school crescent.

Their felicity is only comparative because, in all areas, demand for nursery education greatly exceeds supply. Therefore, some priorities must be worked out. In the past, nursery education has been unmistakably linked with economic and social deprivation, a point of view that is clearly expressed in the Introduction, written by the then Chief Inspector of Public Elementary Schools, to a series of *Reports on Children under Five Years of Age in Public Elementary Schools* by women Inspectors, issued by the Board of Education in 1905:

> If no intellectual result is obtained, should children under five be *excluded from school* altogether? This question is answered in the affirmative if the children have good homes and careful mothers, but if the homes are poor and the mothers have to work the answer must be doubtful . . .
>
> It would seem that a new form of school is necessary for poor children. The better parents [*sic*] should be discouraged from sending their children before five, while the poorer who must do so, should send them to nursery schools rather than schools of instruction.

Even today, priority is still regularly given to some form of social handicap (N.U.T., 1964, p. 13) in deciding which children should be admitted to nursery schools. In the days when nursery-school expansion was possible, considerations of this type undoubtedly affected the distribution of the schools themselves, so that the N.U.T. survey (ibid., p. 22) not surprisingly indicates that four-fifths of nursery provision in 1962 was in 'mainly or entirely working-class' areas. However, the leading protagonists of nursery education have always insisted, as did the Minister of the day (Sir David Eccles) in Circular 8/60, on the importance of nursery education for children from normal homes—those with 'the better parents', as the Chief Inspector in 1905 felt justified in calling them. Indeed, as will be seen from the extract quoted from Circular 8/60, it was the need to extend nursery provision for 'normal' children which impelled the Minister to advocate the two-shift system. But this would fall far short of solving the problem. While shortages continue, selection will be necessary, and it is likely still to be associated in the public mind, and usually in practice too, with social deprivation.

In order to indicate the full scope of nursery-school, as distinct from nursery-class, provision, a brief mention must be made of the few direct-grant and the many independent nursery schools. The official statistics indicated (*Statistics of Education in 1962*, Part I, Table 7, pp. 30–1) that in January 1962, there were 20 direct-grant schools, 10 independent schools 'recognised as efficient', and 205 'others'. According to the Nursery School Association, one-third of the direct-grant schools and one-half of the recognised schools were in the Greater London area; the others were scattered, apart from four direct-grant schools in Greater Birmingham. The location of the 'others' is not stated, though they may well be typical of areas where local-authority provision is deficient or where there are a number of parents able and willing to pay for something that they value on developmental grounds, though perhaps unable and unwilling to send their children to an institution in which deprived children are numerically over-represented.

Pressure to provide further fee-paying nursery schools is likely to be increased since standards of child-rearing are generally rising and are impelling middle-class parents to make more articulate demands for the social education of young children. This is particularly probable now that the population of children under five is growing steadily, so that a frozen absolute number of school places represents a relative decline in places available. The upward turn in numbers of young children is shown in these figures derived from the official statistics (ibid., Table 2, pp. 10–11) and from the *Annual Abstract of Statistics* for 1961 (Table 9, p. 9):

TOTAL NUMBERS OF CHILDREN AGED 2–4
(NEAREST THOUSANDS: ENGLAND AND WALES)

1955	1,973,000	1960	2,031,000	
1956	1,964,000	1961	2,108,000	
1957	1,962,000	1962	2,160,000	
1958	1,969,000	1963	2,223,000	(estimated)
1959	2,001,000	1964	2,286,000	(„)

The same social pressures are also partly responsible for the accommodation of nursery-age children in other direct-grant and independent schools, rather on the same basis as nursery classes in maintained primary schools. The table on p. 29 suggests that in 1962 many more children were accommodated in these classes than in non-maintained nursery schools, a higher proportion, in fact, than in the maintained system. However, the official statistics do not specify which classes in direct-grant and independent schools are nursery classes, so it is not possible to be certain which of these very young children were actually receiving nursery education.

33

D

In all categories of nursery education, the older the children, the more likely they are to be admitted. Thus, by waiting, some children are eventually admitted though (N.U.T., 1964, Table 20, p. 14) some wait in vain and reach the school-entry age before they climb to the top of the priority list. Still others may come from families which organise a pre-school play group in order to fill the gap; but not all parents are able to do this, even as a makeshift. Despite a hostile public attitude in some quarters, there remains an imperative call for extension of nursery-school provision and, until it takes place, some parents will continue to pay fees (sometimes in a rather shamefaced way) while others, unable either to find a fee-paying place which they can afford or to plead misfortune enough to qualify for the few places in a maintained nursery school, will remain outside.

Social Analysis of Nursery Schools

Nursery schools, like other schools, are social institutions, and may thus be considered according to the plan discussed in Chapter I. In this borderland of the Midlands years, the scheme will require some, but not much, modification.

The greatest amendment will be necessary in the discussion of *structure*. For nursery schools minimise structure. The physical aspect of the formal structure is irreducible and exercises a powerful effect, whatever its actual form. It may be an old converted house whose various rooms and alcoves can be designated for different types of activity (large toys in this room, Wendy house in that corner, climbing-frame outside). It may be a gaunt prefabricated building from the darkest years of the Second World War, whose monotony is a challenge to its staff, but which is in fact successfully subdivided into areas of activity. Or it may be a room or two in a cosy but overcrowded private house, where there flourishes an independent nursery school which just contrives to conform to the necessary minimum conditions required for registration. Apart from this physical configuration, there is little formal organisation either of the children or of the time, except for the rather flexible start and finish of the day or half-day and an occasional time set aside for a corporate activity such as music and movement or the watching of a television programme.

Semi-formal organisation (clubs etc.) obviously has no place in nursery schools. Informal structure, on the other hand, is very important, since the informal social relations of children are of central importance in nursery education and constitute the focus of its socialising role. In any well-ordered nursery school, children are to be seen in various group situations: playing in sequence on a slide, or side by side with dolls, or competing, with occasional flashes of aggressive behaviour, for popular toys. Yet even this informal grouping is, from the sociological point of view, very rudimentary. The children's attention is often focused on their own emotional states and on the objects of their play rather than on their relationships with each other, at least among the two- and three-year-olds. As Susan Isaacs (1933) showed, there are times when they display some group cohesiveness and opposition to outsiders, and others when the four-year-olds galvanise the younger ones into a temporary group organisation which often seeks expression in opposition to an individual or collective scapegoat, child or adult; but a considerable time must elapse before the children reach the state of actually choosing friends as friends. Until that happens, one cannot meaningfully speak of informal *structure*, as something independent of adult stimulus or of the whim of the moment. Similarly, role-playing among these very young children is rather rudimentary, being limited to imitation of familial relationships, and in particular the mother-child relationship, or to simple observable adult roles which can be simulated as a part of personal-social development (May, 1963, pp. 54–5 and 94). Role-elaboration within the peer-group is a much later development.

Nursery schools can be more effectively considered in terms of their social *functions*. In the scheme outlined in Chapter IV, the first of these functions to be considered was instruction. However, even in the somewhat austere language of the official Schools Regulations, 1959 (S.I., 1959, No. 364) a sharp distinction is drawn between the 'secular instruction' which must be given for at least three hours per day to children between five and eight, and the 'suitable activities' prescribed for the under-fives. In view of this, it is easy to forget that a great deal of what goes on in nursery schools is, in a broad sense, instruction. Although the nature of the basic programme of activities represents the unqualified triumph of the developmental tradition, a great deal of instruction takes place incidentally, both in day-to-day learning of social behaviour and in adults' response to children's questions. Both of these serve also to extend the use and comprehension of spoken language, at an age when this development may be decisive for education, as Bernstein (1958, p. 173) pointed out. In the course of a discussion of children's language, he claimed that

> . . . a comparative study of middle-class and working-class nursery schools would be invaluable

for it would then be possible to discover more about the early mastery of what he terms 'formal language', the official and highly-structured passport of communication required for free movement outside one's primary-group context. For this purpose it would, of course, be necessary to go to independent nursery schools in order to find the middle-class children.

Much is done, too, in nursery schools to encourage children to experiment with tools and materials, and thus to learn for themselves some of the properties of their environment and to come to terms cognitively with it and with themselves. Opportunities are given for children to become familiar with books and to develop an interest in them so that later some, especially those with encouragement (not pressure) from their homes will learn to read. But in this respect, as in others, the schools vary widely, so that instruction becomes a very flexible process.

It will be convenient next to look at the classificatory role, remembering that some classification has already taken place in deciding which children are to be admitted. Physically, classification may begin as soon as the beginning of nursery education itself, and for the more obvious types of handicap such as deafness and blindness, special educational treatment may begin in the nursery years (see Ch. V). In addition, a nursery school allows children to reveal characteristics of their personalities and interests at an age when both are still malleable, so that prognostic classification is more difficult than at a later age, and the dangers of stereotyping easier to avoid just because the children change so palpably quickly. Nevertheless, some traits which appear at this early stage do persist, so that there is a strong incentive to the nursery-school staff to foster desirable traits as far as they can.

Welfare is the role most readily associated with nursery schools in the public mind. Because of their past association with economic distress and emotional deprivation, there remains a tendency to regard nursery education itself as a regrettable makeshift for a good home. It is often suspected (Dobinson, 1963, pp. 30–2) of being the outcome of a mother's employment, which is either something which she undertakes from reluctant necessity, in which case she and the children are to be pitied, or else something on which she embarks for the sake of a few material possessions, in which case the children are to be pitied but she is to be condemned. The only other circumstances justifying nursery education is often thought to be the absence of the mother, in which case the children are still to be pitied. And since the children are to be pitied in each case, nursery education tends to be associated with misfortune, like National Assistance. This is regrettable, because nursery schools, including independent schools, are well placed to carry out the more positive welfare functions, dividing the field between the Welfare Clinics and themselves.

The socialising role is, however, more essentially linked with the nursery school itself. Instruction and welfare could be provided elsewhere; socialisation could not. The particular combination of children of a limited age-range with suitable apparatus and expert supervision and understanding provides an environment for social learning and development which has no real parallel. It may well be that the experience of learning to live together at this age is of permanent value in personality-development.

However, it is necessary to consider carefully how this operates in practice. If it takes place entirely among children from 'deprived' backgrounds, owing to the method of selection, then some of its advantages will tend to be lost, or at least outweighed, owing to the handicaps already sustained in speech or health or cultural background by the children who are admitted. The most effective means of countering this tendency is for the school to develop a range of intrinsic interests and activities, within the children's range of experience, so that they can become absorbed in its common life, as Montessori's first pupils were (Montessori, tr. George, 1912, Ch. 3). In other words, the socialising role can be most effectively carried out when the autonomous role is also vigorously discharged. When this happens, all that the school does is characterised by a quality of frankness and creativity which is unmistakable, and the children's initial handicaps are well-nigh forgotten.

Social cohesion and control scarcely requires particular consideration in nursery schools. It is usually and efficiently based on wisely-chosen routine and understanding, interspersed with occasional intervention when necessary. Children's norms are at this age rudimentary and ephemeral, while rewards and punishments in the usual sense are obviously inapplicable, though in the psychologists' sense of positive and negative reinforcement of behaviour patterns they are implicit in the process of socialisation. Children learn readily the satisfaction of complying with the group's activities under adult guidance, and this provides the most effective form of social cohesion until they begin to develop an independent society with a role-structure of its own.

Finally, *social change* affects nursery schools both through changes in the contributory population (for example, the advent of a recognisable proportion of coloured children) and through alterations and improvements deliberately introduced by the superintendent and her staff. The latter, deliberate type of change takes place more rapidly than the former, though both would repay investigation. Indeed, it would probably be advantageous if a nursery-school staff were accustomed to developing a systematic method of recording their observations on social development, as was done by Isaacs (1933), May (1963) and others.

In general, nursery schools are simple institutions, though diverse and individual ones. They do not require an elaborate sociological description. It is, however, regrettable that, even within these limits, they have received so little attention from sociologists.

Nursery Classes merit briefer consideration. The difference in age of entry—three instead of two—has already been mentioned. Table 25 of the N.U.T. Report (N.U.T., 1964, p. 16) brings out the rarity of exceptions to this rule, for only 1 per cent of the nursery-class pupils studied in their sample were under three. Of the others, about two-thirds were over four. According to the same survey it also appears that the majority of eligible children, that is, those who satisfy a Local Education Authority's priorities for admission, are eventually admitted though this often involves a wait of eight or more months (ibid., pp. 21–2). Possibly this availability of places is effected by infringing the letter of the Schools Regulations, 1959 (S.I. 1959, No. 364, Sec. 6) according to which the size of nursery-classes is limited to thirty, for in January 1962, 462 of the 2,213 nursery classes in maintained primary schools exceeded thirty (*Statistics of Education in 1962*, Part I, Table 13, p. 44), twenty-three of them being actually over forty in size. It is not clear (ibid., Table 14, p. 45) how many of the 60,689 *pupils* in nursery classes were in oversized classes, but the figure was apparently about 25 per cent. The N.U.T. survey at first sight gives a still gloomier picture for it indicates (N.U.T., 1964, p. 15) that the average nursery class within the survey sample had in 1963 forty-one pupils, and that 5 per cent actually had over seventy. This is because, for some reason, nurseries with two classes are combined for purposes of this Report, a device which can be confusing.

As for the part-time attendance recommended in Circular 8/60, it appears that less progress has been made in nursery classes than in nursery schools, for the N.U.T. survey (ibid., Table 23, p. 15) indicates that only 2 per cent of nursery classes were wholly, and another 5 per cent partly, organised on a part-time basis.

Little information is available about the location of nursery classes: this has already been indicated. However, it appears that nursery classes, like nursery schools, are to be found predominantly in working-class areas (ibid., p. 23).

As social institutions, nursery classes show some obvious contrasts with nursery schools. Not only are their social characteristics more closely confined to those of the three- and four-year-old children, but they are administratively a part of infant schools. Yet in spite of this, they do often constitute quite a separate entity. In one-quarter of the instances quoted in the N.U.T. Report (ibid., p. 20) the nursery classes were actually in separate premises, and in many other cases the different staffing and programme emphasises the separateness of the youngest children. Thus, the description already given of nursery schools as social institutions applies substantially to nursery classes too. Much the same can be said about nursery classes in independent schools, but no official data are separately available about these.

Day Nurseries and Other Approved Nurseries require some comment at this point. Despite popular belief, these are on quite a different legal basis from nursery education. Day nurseries are established and maintained by the Health Departments of Local Authorities under Section 22 of the National Health Service Act, 1946. Others are registered under the Nurseries and Child Minders Regulation Act, 1948: these may be maintained by private individuals or attached as crèches to industrial concerns. In any of these, children may be accepted at an age as low as six months, and they are open for a much longer day than any nursery school or class. The numbers of day nurseries have been falling, and of independent nurseries rising, until on 31st December 1962, the total number of places offered under the 1948 Act (22,591) exceeded day-nursery places (21,876) for the first time. On 31st December 1961, the closest date to the current figures in *Statistics of Education in 1962*, the corresponding totals were respectively 17,618 and 22,259.[4] Although there is no administrative regulation restricting expansion comparable to Circular 8/60, economic and other considerations make it increasingly difficult to maintain, let alone increase, local-authority provision at the level reached during the Second World War and afterwards.

These figures cannot be compared with those of places in nursery schools and classes unless the proportion of children aged 2–4 is known. For this purpose the most complete information is to be found in a survey of day nurseries conducted by the National Society of Children's Nurseries[5] and published in February 1962. From this survey, which did not cover the whole country, it can be inferred that about 13,000 places were available for children aged 2–4. No comparable figure is available for other nurseries, but if the proportion were similar, then some 23,000 children aged 2–4 were in attendance at these nurseries; more than the 20,564 in nursery schools, but many fewer than the 60,689 in 'classes of pupils under five', the nearest available approximation to nursery classes.[6]

In the opinion of the authors of this survey, the distribution of day nurseries reflects local authorities' policy rather than the economic characteristics of different areas. Actual criteria for admission resemble those for nursery education, though they are differently ranked. According to the survey, the status of the mother constituted the first priority, followed by poverty severe enough to oblige her to work, and then by unsatisfactory physical conditions at home. More rarely, the emotional needs of the children are taken into account. By contrast the N.U.T. survey (N.U.T., 1964, p. 13) indicated that in nursery schools the child's own health and general needs carried most weight.

Since they are not subject to the abolition of fees in grant-aided schools, day nurseries and others make a charge. In the case of day nurseries, the Report indicates that this charge is about 5/- to 10/- daily, but varies quite widely and is often adjusted to the needs of individual families. It is almost as though the intention were to underscore the economic basis of day nurseries and their separateness from nursery schools. There is no published information about fees in other nurseries, or about other aspects of these, except that the Ministry of Health is responsible for guaranteeing the standards of premises in nurseries of all types.

The numerical relation of these nurseries to nursery education has already been mentioned. They also impinge upon primary education in three other ways; that is why they deserve mention here. First, nursery assistants usually undergo a part of their training in a day nursery and another part in a nursery school or class, so that some communality of principles and practice becomes established between the two. Secondly, nursery schools and day nurseries are often confused in the public mind, so that both tend to be regarded as child-minding establishments rather than educational institutions, just at a time when day nurseries are themselves developing in a much more imaginative way. Thirdly, a small number of children arrive at their infant school having had some experience in a nursery, so that they have at least been familiar with larger numbers of children than is usual in their immediate habitat, and have also been used to being away from their mothers during the day. Nevertheless, these are not a part of primary education, and if the nursery years ever become a full part of the Midlands of childhood, the need for day and independent nurseries will disappear.

B. INFANT SCHOOLS[7]

With the beginning of statutory school life, the sociological situation alters in many ways. This is the boundary of the Midlands proper, the first great transition-point in the Englishman's life-cycle. Two-thirds of the child population experience their first move away from home at the age of five and make their way into the first formal environment of their lives. Of the remaining third, a large proportion are admitted to infant classes only just before they are five, though the data given in *Statistics of Education in 1962*, Part I (Tables 8, 13, and 14, pp. 32–5, 44 and 45) are presented in such a way that it is not possible to compute just how many under-fives in England and Wales, in primary schools other than nursery schools, are accommodated in classes other than nursery classes, or how many of these are in classes mainly composed of over-fives. What is more, there is a slight overlap because nursery schools continue to take some pupils of five or even six, while in districts where there is an acute shortage of infant-school places or teachers, the entry to the infant school has sometimes to be unobtrusively deferred.[8]

But in the vast majority of cases a start is made at five. In January 1962, the percentage of the estimated age-group in maintained primary schools at the age of five was 94·1 (derived from Table 8, in

Statistics of Education in 1962, Part I, pp. 32–5) and this remained fairly constant at successive age-levels: 94·4 at six, and 94·2 at seven.

The small remaining percentage of children attended other types of schools, not because places were unavailable, but because for various reasons their parents chose for them to attend one of the 'minority schools' to be discussed in Chapter V. Thus it is at the age of five that minority schools begin to appear distinctive.

For those who proceed to maintained infant schools, three further variations may be encountered. They may go to a county or a voluntary school (as at the nursery level); they may go to a separate infant school or a junior-with-infants school, or more rarely to an all-age school; and they may find themselves in a school which transfers children to the junior level at the age of seven or one which defers this transfer until the children are eight. They are however almost certain to attend a mixed rather than a single-sex school, as is shown in the following table based on data derived from *Statistics of Education in 1962*, Part I, Table 7, pp. 30–1 (England and Wales):

Type of School	Number of Single-Sex Schools			Number of Mixed Schools	Percentage of Schools which are Single-Sex
	Boys	Girls	Total		
Infants	3	3	6	5,496	0·11
Junior with Infants	7	96	103	11,992	0·86
All-Age	73	74	147	628	19·0

In respect of denominational status, pupils in county schools in 1962 considerably outnumbered those in all voluntary schools, (see Ch. III, p. 58 below) in primary education as a whole, though separate figures were not given for infants. Pupils in separate infant schools outnumbered those in junior-with-infants and all-age schools as is indicated by these figures taken from Table 8 of the same *Statistics*:

NUMBERS OF CHILDREN AGED 5–7 IN
MAINTAINED SCHOOLS (ENGLAND AND WALES),
JANUARY, 1962

	Girls	Boys	Total
In separate infant schools	408,454	433,320	841,774
In junior-with-infants schools	370,446	388,590	759,036
In all-age schools	16,360	17,167	33,527
Totals	795,260	839,077	1,634,337

However, the proportions are slightly misleading, since some of the seven-year-olds in the 'separate' category were in junior schools (108,170 girls and 114,640 boys, in addition to a very small number of under-sevens) so that the preponderance of the 'separate' group is in fact slightly greater than the figures indicate. As for the age of transfer to junior schools, the end-point of infant education, this usually takes place at seven: in January 1962 (ibid., Table 8, pp. 32–5) there were twice as many seven-year-olds in all-junior as in all-infant maintained schools, and the latter will have included some children who had just reached their seventh birthday but who would not be moving into the junior school until September 1962. This prompts some consideration of the suitability of the eighth year as a stage of transfer and, since this in turn involves examination of the total span of infant education, it almost inevitably implies also some thought about whether five is a suitable age for the start of compulsory full-time education.

The Age-Span of Infant Education

Traditionally, compulsory education in the United Kingdom begins at five. Dottrens (1962, Table 13, p. 58) pointed out that this characteristic was shared by only two other members of U.N.E.S.C.O., namely Ceylon[9] and Paraguay. But whereas many countries such as the U.S.A. and the Scandinavian states offset their late entry-age by providing an extensive network of nursery schools or their equivalent, the British way is to plunge the majority of children into full-time attendance from 9 to 3.30 each day in the term in which the fifth birthday is reached, or as soon afterwards as possible. Sometimes, as already indicated, the delay is considerable; always it is regretted. Yet at the same time, if a parent elects to satisfy the school-attendance requirement by sending a child to an independent school, and if that school decides that a half-day attendance is sufficient for a five-year-old, then the law is satisfied.

In view of these anomalies, suggestions have been made in political (see Vol. II, Ch. V) and educational circles that compulsory full-time education should be deferred until six, while the provision of nursery-school places for voluntary attendance should be augmented. In this way, it is contended, each child can begin school at his own time and pace. This plan has the virtue of catering for individual differences, and in particular of recognising the degree of fatigue which a full day in school may cause in a five-year-old. Some of its protagonists have also suggested that schools and teachers might operate on a shift basis, as recommended for the nursery stage in Circular 8/60, which might also ease the teacher shortage. But the whole conception has been vehemently opposed by many experts on infant education, on several grounds. One is that compulsory education ensures that the web of medical inspection covers all children at the age of five: this argument is not decisive, for part-time education could do that too. It has also been thought that most parents would opt for the morning 'shift', though this does not appear to have happened in nursery schools (Circular 8/60, p. 3, para. 10). Others contend that children from the more favoured homes would establish a greater lead than ever if their less fortunate peers had to wait longer for their full-time education to begin; but here again part-time education might bridge the gap. Again, it has been emphasised that part-time attendance would only be practicable if teachers were also part-time; otherwise the strain on one teacher playing Cox and Box with two large classes of part-timers, and two sets of parents, would become excessive and would involve a radical change in the teacher's role. However, this is not likely to be needed, since in view of the teacher shortage one of the main administrative arguments for the 'shift' system is that it would facilitate the wider use of part-time teachers, especially married women, who would still be 'our teacher' to their half-day flock.

A more radical attack on the proposal to alter the entry date comes from Miss D. E. M. Gardner (1964, p. 61) who roundly declares that full-time attendance at a well-conducted infant school is not too fatiguing for five-year-olds, and suggests that when this argument is put forward, it is really a cover for other and more insidious attacks on English infant education, as though Robert Owen and the Macmillan sisters were being stabbed in the back by the advocates of a leaving-age of sixteen. It seems to me that this is a real danger, but that in her determination to withstand it, Miss Gardner dismisses individual differences too summarily and assumes too readily that every five-year-old is ready for a full day at school. However, Miss Gardner represents an influential and weighty body of opinion, which would resist any attempt to alter the present arrangements other than by expansion of nursery education. Thus, for practical purposes, and in spite of the anomalies already mentioned, five appears likely to remain as the age of entry to full-time compulsory education.

Therefore, even if each child is to have two complete years in the infant school, seven can be the leaving-age. This, too, summons ghosts from the past, for it is the age at which the Standards began. Official opinion has generally favoured the earlier transfer age (seven rather than eight). For example, it is clearly stated in *The Nation's Schools: Their Plan and Purpose* (Ministry of Education, 1945, p. 11) that transfer at seven-plus, previously sanctioned by the 1931 Report on *The Primary School*,

... may be expected to be the general rule.

It might also be justified because it coincides with a minor growth spurt and approximately with second dentition, a scarp, as it were, dividing the earlier part of the Midlands from the years from seven onwards which, as was mentioned in the Introduction, Rudolf Steiner calls 'the heart of childhood'. However, Ross (1960, pp. 61–2 and Ch. 10) points out that seven-plus as an age of transfer can severely truncate infant education for some children, especially if they are afflicted with an awkwardly-placed birthday, and adds that there may be a positive value in postponing transfer until after the growth-scarp is climbed.

Thus there is no unanimity of opinion either about the start of infant education or about its termination. The Plowden Committee may accumulate important new evidence on this point. Meanwhile, five to seven remains the predominant pattern.

Social Analysis of Infant Schools

Although research findings are still limited in extent, it is possible to apply the scheme of analysis more systematically at the infant than at the nursery stage.

As regards *formal structure*, every infant school has its physical premises, which influence much of what goes on within the school. The tendency in recent years has been towards the erection of buildings which can be converted from one purpose to another, and rooms whose divisions are movable or imaginary, so that the conception of a school as a series of discrete learning environments is now outmoded, though the heritage of buildings ensures that it remains widely commemorated. Flexibility in structure encourages flexibility in teaching; rigidity of structure operates in the reverse direction, though it can be resisted by leaving doors open and using corridors and corners of halls and playgrounds. However, the physical layout of a school constitutes an initial circumstance which must be taken into account when assessing the formal structure of any infant school. In addition, whatever may be the actual shape of the building, its features can take on a particular significance for individuals. A corner may figure as a retreat for the timid or for the child who depends unduly upon phantasy-life, or perhaps for the mischief-maker; and a teacher may need to be on her guard to prevent this place-identification from becoming too stereotyped and ingrained.

Among the children, the principal characteristic of the formal social structure is simply that it *is* formal, not in the sense of formal teaching, but because it involves contact with other children in a large, structured, imposed group situation, quite unlike any of the face-to-face groups with which most of them are familiar. The first step, that of the *reception class*, is thus in many ways the most important. Here, children with a wide variation of social experience come together under the stabilising influence of one teacher, who inevitably figures at first as a mother-substitute (see Ch. VII) and who must gradually divest herself of that role. The fact that she is everybody's 'mother' itself constitutes a contrast to home, and this situation may involve, for some children, a temporary regression to babyish behaviour, of which desolate crying is the most obvious example. All of this makes big demands on the teacher's own emotional maturity, as she patiently creates a new colony of formal organisation on the frontier of the Midlands. It may be possible to mitigate the impact of this situation by admitting small groups of children at any one time, as suggested by the National Association for Mental Health in *Periods of Stress in the Primary School* (1955, p. 6) but this is not always administratively practicable. A more effective method, to be considered shortly, is that of vertical grouping in the school as a whole, whereby the newcomers are welcomed into existing 'families' of children of different ages, but this is only possible if the entire infant school, or at least the younger part of it, is organised in that way. If it is not, then the reception class or classes must remain in some measure distinctive.

In the usual pattern of organisation, differentiation begins when the children leave the reception class. It is usually based on age, the most important of sociological variables among children. Yearly or half-yearly promotion is widely practised, partly as a legacy from the days when infants were pushed relentlessly forward towards the examinable bounds of Standard One. But in addition, and progressively, differentiation is also based on ability, or at least on presumed ability. In its most blatant form, according to observers such as Michael Young, this involves the allocation of children to 'tables', with about six children at each, at least during the times allocated for reading and number work, so that the 'top table' soon begins to draw ahead in formal attainment and to become the nucleus of the 'A' stream in the junior school. Where this procedure is established, it is often reinforced by the segregation of classes within separate rooms, and also by a progressive formalisation of the time-table, even though the teaching within the time-units remains flexible. The operation of this differentiation by ability is of course masked and qualified by the grouping of children in different ways for the large part of the school's activities which fall outside the 'formal skills', but it sometimes happens that children absorb, from school and home alike, the impression that these ability-based activities are the important ones, and that therefore the classification associated with them is also important; as, in a sense, it is.

In addition to the 'table' principle, there is another by which age and attainment are combined as a basis for differentiation in the formal organisation. One is told, for example, that a certain class contains 'the bright sixes and the bottom sevens', that is, the children are really grouped by a crude assessment of mental age. This may facilitate teaching, but it carries implicit assumptions, for example that age-status is to count for less and less as children grow older. It also implies, frankly, a danger that the 'bright sixes' will gladden their teacher's heart more readily than the 'bottom sevens', with results that belong more accurately to the school's classificatory and socialising roles than to the formal structure itself.

Other schools have deliberately abandoned division either by age or by attainment. Prominent among the alternative methods of organisation is that of the family system or vertical grouping, which attempts to maintain within large schools something of the intimacy of primary-group relationships between children of different ages which are characteristic of small rural schools.[10] When schools are organised in this way, the children are grouped in vertical units within which the older children help the younger, and the abler the less able, so that ability is abandoned as a basis of differentiation and age figures in a different way. Newcomers are welcomed into a living unit, perhaps already including one of their own siblings, instead of a new 'reception class'; and all children, however limited in ability, have a prospect of becoming in due course one of the trusty sevens who can look after the newcomers. An experiment in organisation by vertical grouping at Rolls Road Primary School, Camberwell, was watched by the Plowden Committee. Sometimes a modified pattern of vertical grouping is used, in which the seven-year-olds are age-graded as a preparation for the usual junior-school organisation. Of course, there are big difficulties in working within a vertical pattern, especially for teachers with a lifetime of experience in an age-graded school, but it has perforce served the countryside well for generations, and its applicability to larger city schools with a less generous staffing ratio deserves serious examination, though it cannot be automatically assumed that it is equally effective in large classes where its essentially familistic character is contradicted by the scale of the formal unit.

Within horizontal or vertical units, the beginnings of role-taking are officially encouraged. By the age of six, some children are ready to act regularly as helpers, boys often preferring apparently man-size jobs while girls are ready to prove their own maturity by looking after the younger ones. (This, too, is facilitated by vertical grouping.) But it is important to prevent individuals from establishing too early a monopoly and from excluding others from a share. Premature stereotyping of individuals as 'trusty', 'clever'—or 'scatter-brained' —is easy and is deplorable.

Formal structure cannot be considered without some reference to the social background of the children. Although the immediate habitat is important to infants, there is little evidence that rural-urban differences are very important at this age, mainly because few infant schools are large enough to include town and country children. But *within* rural infant schools there may be an important difference

46

between children who can walk a short distance to school and those who have a longer journey, especially if it involves travel by bus. Lee (1957) carried out a very interesting pioneer study in Devonshire in which he indicated that those children, especially boys, who were transported considerable distances daily showed a poorer level of emotional adjustment than those who lived nearby. This he attributed to the decisive separation from their mothers which the journey symbolised. This important and precise study has, unfortunately, no parallel.

There is more evidence about the importance of social class in infant schools. Basically, it stems from the different family environments characteristic of different social levels. The critical difference as will be further discussed in Volume II, Chapter V, is between the lower or unskilled working class on the one hand, and all other levels on the other. The latter, who to some extent wield Bernstein's 'formal language', confer from the very outset a triple advantage on their children. First, they ensure a built-in superiority of ˙cognitive equipment, by dint of early language training. Second, they encourage them to take full advantage of the learning environment provided by the school. Thirdly, they furnish them in countless small ways with the patterns of social response which a school expects and values. As Bernstein puts it, in an excellent phrase (1958, p. 163) they are

. . . oriented to certain values but individually differentiated within them.

and this in turn makes them likely to stand out as more 'visible' to their teachers. They are often bright, definite, saucy little individuals, as the teachers possibly were in their own day, and it is probably the cumulative experience of such children which induces the consensus of teachers' perception of home background which Goodacre (1961) discusses. Although there is nothing necessarily invidious in this, it may be important in its effects on the classificatory function of the infant school which is to be discussed later.

As in nursery schools, *semi-formal organisation* is unimportant in infant schools; but *informal organisation* is very significant and already begins to show interesting developments. The children are now more numerous than in nursery schools, and have also reached an age-level at which they can elaborate their social relationships. At first, for those with no previous experience of life in a formal organisation, the initial adjustment is itself sufficiently difficult to absorb their social attention. But, just because the new environment is formal and the teacher is not a real mother, the children are in due course impelled to respond to the second social stimulus in their new environment, namely the other children. However, the quality of their response depends substantially on the teacher, for five-year-olds are not developed enough to sustain a fully autonomous society. As in nursery schools, teachers have for a long time realised this, and have been accustomed to observe and assist the social development of children.[11]

The general tendency appears to be for experiments in pairing or 'dyad-formation', as it is sometimes called, to take place first, followed by more ambitious groups engaged in classroom activities or in traditional games in the playground whose importance as a socialising influence has been stressed by the Opies (1959). In this way, the first steps are taken towards the formation in the school environment of social organisations comparable to those found in peer society outside, as will be discussed in Volume II, Chapter III. Once again the most important unit is the group, which comes to be the embodiment of friendship as the children grow older. Alongside this there develops what might be called gangship, as the various groups coalesce into larger, more ephemeral units for particular purposes.

At the five- or six-year-old level, friendship is still a very unstable affair. Today John proclaims that Robin, or Linda, is his 'friend'; tomorrow there is someone else, and if John is asked what has happened to Linda and Robin, he replies conclusively that they were his friends yesterday. All the same, while it lasts, this is real friendship and is regarded as such. It often develops on a basis of shared interests and activities, or of mutual dependence, and extends, as in the case of Robin and Linda, to either sex. Sometimes, however, the sex-choice is conscious, for infants are already aware that some activities are typical of one sex rather than of the other and may allow football or needlework to affect their choice. Conversely, there can be a protosexual element in the choice: for a day or so, Linda is John's sweetheart. As the infant-school years come to an end, the monosexual pattern tends to assert itself at the expense of the other.

Gangship among infants is an even more precarious phenomenon. To some extent it is fostered by the formal organisation of the school itself, for activities such as singing and 'story' and movement are inevitably conducted in a gang context. Educators such as Froebel and Montessori laid considerable stress on the value of this extended collective experience and made provision for it in the school's programme. It tends also to create a we-feeling in the class and to enable it to spill over into the playground, where infants combine in some rudimentary game, or join hands in a long line in order to run shouting across the middle. Here, too, there may be some recognition of sex-differences because some activities are considered more appropriate for boys than for girls.

There is little direct evidence that friendship or gangship at the infant stage is affected by social background. Within a school's catchment area, neighbours' children are likely to come to school together and to associate within the school to some extent, and sometimes neighbours within particular streets or hamlets or avenues are distinctive within the community as a whole; but that is as far as it goes. On the whole, infant schools have catchment areas small enough and homogeneous enough to make it likely that differences between schools are greater than differences within schools. However, as they grow older, the children may begin to notice the conventional indices of brightness and neatness in each other, so that the process of classification, accelerated sometimes by the teachers' attitudes, begins to affect the informal organisation, bringing the brighter children together at the top. Here the familiar figure of speech about the 'cream' has more point than usual.

Turning now to the *social roles* of infant schools, one finds that *instruction* occupies a central place in most people's conception of what should be done. Indeed the primacy of the instructional role is often reflected in the formal structure itself. In actual fàct the definition of this role could be made still more precise, for it is the basic skills of number and language, especially reading, which figure most prominently within it. It is no accident that the principal controversies about infant education have centred on this aspect of instruction, just because it is widely regarded as important. It is not possible in the present context to attempt any complete discussion of the instructional role, for that would soon degenerate into a tabloid and indigestible summary of infant-school method, a subject on which there are excellent books (e.g. Mellor, 1950: Hollamby, 1962). All that can be done is to comment on the sort of instruction which takes place, and on its social significance.

For example, it has been in the discharge of the infant school's instructional role with regard to language and number that the developmental tradition has gained its principal victory in English education. The use of groups and of individual work, the making of number and reading apparatus, and the development of the basic skills in relation to children's growing experience of their environment has become characteristic of the stock-in-trade of infant school teaching, while the older traditions of formal class teaching, even in the relatively enlightened form which they took under the influence of Pestalozzi and Froebel, are now retreating. It is true that within the modern approaches there is room for disputes, such as between the adherents of phonic and look-and-say methods or over the introduction of the i.t.a., but collectively all these methods symbolise the triumph of the developmental over the elementary and the preparatory tradition alike. In fact, infant schools are often characterised by the atmosphere of a successful, though very gentle, revolution, and those who are associated with them still have enough revolutionary fervour to be willing to convert those

49

parents who appear to harbour some lingering preference for the *ancien régime*. Occasionally this is linked with a socio-economic attitude, for resistance to activity methods has tended to come from articulate middle-class parents who learned successfully by the traditional means and have given their own children every chance, and perhaps some pressure, to do the same, while teachers have tended to feel that informal methods of teaching are particularly valuable for infants from unfavourable home backgrounds (Morris, 1959, p. 54). Thus, in several ways, the implementation of the instructional role in the basic skills can have important sociological consequences. At the worst, it can produce a situation in which parents and teachers despair of each other; at best, it can result in positive co-operation between teachers and parents of all kinds.

Despite this centrality of reading and number, there are other important aspects of instruction, extending through the rest of the curriculum into the field of social learning. These are also important, and it is a part of the modern approach to infant education that their importance should be stressed. They usually constitute an extensive part of the 'at least three hours of secular instruction' which the Schools Regulations, 1959 (S.I. 1959 No. 364, Sec. 10/1) require daily for children between five and eight. In this part of their instruction, most of it derived in the course of play and story and other kinds of activity, children make their first steps towards skills in art, craft, music, physical development, and towards rudimentary scientific knowledge. Concurrently, they continue to experience a widening world, which becomes more intelligible as sensory and perceptual development proceeds. Here too, as in the formal skills, there are disputes among teachers and in society at large about the value of these activities and of the ways in which instruction, thus conceived, is in fact carried out. For example, a 'traditional' infant teacher is likely to concentrate on a wise choice of material mediated in a kindly atmosphere, whereas her 'modern' counterpart would more probably interpret instruction not only as the selection of material for presentation, so that the children may make their own choices within it, but also as the active stimulus of individual children by question, suggestion, example, comment or restraint, interspersed with discreet withdrawal, during the actual time when the children are interestedly engaged in their chosen activities.

A special case of the instructional role is the one specifically excluded in the foregoing Regulation, namely religious instruction, which is separately required under Section 25(2) of the Education Act, 1944. Its actual nature is determined in any particular case by the denominational status of the school, but nevertheless it gives rise to disputes among teachers and among parents, especially those who feel strongly about the subject. Some object to any instruction in what appears to them an outworn superstition; others resent the lukewarm way in which teachers convey to children what they regard as the pearl of great price. The statutory requirement is of course the result of a series of compromises between differing and strongly-held points of view, but it has left a legacy of difficulties and these are sometimes regarded as at their greatest in the infant school, where children are prone to accept their teacher's word and to be bewildered if it differs from their parents', but where their capacity to understand anything in the nature of doctrinal statements is at its minimum. There is also a further complication, for many parents and teachers regard religious education as valuable rather for its social-ising than for its purely instructional significance; and this leads to a consideration of the second of the infant school's roles.

The *socialising role* does, as indicated in Chapter I, involve basic considerations of belief and of procedure. In addition, there are specific differences between schools which reflect differences in background. There are some aspects of the common life which are fostered in all schools, but denominational schools may lay particular stress on specific practices, and schools in predominantly middle-class areas may, even at the infant level, emphasise especially certain aspects of politeness and good manners or such external symbols as uniform.

The actual methods used to develop the social attitudes considered desirable may also vary from school to school. Sometimes the main stress is laid upon verbal precept which, as Piaget (1932) showed, can be elevated by infants to an almost supernatural status. Other schools rely heavily on what is termed 'atmosphere', which can mean anything from the impressive togetherness of a bright, orderly morning assembly with carefully-chosen devotions, to a mystifying agglomeration of piety, or to the ponderous manipulation of group approval and disapproval in order to shame and shape a deviant child into the accepted mould. Others again prefer to reason with children, as Rousseau (tr. Foxley, 1911, pp. 53–4) refused to do, and a still larger number use a judicious blend of methods, adapting them to individual children and particular situations and bearing in mind that infants envisage their social relations very much in simple, inter-personal terms. Still others, perhaps remembering their Plato, make a careful selection of stories and games and other means of influencing young children. Whatever methods are used, the children normally regard socialisation as desirable. They want to learn to live together, and regard the acquisition of this skill as characteristic of the pupil role. Thus the average seven-year-old is much more a social being than he was two years previously.

The *classificatory role* has also been discussed implicitly in relation to the formal structure, for the primacy accorded to instruction has an effect on classification too. As Talcott Parsons emphasises, the main dimension of classification is that of achievement (Parsons, T., in Halsey, Floud and Anderson, 1961, p. 440), but this is not the only kind of differentiation that takes place. For one thing, this is the first stage at which systematic physical records are begun, since compulsory medical inspection starts at the beginning of compulsory education.[12] Again, in many cases schools begin to keep records of social and emotional development, though these are scarcely suitable for reliable prognosis. In addition to these means of formal classification, teachers are constantly busy assigning children to various categories, and here again there is a danger of premature stereotyping.

The children themselves are not yet fully aware of the significance of these various kinds of classification, nor indeed do they always appreciate that they are being carried out. Probably they come to realise first the more obvious types of physical difference, so that infants with the more extreme kinds of physical deviation can be treated with what, in older children, would be regarded as heartlessness. Then, owing to the nature of the formal organisation of the school, differences in attainment become apparent, particularly in the basic skills on which so much time is spent, but also in physical movement and in social behaviour. The practical implication of this is that children should be given opportunities of doing something at which they can be relatively successful: easier said than done, in many cases. In fact, the reverse is often found, for the definite little people who achieve most in the formal and physical skills, and mature more quickly, often thrust themselves into the forefront socially too.

Children may be more aware of the social classification which goes on among themselves. As the elements of friendship become established, they begin to sort themselves out into various social roles that become increasingly stable as time goes by. At first, only the most obvious differentiation of admired and rejected roles takes place, some boys figuring as leaders or fighters and some girls as stars and protectors,[13] while children of both sexes who are dirty, aggressive or unduly egocentric or babyish or physically incompetent are already on the way to becoming isolates or rejectees. What is more, as a class or a vertical group develops a we-feeling and a series of norms of conduct, it also evolves, in partial association with the teacher, techniques of social exclusion and social control which bring home to the deviant children the fact of their deviance and rejection. As this process gains momentum, some children may earn an adverse stereotype which survives many pathetic attempts to overcome it. Conversely, those who gain an initial advantage may retain it after they are objectively entitled to it, though this is less certain, because the majority of infants find it to their advantage to promote change in the leadership and to make 'room at the top', while they work to stabilise the tenancy of the rejected roles. Their informal social system promotes upward, but not downward, mobility.

Within it, by the end of their sixth year, children have usually developed some degree of self-picture (Staines, 1958) and a picture of others. Jane is a good girl; Peter is stupid; Sonia is pretty; Harry hits you; Billy is a clown (Mellor, 1950, p. 180); Mary is nice; and I —well Mrs. Smith says I never have my hair tidy.

So teachers and children alike develop their own view of the process of classification. It may even constitute a part of a larger social process, for the middle-class, flying-start children described previously may pick themselves out already in the infant school as claimants for places in the junior-school 'A' stream, the grammar school, and higher education. Like the professional contenders in an all-comers' mile race, they may move to the front almost immediately; and it requires more than a reorganisation of the formal structure to produce any other implementation of the classificatory role. It is hardly necessary to say that stereotyping is particularly liable to take place in this connection, or that it should be avoided strenuously.

The *welfare role* has no specific characteristics in infant schools, except that this is the stage when the majority of children and their parents first come to associate the school with social welfare. For example, school dinner may be the first occasion on which the children eat regularly away from home, and the School Medical and Dental Services may bring them into contact with preventive medicine for the first time. Beyond this, however, an infant school may become, like any other school, an unofficial advice bureau and even a spiritual power-house for an entire district.

The *autonomous role* of an infant school is more difficult to define. It is often associated in the parents' eyes with plays, parties and Open Days, but basically it depends on a 'tone' arising from the particular skills and devotion of the teachers, an 'atmosphere', to use the term mentioned in connection with socialisation. Thus, one year North Street Infants' has a memorable Carol Service; thereafter, North Street Infants' has a Carol Service every year, and it becomes not only a focus for a wide range of new and varied activities and interests for which the school is well known, but also a part of the Christmas tradition in the neighbourhood. Similarly, South Street has a reputation for the poise and courtesy of its children; and St. Peter's is just a happy school, though it is difficult to say exactly why, except that it has a wise Headmistress, two assistants who have been there long enough to have taught some of the children's mothers, and two pleasant young married women with fresh ideas and children of their own. Incidentally, St. Peter's has a simple uniform, just a badge with crossed keys which the children like to wear on their cap or beret, while South Street has never thought of any external symbol at all. In their different ways, each of these schools is carrying out its autonomous role, its obligation to be more than a mere reflection of the surrounding society, and is paving the way for the more ambitious autonomy which becomes possible at the junior and secondary levels. In this task, the schools can usually count on the firm if slightly uncomprehending support of the majority of parents.

A closer look at autonomy in infant schools reveals another feature. Despite the differences between them, one thing is common to all three of these schools, namely that somewhere in their curriculum they allow free play to the spontaneity and creativity of the children. Not every nativity play, or manifestation of good manners, implies this. On the contrary, it may be a symbol of starchy artificiality. Genuine 'autonomy', in the present sense, involves both an accepted and distinctive tradition, and the fostering of spontaneity within it. This spontaneity may be shown in art, or in craft, or in music, or in movement; but somewhere the children can be their best selves without constraint. Education, at every level and in all ideological settings, can and should endeavour to conserve this spontaneity, for it is childhood's unique gift to society.

The maintenance of *social cohesion and control* was considered in general terms in Chapter I, and reference has already been made to it in the discussion of socialisation and classification. But in addition, it is necessary in practice to establish certain specific mechanisms for the day-to-day conduct of the school's corporate life. These are the school's formal rules and routine. It is a commonplace of child psychology that infants love routine, and that it is beneficial to individual and group alike that a basic similarity of procedure should be followed each day. This, and notably the assembly and the start of the day[14] in each room, can be used both to stimulate the sense of belonging and to reinforce the socialising process. The simple principles of conduct that are established in this way serve also to range the school alongside the forces of social cohesion working in the larger society.

Where this is effectively done, the need for formal rules is minimised. They need apply only to matters of practical convenience which promote the efficient functioning of the school. For example, there may be rules about the use and drying of clothing, about walking in corridors, about opening doors, or about playing outdoors and especially on grass in bad weather. Such rules can be respected because they are simple, evidently sensible, and almost devoid of moral content. Sometimes one still finds more elaborate rules, almost Pharisaic in character, and of course even the most morally neutral of rules can be enforced in a moralistic way; but there is no need for anything more than simple, enforcible rules.

Education must be adjusted to mental age, for it must also be, like Bismarck's politics, an art of the possible.

At the infant-school level, little importance can be attached to the maintenance of social cohesion and control among the children as a process separate from the social ordering of the school itself. Since most of their informal relations are derived from the formal structure, they cannot be said to develop what Homans (1950) called an 'internal system' ancillary to the external work-relationship in which they find themselves. Their presence in the school is legally required; once there, they basically accept its organisation and sanctions and learn the pupil role itself with some eagerness. When, as individuals, they come into conflict with the school's established order, they react in various ways according to their individual psychology; but it is as individuals that they react, and not as groups opposed to the formal purposes of the school. Thus the maintenance of social cohesion and control is not a difficult matter, for everyone wants it to be that way, and this constitutes the essential prerequisite of an effective social organisation.

This also colours the *separate culture* of the school and its divisions. Here, too, routine and stability are characteristic, and form the basis on which the school's autonomous functions are erected. It is in fact by discharging its autonomous role that an infant school develops a separate culture. Within this general framework, however, particular classes may cement their own solidarity by developing pleasant but distinctive features such as a special kind of nature table, or an effective type of decoration, or even a private joke about the teacher's cat which can be repeated infinitely within the classroom but never outside. In such ways the children gain the experience of being on the inside of society. This has role-implications of its own. For the ascribed role, that of being in Mrs. Smith's class at Downland Road, is supplemented by a range of achieved roles as the weeks go by. In this way the socialising role of the school is promoted by the wise fostering of a separate culture in each class or vertical group, and the responsibilities of the teacher in this connection are evident.

The final element in this social analysis of infant schools is that of *social change*. Internal changes are always taking place here, as in other types of school. The relative smallness and homogeneity of an infant-school staff facilitates collective change, though there are obvious exceptions to this. As for the children, their relative immaturity exacerbates the impact of any social change, for they have not yet learned to distinguish persons from roles, or to dissociate themselves from the immediate framework of social supportiveness. So if a Headmistress retires, or there is a change of teacher, or even if the friend of the moment suddenly moves to a new housing estate, the impact can be temporarily shattering. On the other hand, this same immaturity enables them to recover rapidly from such upsets, provided that their home environment remains stable. Even if some new procedures are introduced into the actual work, a development which at first deeply offends their sense of propriety, the associated novelty eventually tends to triumph, and a new routine comes to be established in its turn.

External changes also make their impact, notably when they are due to large-scale movements of population. Even in the infant years, children are aware of the substantial impact of widely differing patterns of social behaviour. The advent of a large slum-clearance population may let loose a flood of boisterous high spirits expressed in a manner which may appear threatening to a small assembly of demure middle-class children already established in a school. Conversely, newcomers who display extensive material possessions previously unfamiliar in a community, or social customs character-istic of a recognisable immigrant population such as Irish or Jamaicans, may also make an initial impact of a disturbing kind. But if the teachers do not feel threatened (or immoderately gratified) at such developments, they can be made the occasion not for insecurity but for a piece of social education in which mutual understanding is fostered together with a general raising in standards of considerate behaviour. The plasticity of attitudes, and the ready acceptance of adult suggestion, which are characteristic of infants operate both to heighten the responsibilities of teachers in the face of social change, and to make their task in some respects easier.

Infant schools are genuine, though rudimentary, social institutions. Their autonomy, though important, is inevitably limited. More than schools for older children, they take on the protective colouring of their environments, whether they nestle in a leafy suburb, or face the gasworks across an empty croft, or brave the wind on the moors or the sea-coast. Almost universal as they are in the educational experience of the adult population, it is strange that they have been so comparatively isolated from the main currents of investigation in educational sociology. However important it undoubtedly is to study the physical and psychological development of young children, the sociological study of their educational environment is a separate and valid intellectual activity without which, indeed, the physical and psychological studies must remain incomplete. It is to be hoped that infant-school teachers, like nursery-school teachers, being uniquely well placed to undertake studies of this kind, will do so and will thereby not only provide invaluable information for others, but also reap an abiding satisfaction for themselves.

III

The Social Structure of
Junior Schools

SOMEWHERE between the ages of seven and eight, the majority of
England's children move into a junior school. Some stay a little
longer, some make no move before eleven, and a few wait in an
all-age school for all, or nearly all, of their remaining schooldays.
The actual figures derived from *Statistics of Education in 1962*,
Part I, Table 8, pp. 32–5, are as follows:

NUMBERS OF CHILDREN AGED 7–11 IN
MAINTAINED SCHOOLS, (ENGLAND AND WALES).
JANUARY, 1962

	Girls	Boys	Total
In junior-with-infants schools	526,240	540,686	1,066,926
In separate junior schools[1]	653,604	694,534	1,348,138
In all-age schools	45,278	47,978	93,256
Totals	1,225,122	1,283,198	2,508,320

Thus, as at the infant level, the separate junior schools outnumbered
the others slightly.

The separate junior school may be at a considerable geographical
distance from the corresponding infant school, or it may be so close
that it cannot be distinguished in practice from a combined school.
But whatever the nominal position may be, and whether the transfer
takes place at seven or (as it does for some 120,000 children) a year
or so later, there is invariably a change of educational climate when
the junior stage is reached. As indicated in the preceding chapter,
this has traditionally been one of the great divides in English
education, the door to 'the heart of childhood'.

It is also, in numerical terms, the door to the heart of English
education. There is much greater uniformity in education in junior
classes under the three different patterns of organisation than in the
three intentionally different types of secondary school. In January

57

1962, the combined number of children aged 7–11 in attendance at the three types of school—2,508,320—considerably exceeded the total number in secondary modern schools, which constitute the largest category of secondary schools, and indeed approached the total for all secondary schools. This total also greatly exceeded that for infants in all types of maintained school, so that junior education stands out as the most impressive common educational experience for the vast majority of English children. Moreover, 1962 was a year in which the child population in the age-cohorts 7–11 was relatively smaller than among infant or secondary pupils, so that the juniors' numerical importance would normally appear still greater, at least until the tendency to 'stay on' in secondary schools develops further or until the leaving age is raised to sixteen.

As in infant schools there is, of course, a further line of division between county schools and the various kinds of voluntary schools. Pupils in county schools considerably outnumber all the rest in junior and infant schools, but in all-age schools the position is reversed. Separate figures for infants and juniors are not given, though they are shown for Roman Catholics in *Catholic Education: A Handbook*, 1962–3, Table 6, p. 174. The Ministry statistics give the following picture: (*Statistics of Education in 1962*, Part I, Table 15, p. 46):

· SUMMARY OF DENOMINATIONAL STATUS OF PRIMARY-SCHOOL PUPILS
(ENGLAND AND WALES), 1ST JANUARY, 1962

Status of School	Numbers in Junior and Infant Schools	Numbers in All-Age Schools
County	2,884,215	51,355
Voluntary:		
Church of England	720,531	26,401
Roman Catholic	333,097	90,997
Others	21,270	1,712
Total Voluntary	1,074,898	119,110

(Fuller data are given in Volume II, Chapter V, p. 114).

There is slightly more likelihood that a single-sex school will be attended at the junior than at the infant stage, at least by those who are not in junior-with-infant schools, for 649 separate junior schools (353 boys', 296 girls') were single-sex as against 4,170 mixed: 13·5 per cent of the total (ibid., Table 7, pp. 30–1). As previously mentioned, 19 per cent of all-age schools were single-sex, but only 0·86 per cent of junior-with-infants schools, and 0·11 per cent of separate infant schools.

The transfer from infant to junior school or class is a step which involves both a new institutional pattern and a popular expectation that 'proper schooling' is now to begin. Some teachers, and some parents, and therefore some children, still tend to regard this transition as basically one from play to work, and for some the experience is painful, all the more so because its impact is not always fully appreciated.[2] This contrast is likely to be all the sharper when a junior school is organised and conducted in such a way as deliberately to emphasise its differences from an infant school. It is especially acute if a first-year class is taught by a teacher who has had little experience of infants and has scant sympathy with modern trends in infant education, but who is very conscious of the demands of the formal skills and of the virtues of orderly work-habits among eight-year-olds and assumes that modern methods are not conducive to their establishment. Occasionally, and regrettably, adjacent infant and junior schools come to symbolise contrasted approaches to primary education. In such circumstances it appears inevitable that the height of the hurdle between them which the seven-plus children have to leap will be increased. But irrespective of its height, it constitutes a change, which is sometimes symbolised by the designation of the first-year class as a 'transition class', the junior-school analogue of the reception class for infants.

Beginning from this, the junior school develops an institutional pattern of its own, which will be considered by means of the analytical scheme outlined in Chapter I and already used at the nursery and infant stages. However there is greater social complexity in junior schools than in the earlier primary years, and partly for this reason there is also a greater range of empirical information about them. Therefore the study of junior schools as social institutions will be spread over two chapters, the first being confined to the social structure of junior schools, their 'anatomy' as it were, and the second covering the more dynamic or 'physiological' aspects, which sociologists often describe as social process.

The first aspect of structure to be considered is that of *formal organisation*. Within this general topic, it is again possible to distinguish between the physical and social aspects. The former will be discussed first, since they set the stage for the development of formal organisation among the children themselves.

Since junior schools are generally larger than infant schools, and much larger than nursery schools, there is more scope for subdivision in their architecture. This is true whether they are experimental buildings which catch the imagination of an entire continent or, as is more often the case, when they are the remains of old Board Schools from which the seniors have been removed to a secondary modern school, and perhaps the infants also to a place of their own. Indeed, the existence of these two extremes itself conveys something of the story of junior education in England, for until very recently it has been the practice to assume that if anyone must make shift, it should be the juniors. Where there are older buildings, they often emphasise both the separation of classes by corridors and the focal significance of the school hall where assembly, meal, music and physical education all have to be held, thus at least emphasising that these are activities which bind the school together, but at worst conveying the impression that they must all be carried on in the same noisy, overcrowded spot, impinging on the quiet of as many other classes as possible. Some schools are too small or too old to allow of even this division of labour, and can only embrace all their activities within the same dim religious light. Others, built in the present century (about 60 per cent of the total—N.U.T., 1963, p. 38) permit easy access to asphalt and in some cases grass, and allow fresh air to come in readily: too readily in fact, if they were built during the inter-war years when there was a strong reaction against the earlier, more enclosed, patterns. These more modern schools also convey a greater sense of communication between rooms without causing too much acoustic interference. In the most recent phase,[3] this development has been carried still further through a more imaginative use of space, allowing more flexibility of organisation within and between classes, while there is also a striking and welcome concern that a junior school shall be a thing of beauty. The less fortunate result is that the contrast between these and the oldest schools becomes more poignant than ever.

The furniture and arrangements within classrooms is also an important feature of the formal structure. The most marked development has been the decline of the desk-and-aisle pattern in favour of lighter equipment and greater flexibility. In this, the junior school is the disciple of the infant school. Where possible, tables in some schools are now arranged in various ways according to the needs of the work, or stacked away altogether in order to make full use of the floor-space. Here again, there are contrasts between old and new, for the backlog of heavy furniture is considerable and it is frequently necessary to overcome this by moving the children, who are more adaptable than their desks and can overcome formidable difficulties by their ability to turn and squat and close up. However, they are less encouraged to do so than in modern classrooms, especially since some at least of the schools which have to endure the oldest premises and equipment are favoured with some of the largest classes. Thus the physical setting of a school, even when mitigated by the devotion of teachers and the energetic if belated generosity of local education authorities, is bound to exercise some influence on the working of a school. It is probable that this differential influence is reinforced just because the oldest and least well-equipped schools are often also in the drabbest and least aesthetically inspiring districts, or (ironically) in areas where children have been re-housed in modern flats which still lack the one amenity—adequate play-space—which these old schools are least well equipped to supplement.

Meanwhile, as with infants, the physical structure of the schools may also have particular significance for individual children, and for the development of informal social relations in the community as a whole, as will be mentioned subsequently. The more sequestered corners and spaces form a possible retreat for minorities: collectively, they can be designated *minority spaces*. Some schools have more of these than others.

The second aspect of the formal structure concerns *social organisation*. At the junior stage, this usually becomes overtly functional. In the majority of cases, subdivision takes place primarily in terms of age, and then according to assumed ability. Except where numbers are few, classification by age is almost universal: family grouping on the vertical pattern is rare. Annual promotion is also almost universal, in contrast to the quite prevalent half-yearly transition practised in infant schools. Few voices are raised in protest against this pattern, and the children tend to welcome the recognition given to their age-status. On the other hand, ability-grouping has become one of the principal areas of contention in junior schools, and has recently been the subject of considerable research.

The motive for this was probably the suspicion that junior-school streaming involved three half-concealed social processes. In the first, middle-class seven-year-old children might by their comparative verbal precocity and their eager espousal of the good-pupil role earn themselves a disproportionate share of places in the 'A' stream, especially if allocation to streams were carried out by teachers of middle-class origins or outlook. In the second process, the 'A' stream children would tend to regard themselves and to be regarded by others, as the 'bright' children, who would thus set each other a quicker pace and would receive a more stimulating type of teaching than the rest, thereby widening the gulf between streams and effectively minimising the possibility of transfer between them even when this is nominally encouraged. In the third, most obvious, process these 'A' stream children would enjoy a disproportionately high chance of selective secondary education. The raising of these essentially social questions shows how sociological considerations are necessarily involved in the very basis of a junior school's formal structure.

The first major investigation into this problem was by Daniels (1961a, b). He showed that primary-school teachers, even those following courses of advanced study, assumed for the most part that junior-school entrants should be grouped according to some blend of ability and attainment and that such grouping was beneficial both to the brighter children, who needed every chance to ensure their success in secondary-school selection, and to the least able, who could be taught in small relatively homogeneous classes by appropriate remedial methods. He also pointed out that most teachers favoured transfer between streams but assumed that it was more prevalent than is in fact the case. In his second article, Daniels compared children's educational progress in four junior schools, two, of which were, on educational grounds, in favour of streaming and two against. As far as possible—and that may not be very far— the child population and educational experience were equated between the two patterns of organisation. Within the rather narrow limits of this study it appeared that the attainments *and intelligence-test scores* of the children in the unstreamed schools underwent greater improvement, especially among the initially less able children, than those in the streamed schools. Thus the relation of the formal structure to the instructional as well as to the classificatory function of the school must be considered important.

More recently Jackson (1961)* has presented some ancillary information about teachers' opinions on junior-school streaming. His informants were few but presumably representative, and his results run generally parallel to those quoted by Daniels. He also probed into his subjects' views about the distribution of ideas on streaming and found some tendency for them to think that streaming was favoured by the middle class, by supporters of grammar schools, and by the majority of practising teachers, but opposed by the working class, by educational theorists and by the Labour Left. It was also apparently believed that non-streaming would result in social gains but academic losses. (Daniels's study, within its limits, argues against this last point.) More unusually, Jackson suggests a possible nexus between age- and ability-classification, because the youngest children within an age-group, who had had less duration of infant schooling (Ross, 1960, pp. 61–2 and 147), tended to be placed in the 'C' stream, and the oldest in the 'A' stream. Finally, Jackson hinted that those teachers who were in favour of streaming were more likely to be articulate and to set the norms in schools, as well as being 'elitist' rather than 'egalitarian' in social beliefs. This observation was based on impression rather than specific study, though there is no *prima facie* reason to regard it as unrepresentative.

A more extensive, and rather more weighty, piece of evidence about the effects of streaming in junior schools is to be found in the study of a nation-wide sample of children at the junior level described by Douglas (1964). He corroborates (Ch. XIV) much that Daniels

* Since this book was written, the interesting and important results of Jackson's further survey have been published. They should be read in conjunction with the following pages. *See* Jackson, B. (1964): *Streaming: an education system in miniature.* London: Routledge and Kegan Paul.

and others have previously enunciated. For example he points out (p. 113) that only 2·3 per cent of children per year were moved from stream to stream, and (p. 114) that between the ages of eight and eleven.

> At each level of ability the children in the upper streams improve their scores while the others deteriorate.

In addition he shows (p. 115) that when ability was held constant in his analysis, there was a tendency for middle-class children to be allocated more readily than working-class children to the upper streams and (p. 117) for working-class children in the lower streams to deteriorate severely in performance. Like Daniels and Jackson, Douglas found (p. 118) that the teachers themselves were generally in favour of streaming as a means of formal organisation. This evidence, drawn from a very much larger population than in Daniels' study, must be regarded as authoritative, though it is deficient in one important respect, namely that it refers only to schools with two streams, not more.

None of these studies makes direct reference to the social consequences of streaming, which are much more difficult to assess. It is often claimed that it causes unhealthy segregation, and that non-streaming has social-ethical advantages because it obliges the abler and more advanced children to share their expertise with others in pursuit of a corporate goal instead of husbanding it for the sake of individual prowess and advancement. One of the few specific studies of this aspect of streaming is reported by Willig (1963). Within the limits of a fairly small-scale study in London he found evidence in support of a general social advantage in unstreamed schools:

> Considered as a whole, the evidence emphasises the social advantages of mixed ability grouping over streaming by academic attainment. It was established that there was a tendency, in some cases a strong tendency, for children in unstreamed classes to be superior in social adjustment as defined by Stott's Scale, and superior in social attitudes to children in streamed classes. This may well be the result of a classification procedure which allows pupils of all ability and social class levels to become acquainted with children of superior intelligence and socio-economic status who normally set and maintain generally accepted social standards (p. 153).

However, he also indicated that for some children, for example middle-class boys (p. 154), unstreaming might lead to greater anxiety, and that some schools might find a streamed organisation more appropriate. The implication of *bourgeoisie oblige* in the quotation is of course important and will be further considered in Chapter IV.

In general, streaming remains an open question, with an increasing weight of countervailing articulate opinion opposed to the existing practice. Appeals to its efficacy may elicit the comment that this efficacy is itself the outcome of a self-fulfilling process (Douglas, 1964, p. 115). On the other hand, there is some danger that the opposition to streaming may develop into a political touchstone and may result in undue concentration on this one aspect of the sociology of primary education.

It is worth while at this point to consider briefly what other patterns of formal organisation could be developed in place of streaming. Daniels (1961b) examines some of these. One is age: an intake could be divided according to birthday. But according to Jackson this might develop into a covert form of streaming, unless the pattern of infant education was altered. Friendship might also be considered, but this might again lead to separation along ability and social-class lines. In any case, as will be seen when the informal structure is discussed, friendship is too subtle and fluid a matter to be made the basis of formal organisation. Sociologists would not be surprised at this, for it would involve the subordination of the formal to the informal organisation of an institution. Even when, as sometimes in industry or in military organisations, informal relations are taken into account, they are not given primacy; and that would be particularly inappropriate in the Midlands years when inter-personal relations, though intensely important to the children, are necessarily distinct from the adult-ordered world. A geographical classification would also be unsuitable, for it would accentuate the social differences within a school's catchment area and would thus again result in implicit streaming. So would classification by personality-type which Daniels (1961a, p. 73) mentions as a half-serious possibility, in addition to which this would seriously limit the value of interaction among 'all types', which is claimed as a virtue of non-streaming.

The use of half-yearly promotion, or termly promotion, would be a bold solution but it is highly doubtful whether it would be advantageous for children to pass through the social units presided over by eight or even twelve teachers during their junior-school course. The fact that this may happen anyhow through rapid turnover of staff cannot justify its official adoption. It has been found, too, that 'setting' for different subjects, though valuable at the secondary stage, also involves too much instability and change of teachers for juniors, while its academic advantages at this level are doubtful: so that, too, is unsuitable as a method of organisation.

So it appears that nothing can effectively replace streaming except a random allocation of children, or else a deliberate equalisation of classes in terms of measured ability or (better) of attainment in the most basic of skills, reading. Even this would not ensure complete equality, and if it did, the differences between teachers would soon bring it to an end. In any case, some teachers might, as

Vernon (1957, p. 44) suggests, introduce rigid grouping within their class; an internal streaming, in fact, sometimes indicated by a remark such as 'The children over there are all "C"s really'. For any individual school, it is necessary to consider the various consequences which appear likely in view of the evidence.[4] There may be complete streaming, or complete non-streaming, or a compromise of the type suggested by Ross (1960, pp. 64–5) and Vernon (1957, p. 48) whereby streaming should begin, with modifications, at the age of nine. Exceptional circumstances, such as the presence of a large number of non-English-speaking children or of backward children, may in any case require exceptional measures. No solution will be perfect; the choice of policy in any particular instance will indicate what a school regards as important, and what its teachers are prepared to do. For most schools where numbers require sub-division, random or 'equated' allocation may bring the best balance of advantage.

The mention of backward children and their needs calls for a further comment on existing practices. In line with the teachers' opinions assessed by Daniels, in a streamed organisation the 'C' stream is often kept deliberately small and given special attention of remedial nature. In addition, some schools have special teaching groups for children with specific or general retardation, and occasionally also for children with other handicaps for whom places cannot be found in special schools, or for whom it is considered possible and desirable that they should be retained within junior schools to share in the common life. This feature of formal structure cannot be regarded as 'exceptional', in the way that inability to speak English, or a high concentration of backward children, is exceptional. Nevertheless it represents an aspect of junior-school work which requires a definite place in any unstreamed organisation, probably through the withdrawal of some children for some of the time, their degree of separateness being kept to a minimum. For this purpose, incidentally, part-time teachers including retired teachers can be invaluable if administrative provisions make it possible for them to come in. Unless these relatively handicapped children are withdrawn sometimes, however, both the minority and the majority may suffer, the former through the overlooking of their special needs, and the majority through the possible depression in the general standard of achievement, especially where a teacher lacks skill in the appropriate organisation of individual and group work.

So much attention has been paid in recent years to this question of streaming that the remaining aspects of formal organisation in junior schools have been comparatively neglected. However, it is also important to consider the distribution of positions of individual prestige and status; indeed, these may help to reinforce or to counteract the effects of streaming. There are some of these positions in most

65

classrooms: individuals responsible for particular functions such as filling inkwells, fetching milk or carrying registers. There are others in schools as a whole, exercised particularly by the ten-year-olds. Also, in schools which place great emphasis on semi-formal activities such as games, the captains and members of schools teams may carry considerable formal status. A sociological consideration of these positions involves both an enquiry into their significance and an examination of the personnel which occupy them.

It is noteworthy that these are usually the first social positions in which children develop achieved rather than ascribed status. A boy is football captain ostensibly because he is a good footballer and can lead his team, and not because his father is a well-known local figure. In English schools this is taken for granted. Indeed, many teachers would consider it impertinent to enquire whether ascriptive influences were at work, and it seems to me that in most cases they are not.

However, it does happen that the children who are prominent in the semi-formal positions such as a school team differ slightly from those who are the leaders in formal attainment or in formal organisation. Games can represent an alternative value-system, approved by the school and yet not identified with its central purposes. So some children who are quite content to remain inconspicuous or even antagonistic in the parts of the status-system which depend on standards of formal achievement or approved conduct are nevertheless prepared to represent their school enthusiastically on the games field. Perhaps this is the beginning of the value-divergence studied by Coleman in its extreme form in the American high school (Coleman, 1961). It is possible that those junior-school teachers who spend a considerable amount of time and effort in the coaching of teams do not always realise the social consequences which their activities may entail for the formal organisation of their schools.

This raises the general question of the significance of status-positions in a school. The children are socially aware enough to realise that they are an index of the relative importance attached to different types of activity. For example, the relative numbers of prefects, team members, librarians and choir convey a clearly-understood meaning. In addition to their relative importance towards each other, these status-positions have a collective significance because they indicate the amount of genuine responsibility which the Head Teacher and staff consider appropriate to delegate to the children. Its extent depends both on the cognitive powers and on the social-emotional maturity of the children, as well as on the social attitudes of the staff. Piaget's studies would suggest that even the ablest junior-school children think in terms of particular situations and procedures rather than of general principles. They understand the necessity for simple rules such as 'no playing outside on wet days', and also the significance of *meum* and *tuum*, so that they realise that personal possessions are not to be treated as communal property. They are also capable of developing a devotion to the well-being and appearance of the school itself which can be quite moving. But they cannot understand the issues involved in a general concept of justice, or the situational factors which may extenuate the conduct of individuals (other than themselves) in particular circumstances. They tend to see conduct in terms of black and white, and to judge their peers on that basis with more zeal than compassion. Moreover, they are prone to allow the general stereotypes acquired by their classmates to colour their interpretation of particular incidents, so that Jennifer, who is 'nice', may be excused minor aberrations that would be seized upon as typical and blameworthy if committed by Albert, who is 'daft'. More will be said about stereotyping in the consideration of classification in Chapter IV, but it must be mentioned here as one of the reasons why formal status-positions should be confined to clearly-defined and circumscribed functions.

These may comprise a whole range of specific positions such as librarians, monitors of various kinds, canteen servers, and bringers-of-cups-of-tea-to-members-of-staff-on-duty, and also prefects with limited powers. In addition they may include the captains and members of teams, provided that their prestige is kept within bounds, for the very fact that games are organised according to rules which children respect itself guarantees that the powers of these status-holders will also be limited by customary agreement. There may be a place for one school captain, or in a mixed school two, who can achieve a personal relationship with the staff and particularly with the Head Teacher, rather like the eldest child in a large family who identifies himself with the adults as well as with the children in the community. It is quite usual in a junior school to find a mature-looking boy carrying keys as though he were the caretaker, or a poised girl coming in to discuss some point of procedure with the Head.

The actual choice of these status-holders throws an interesting light on the school and its values. There are disadvantages both in autocratic appointments by adults, and in popular election which is open to demagogy especially because the children are too young to distinguish the particular attributes required for the discharge of specific functions. In one junior school I found (Blyth, 1958) that the results of a sociometric survey (p. 73 below) made it possible to choose prefects with reference to the informal social structure of the school and thus to make realistic choices without resorting either to open voting or to unfettered staff selection. Moreover, a subsequent appraisal of their performance substantiated the validity of this method of choice.

Less sophisticated methods may be adequate for the selection of children for more specific tasks than that of prefect. This is especially true of tasks within one classroom, such as looking after the nature table, or games positions which must be to some extent the prerogative of the teachers responsible for training the teams, and thus qualified by superior acquaintance and expertise to make the selection. In practice, there are variations from school to school and from situation to situation. Some children plead 'Please, *you* decide'. Others resent any decisions by teachers who have forfeited their confidence; but on the whole there is general agreement that the staff must play some part in the final decisions. It is more important, in a junior school, to develop self-confidence in children, and the capacity to co-operate in specific situations, than to injure their development as democratic citizens by premature imposition of responsibility. 'After all,' say teachers, 'they're only juniors': and it is true.

A description of the formal structure of a junior school would be incomplete without some reference to its relation to the social background of the children. In two respects this has already been mentioned, once negatively when it was pointed out that background influences rarely affect the choice of status-holders in schools, and once positively, in connection with Douglas's comments on the relation between social class and streaming. In combination, these two observations probably give a fairly accurate picture, for it is likely that social background plays a greater part in classification than in the distribution of status. From my own researches in junior schools I should infer that there is a fairly steady relationship between stream and social class, the phi-correlation between the two being about 0·5 when there are two streams, and between 0·6 and 0·7 when there are more and thus a greater opportunity for subdivision. It is not, of course, surprising that social background should be more influential in classification because that depends basically on estimated abilities which are in practice related to social class, whereas the duties of status-holders are less obviously dependent on measured ability or attainment.

When these correlations are considered, it should of course be borne in mind that they are global, uncorrected for any intervening variable. One of the significant points already quoted from Douglas's study (p. 63 above) is that there is often a tendency for middle-class children to be allocated to upper streams even when equally able working-class children are placed in lower streams. In other words, in addition to relatively high overall correlation between social class and stream, there is an important low partial correlation when ability is held constant. Thus there is some evidence that social class operates as an independent factor in the formal organisation, but only in particular ways. (Its relation to social processes in junior schools will be considered in Chapter IV). As for other background factors, in the course of my own investigations it became apparent that habitat might exercise a distinctive influence on the formal organisation of schools, and one could expect that broad ecological differences such as that between town and country, or between one village or hamlet and the next, might also be important. Some current researches are directed towards the exploration of questions such as these, but at present the only definitive information at the junior-school level is on rather too small a scale to warrant any generalisation.

One other aspect of formal structure is sometimes found in junior schools or in parts of them. This is a house or team system. It bears some resemblance to similar features in secondary schools, but little is known about its effectiveness. Since it appears to be introduced principally in order to provide additional incentives, it will be mentioned again in Chapter IV in the discussion of rewards and punishments.

In junior schools, unlike infant and nursery schools, there is some place for *semi-formal organisations*. The importance of school teams has already been mentioned in relation to the impact of games on the formal structure. It is perhaps worth adding that they may easily develop into a privileged élite. For a long time, boys' football and cricket have shown this propensity, and now girls' netball and rounders are sometimes in a similar position. Moreover, this redress of the sex-balance may result in a reduction in opportunities for physical education for the rest of the girls, just as it has often done for the rest of the boys. There is certainly something delightful about the enthusiasm, camaraderie and physical poise of these teams, which show both girls and boys at their best, even when they come from the most unpromising surroundings. Swimming teams have much the same social function. All of these can help to stimulate respect for vigour and grace of physical movement throughout the school, thereby perhaps introducing a Greek ideal into English towns whose Hellenism is often confined to the façade of the Town Hall. But it is important to remember that this emphasis in the semi-formal organisation, however beneficial it may be in some ways as a part of the process of socialisation, is always prone to have unforeseen repercussions on the formal and informal social systems too.

Some schools also find a place for other semi-formal activities such as model railway building, stamp collecting, chess, bird watching, and even quite ambitious youth hostelling. These give the lie to the suggestion that such activities are beyond the capacities and interests of children under eleven. They tend, like the teams, to draw their membership mainly but not entirely from the older children, and they depend for their success both on the enthusiasm of the staff and, less essentially, on the cultural traditions of the district. Chess, for example, is more likely to flourish when there are some fathers who are actively interested. A choir has a particularly good chance of succeeding in an area such as County Durham. A club requiring technical skills is likely to make a good start in a district with a high proportion of skilled workers. But there is very little direct evidence on these points.

Informal relations among junior school children have been rather more adequately studied, partly because of the opportunities made available through the development of appropriate theoretical approaches and techniques of investigation. The theoretical basis for the elaboration and crystallisation of informal relationships in middle childhood is clearly enunciated by Moreno (1953) and Fau (1952). They both see the junior-school years as a time when the focus of children's social life is to be found in the school itself. Whereas infants have first to learn how to adjust themselves to the secondary-group situation in schools, juniors use this now-familiar environment for further social experimentation, first under the aegis of the teacher but later to some extent in opposition to the teacher. At the same time the social integration of the classroom group (to use the customary, if slightly pretentious, terminology) becomes more complete, as individuals and pairs or trios of friends are drawn more closely into the general structure of the class as a whole. The class group figures as a gang, in the sense in which that term is used in the present volume, and at this age, more than before or after, friendship tends to merge into gangship and the class-as-a-whole becomes the focus of allegiance. Of course, this general theoretical picture allows of much modification in view of the influence of other sociological factors, so that individual cases are likely to diverge from the simple pattern on theoretical grounds, while in practice the situation may be still more complex. However, it remains a useful guiding hypothesis.

The investigation of particular instances depends also on the use of appropriate techniques, notably *sociometry*,[6] of whose applicability to junior schools I have had some experience. It comes into its own at this stage because children over seven, and especially those over nine, are more capable of verbalising and conceptualising their social relationships than infants are, and also because the relationships themselves are more stable and therefore more open to systematic study. Basically, sociometry is a method of detecting the choices which children (or adults) make when selecting associates for real or imaginary activities. For example, children may be asked to indicate who, in their class, they would most like to have as a partner during the physical education lesson, or to sit with at dinner-time. From simple data of this kind it is possible and legitimate (Blyth, 1961, Ch. 9) to build up a valid picture of the informal social structure of a junior school. The best general accounts of sociometric methods are by Gronlund (1959) in the U.S.A. and by

Evans (1962; 1963–4) in the United Kingdom. Northway and Weld (1957) have written a useful handbook for beginners. In a survey prepared a few years ago (Blyth, 1960) I indicated the extent of sociometric studies in English schools, including junior schools, up to that time.

In combination with other research methods, sociometry makes it possible to amplify and extend the theoretical picture of informal social relations in junior schools which has already been sketched. At the age of seven, the detailed patterns of social relationships still tend to be rather shapeless and unstable, as they are among infants, though there is sometimes evidence of the beginnings of something more structured. The two sexes are also noticeably beginning to concentrate their choices within their own ranks. One year later, when they are between eight and nine, this tendency has already become marked, and thereafter it continues to intensify. At the same time, though less invariably, there develops especially among the boys a more closely articulated structure so that they almost all focus their choices on one outstanding leader and his trusted henchmen. When this happens, there is usually a close relationship with the formal and semi-formal structure, since the same few stalwarts are to be found in the school teams, in the upper ranges of ability and attainment, and participating centrally and with a jolly and confident bearing in whatever is going on. This interplay between the different social systems helps to maintain social equilibrium. Meanwhile, as Dahlke (1958, p. 359) found, the less prominent boys tend to arrange themselves round the edge of the leading group in a series of pairs and trios. Among the girls this concentration of leadership and popularity on a few individuals is not always so marked. Sometimes there is a bunching of girls in the social centre, but the marginal girls are more likely to dissent from the dominant pattern and to form a minority or 'opposition' element of their own. Here, and among the majority, the persistence of close-knit pairs and trios is more marked than among boys, so that the whole-class gang is less in evidence on the distaff side of the social pattern. Thus the most usual situation is that at the end of the junior-school years a marked focal group of boys, and a less marked group of girls, hold the centre of the social stage, while minorities, especially of girls, occupy the periphery. Incidentally, it is often these minorities who, mingling with their counterparts from other classes and perhaps from the same habitats, occupy the 'minority spaces' in the school premises (see p. 61 above).

Another feature of the informal structure which is often noticeable is the degree of persistence shown over a period of time by the children's patterns of choice, at least of their 'special friends', and also by their general choice-status in the class. Children who reach the highest levels of popularity rarely lose their position entirely. I have several times followed a girl or boy 'star' through one year or more without their once slipping down from the highest rank-positions, and one memorable little girl, who was undisputed queen of her half of the class at the age of seven, actually held her throne of popularity throughout the whole of her junior-school life. This tendency is accompanied by a quite disproportionate concentration of choices on a few individuals, a tendency which Moreno (1953) termed 'sociodynamic effect', and it is difficult to resist the impression that very popular children acquire a favourable stereotype which sustains them year after year. Shaw (1954) indicates that at the age of ten or eleven such children are gay, outgoing and well-adjusted, a finding which has many parallels in the U.S.A. This applies irrespective of sex, though apparently the ideal girl is a little quieter than the ideal boy at this stage. Both sexes, incidentally, seem to like their leaders to be good-looking.

It may even be that popularity itself evokes the very traits which lead to popularity, so that the children who start well experience the working of a virtuous circle. Their initial social success must tend to smooth their path and act as a signal that the traits which they manifest should be developed. Moreover, since cheerful gaiety is itself approved, the very fact that school and its peer contacts is so rewarding to the already popular children renders them likely to gain further popularity. On the other hand the least popular children, the 'isolates' and 'neglectees' of the sociometric literature, are, fortunately for them, not certain to retain their lowly status. Some do: for them, school must be a wearisome agony, unless they withdraw psychologically from the conflict situation altogether and invest their hopes in their habitat. But for most, sometimes on the basis of a shared interest, or just through the passage of time, there comes a stage at which, perhaps through the judicious help of a watchful teacher, they are accepted by somebody and then gradually become absorbed in the class social system, though they are unlikely to rise to the heights. Meanwhile, in the middle ranges of popularity there is considerably greater fluctuation of status. Occasionally, perhaps through moving to a distant address or through committing some unusually serious breach of the class norms, a child may suffer catastrophic loss of status. When this happens, it must be a very painful experience for a child to become gradually aware of this estrangement: but it is not a common one.

These general patterns are subject to modification in every individual school context. In order to indicate the possible nature of this modification, some specific examples of empirical studies will be mentioned. They include instances both of the impact on informal relations of the formal structure and social processes within the school, and of the effects of external factors.

As regards the impact of social processes Wilkie (1955—see

Evans, 1962, p. 77) indicated that social integration within upper junior classes was improved when group work was introduced into some aspects of the curriculum and children were allowed to work with others of their own choice. Connor (1960) suggested that junior classes (in New Zealand) with a genial teacher-pupil climate were likely to have fewer 'isolates' but also fewer 'stars' than other classes where teacher-pupil relations were more strained, as though the presence of tension within the classroom induced the children to develop the social equivalent of a siege economy within their informal system. Other studies, published and unpublished, some at least of them conducted in English schools, support Wilkie's and Connor's contentions and suggest that the teacher's behaviour is an important formative influence on informal relations among children in school not only between seven and nine, but also up to the age of eleven and beyond.

Willig (1963), in the study already quoted, showed how the formal structure of the school may itself affect informal relations. Though he based his observations on very small numbers, he indicated (p. 152) that in the more open situation afforded by non-streamed organisation there may be a tendency for socio-economic influences to affect children's choices, though he was careful to point out that there were marked exceptions to this tendency. Where it did appear, it was noticeable in two ways, first, that children in the lowest socio-economic strata tended to be underchosen, and second, that

> When the social class range was wide and numbers of subjects falling into extreme social grade categories were approximately equal, a tendency was noted for children to choose those of similar socio-economic status to themselves . . .

I have personally observed both of these tendencies several times among older junior and younger secondary pupils.

Willig's results raise the question of the second type of social influence which may modify the informal structure, namely those outside the school. The first instance of such influences is drawn from a study of my own in an average upper-working-class district, in the school already mentioned when discussing the appointment of prefects. Here, there was some evidence of trends which may be at work elsewhere. For example in one fourth-year 'A' stream it appeared that, after the eleven-plus examination results had been published, some of the girls allocated to selective secondary schools formed a group of their own; but this tendency had no parallel in other similar classes. In the corresponding 'B' stream the girls' pattern showed one of the distinctive minorities already mentioned, and in this case it was clear that the girls who composed it came from an ecologically-distinct area, were more mature than the others, and abstained from participating in the school's main value area

73

though they did support netball, a prominent feature of the alternative approved value-system of athletics. Unlike the 'A' stream grouping, this 'B' pattern did reproduce itself in a subsequent class, where it was evident that their values differed from those of the rest.

The boys showed less subdivision, as would be expected in view of the general developmental pattern already outlined, but with one marked exception. The nine-year-old 'B' class in one year showed a deep and persistent cleavage among the boys, which lasted throughout the remaining two years of their junior-school life. This cleavage separated from the rest a minority of boys who were significantly less intelligent (as far as measured intelligence indicates this), had significantly fewer friends outside school, mostly lived on one part of a Corporation estate, and appeared also to attend a particular church and its youth organisations. In socio-economic status, however, they were not distinguishable from their classmates. The most interesting thing about this cleavage was that the minority boys were well aware of their own solidarity, which they expressed by an interchange of gifts almost on a ritual basis and perhaps by colonising minority spaces in the school (though I was not in a position to observe this) while the majority appeared genuinely oblivious of the existence of the cleavage, as were the teachers. The whole phenomenon appeared so interesting that I discussed it in detail in the latter part of an article about the school (Blyth, 1958).

Although this cleavage appears to be a rare phenomenon at the junior-school level, it indicates two important points. First, it shows which factors may discriminate among children even in a district which appears socially homogeneous at least in socio-economic terms. In addition it suggests that the more social features which a minority shares but which a majority lacks, the more distinctive the minority will become. This overlap or *aggregation* of factors can be very important at the primary stage (and even more so at the secondary stage) and can powerfully amend the normal developmental pattern in the informal structure of a school. In the same piece of investigation I was able to identify slight traces of aggregation elsewhere, notably among the girls. In general it appears more typical of girls than of boys. If Susan and Jacqueline both live in Gallipoli Crescent, run in and out of each other's gardens, go to the Methodist Church on the corner and belong to its Sunday School and Brownies, then they will be thrown together so much in the children's world and their life-spaces will overlap so considerably that they will also tend to walk to and from school together (they go the same way anyhow) and may well become inseparable in school too. In that case they may both be monitors, or members of the netball team, thus reinforcing their solidarity by prestige-bearing activities associated with the good-pupil role, and perhaps joining with two other girls who do the same. The fact that Susan's father is a welder and Jacqueline's works in a bank makes no difference, unless some adult impresses it upon them. However, they are less likely to form such a close link with Lynn, whose father is a fitter but who lives half a mile away in a terraced house in Mafeking Street and who has to play either in the 'rec' or in the street. As will be shown in Volume II, Chapter III, the children's world is largely a world of ecological, local ties, and these spill over also into the school, sometimes for boys but more especially for girls.

In fact, as I found through subsequent research (Blyth 1959; 1961), there is evidence that children's neighbourhood peer-groups themselves influence informal relations within school, and project value-systems into the school situation which, as will be seen in Chapter IV, influence the norms which are established in its various classes. Thus, in addition to the twos and threes of children with high aggregation who are virtually inseparable (apart from temporary tiffs and permanent moves of residence) there may be larger groups or even gangs from particular areas, almost all of whose members bring particular values and social patterns to school with them. At the school already mentioned, one such group of girls maintained its cohesion and characteristics throughout the three years during which I was associated with the school. Its focus appeared to be a little park with a recreation ground to which its members may well have been first brought by their older sisters and friends to experience the initial widening of their world. On one side of the park was a group of streets consisting entirely of substantial terraced houses with a fairly stable population: across the park was another group of well-maintained terraced streets which stood out from the Corporation housing beyond. The girls in this group were almost all neat, steady and reliable, hard workers in school and enthusiastic members of teams, thus supporting both the main and the alternative value-system of the school. When the homes of the pupils successful in gaining selective secondary-school places were plotted on a map, it was clear that the girls were drawn disproportionately from the area where this group lived, and indeed it was fairly evident that they encouraged one another much as middle-class children are expected to do, though most of them were skilled workers' daughters. (However, as will be noted in Chapter VI, they did not always maintain their impetus inside the secondary schools.) Here and there, traces of similar reputations could be found in other parts of the school's district, while on the Corporation estate one or two roads earned an opposite notoriety especially for the boys. Teachers in junior schools often give vent to comments about the characteristics of children from different parts of their 'catchment areas': here is some evidence that their impressions are in part substantiated.[6]

Another junior school which I studied sociometrically, in a district with rather more middle-class owner-occupied housing, affords some further relevant data about the development of informal social structure. In the 'A' stream (there were three streams in all) it was clear that high, rather than outstandingly high, academic ability carried prestige. In the 'B' stream, and to some extent in the 'A' stream too, the few girls who had been promoted from lower streams clung closely together as if overawed by their new status, as happens quite frequently in secondary schools, though in this particular school this effect of the formal structure may have been reinforced by differences in socio-economic status between the promoted groups and the other girls (in one case they were of superior, and in the other case of inferior status). Finally, in the district as a whole it was clear that the same ecological influences were at work as in the other school, especially again in the case of the girls, and in particular of some girls mainly from professional families and living in a part of the middle-class housing area, whose energetic espousal of the good-pupil role and prominence within the girls' part of the informal system lasted within an 'A' stream throughout their junior-school life.

Another external factor, and one which causes more excitement when it is mentioned, is that of colour. I have had some opportunity of examining its influence within junior schools and find, like Silberman and Spice (1950) that when the numbers of coloured children are small, they accept the native white children and are accepted by them unless, as does sometimes happen, they are among the dirtier and less intelligent children who, white and coloured alike, tend to under-chosen. However, the general literature on race relations suggests that the situation may be different when there are many coloured children, while in any case the problem enters a new phase when secondary education begins.

A more specific cause of cleavage in the informal structure of junior schools may arise when, as in the case of some Asiatic children, they do not or cannot speak English. Difference in speech then powerfully reinforces difference in colour. In such cases it may be necessary for the formal structure itself to be adapted to allow for remedial teaching, as already indicated (p. 65 above). Even then, cultural pressures may continue to prevent the full absorption of the minority children in the informal structure.

The problem of the low-intelligence children deserves particular mention because, as in Willig's study, they so often stand out (or rather hold back) in a class, perhaps because they are less able than the rest to appreciate and pursue the common interests and objectives of the class, and also perhaps because the others find them on that account less interesting persons. Where, as in some schools in the slums, these children are disproportionately numerous, and also less well cared for than they might be in a more delectable environment, they may through aggregation of negative characteristics form recognisable minorities, though there is little specific evidence of this.

Informal structure in rural areas has received less attention from investigators. Therefore I am indebted to two advanced students of the Department of Education in the University of Manchester, H. Stockton and C. F. Smith, for allowing me to refer to their recent investigations. Stockton's study is in an overspill area to which most of the existing population has moved during recent years, so that this particular instance is that of an urban outlier in a rural area rather than a basically rural community. Within this interesting and increasingly frequent social situation he has been able to demonstrate that neighbourhood groups form just as they do in cities, and that they conform noticeably to particular ecological divisions of the area which to some extent reflect physical boundaries such as main roads. He has also been able to show how these neighbourhood groups project their stability and their values into the school situation. In addition he has found some evidence in support of an hypothesis which, if widely upheld, will add significantly to the general picture of neighbourhood-group influence on schools. This hypothesis will be outlined after discussion of the other specific pieces of field work.

The second example is drawn from a genuinely rural area, in South Shropshire. Despite the absence of comparable studies in England, there is some basis for comparison in the work of Hetzer and Morgenstern (1952) in Bavaria which indicates that in very small rural all-age schools the children have such a limited choice of companions that subdivision even on an age-basis is limited, though sex-divisions remain fairly complete. Smith's study is not strictly comparable to the Bavarian results because all of his small rural schools are separate primary schools, but he has found many situations similar to Hetzer and Morgenstern's, though the sex-cleavage appears less marked in very small Shropshire schools than in the Bavarian instances. One larger, two-stream school in a small town is included in the same study, and it is interesting to note that here the patterns usually found in city and large-town schools begin to emerge.

In reviewing studies of the impact of the external social situation on informal relations among children, a mention must be made of Castle's (1954) study of girls from a children's institution in a girls' junior school. Although her analysis was not strictly sociometric, it showed something of the way in which these institution girls fitted into the school. They formed a rather hesitant minority in the 'A' stream but a majority in the 'B' stream where they set the predominant tone, with the result that in both streams there were cleavages and tensions. Such a development may be unusual, but when it does occur it, like the more strictly ecological influences, can override the usual pattern of development to a considerable extent.

At present, a considerable expansion of studies of the formal and informal structure of junior schools is taking place. From these, a more complete picture should emerge, and may well amend and amplify our general knowledge in this field. For example, it would be valuable to consider the suggestions made by Thorpe (1955) and Douglas (1964), mentioned in Volume II, Chapter III, about the impact on children's social acceptability of their place in their families. It would also be interesting to examine the validity of the hypothesis already mentioned in connection with Stockton's present research. He indicates that in any junior school it may be possible not only to locate neighbourhood-group influences, but also to show that some groups in school are based on neighbourhood affiliations and some are not. The latter, school-based groups may thus be more open to school influences, the extent of these perhaps depending in its turn on the nature of their habitat, as discussed in Volume II, Chapter III. If this is generally true, it could have important implications not only for the informal organisation of primary schools, but also for socialisation and other aspects of social processes within them. In this, as in many other ways, the interaction between social structure and social process is manifold, however convenient it may be to separate them for purposes of analysis. This will be apparent in the following chapter, when the foreground will be occupied by the social processes in junior schools.

IV

Social Processes in Junior Schools

A. SOCIAL ROLES OF JUNIOR SCHOOLS

THE first aspect of social process to be considered is that of the social roles of junior schools, beginning as before with *instruction*. Here in the later Midlands years, school is the focus of life, and the purpose of going to school is seen primarily as that of learning. Indeed, more learning is generally expected than in infant schools. According to the official Schools Regulations, 1959 (S.I., 1959, No. 364, Sec. 10(1)(c)) four hours of 'secular instruction' should be given daily to children over eight, as compared with three hours for those below that age. Within that official compass, there is plenty of room for disagreement about what should be learnt.

However, there is general agreement that the basic skills of language and number are indispensable elements in the learning programme. As in the infant school, disagreement is concentrated on the means by which these skills are to be attained. The triumph of the developmental tradition, already mentioned in relation to the infant school, is considerably less certain at the junior level. Sometimes there is a sharp discontinuity between the two schools, the junior school regarding itself as fulfilling a rigorous remedial function after the allegedly insipid approach of the infant school, with unfortunate results on the smoothness of the transition, as was suggested in Chapter III. Usually the contrast is less stark, though a greater sense of pressure often permeates the whole of a junior school because of the externally-imposed standards expected at the age of eleven, when the instructional role tends to be subordinated to the classificatory role under the influence of secondary-school selection, or to be affected by preparation for the kind of specialist instruction which primary-school teachers suspect, often with reason, to be the reigning pattern in secondary schools. In this way the instructional role of the junior school tends to differ from that of the infant school, even though the backwash of secondary-school selection may be felt to some extent from the age of five onwards.

The nature of instruction in junior schools is further complicated because both of the older traditions—elementary and preparatory—exercise some influence. Concentration on the basic skills, largely by

79

rote and drill methods, has been characteristic of the former, while the latter is represented by something like an *hors d'oeuvre* of secondary education mediated by generally humane and scholarly, sometimes 'progressive', but essentially didactic methods. In areas in which junior schools have taken on something of the colouring of private schools, and especially where they regularly compete for places in direct-grant and independent schools whose entrance examinations make demands of the *hors d'oeuvre* pattern, the preparatory tradition has continued to show some influence, while in the most culturally deprived areas, such as slum districts and some rural villages, the problems of ensuring a minimum of language and number skills adequate for social communication and for any kind of secondary education has given some impetus to the perpetuation of the elementary ethos. The developmental tradition, while embracing a considerable amount of the same skills and subject-matter, take its stand rather on the readiness of children in the later primary years to be introduced to a wider heritage and to explore their environment (wherever it is) and their own capacities for individual and collective activity and creativity.

The interplay of the three traditions results in some degree of variability in each area of the junior-school curriculum, and in the balance between the various curricular elements. The learning of the mother tongue and its use, beyond the bare acquisition of skills, can be characterised by manipulation of formal rules, by introduction to formal literature, or by individual or group creative writing. It is likely that all three will be represented, but the predominant emphasis will reflect the type of educational climate prevailing in the school. Similarly with arithmetic; one class is on its toes with mental arithmetic involving rapid and accurate mastery of the multiplication table, one with problems about fitted carpets and garden paths, and one with the dimensions of the timber required for the rabbit hutch which they are actually building. At least, these are three 'ideal types' of numerical work whose relative prominence affords another index of the prevalent ethos, and perhaps of the social influences which determine it.

Outside the basic-skill area there is perhaps more scope for variation. In the study of heritage and environment this is shown with particular clarity. The extreme or 'ideal type' cases here would be that in the elementary tradition the study of both would be severely curtailed, a pale reflection of the preparatory tradition in which the time-table would offer 'history', 'nature study' and 'geography' *tout court*, while the developmental counterpart would be entitled 'environmental studies' or something similar. Here again, each school evolves some solution of its own, usually a compromise. Actually it appears that the developmental approach is more characteristic of districts in which children are less likely to learn about their social environment in their home life (Kendon, 1954, pp. 145–6), though it would be difficult to generalise about this. Incidentally, it appears that this area of the curriculum, in which formerly there was considerable enterprise, has in recent years become rather stabilised and remote from the winds of change.

This is least true of one aspect of it, that of traditional 'nature study' which has come to be merged in primary-school science. Here, a great deal of recent change has taken place. Partly in response to the growing prestige of scientific studies, and perhaps to some extent in recognition of the achievements of scientific education at the primary level in the Soviet Union and elsewhere, it has become quite usual to see, in junior schools, experimental work on subject-matter which until recently would have been regarded as beyond the powers of primary-school children. Not only 'nature study' but aspects of the physical sciences figure in this way. In conjunction with this development goes the astonishing expansion in modern mathematics which has translated into the junior school, almost overnight, some principles which were formerly regarded as appropriate only to a few senior pupils in secondary schools. And if this explosion of mathematical and scientific studies has transformed the instructional role in one respect, it can be paralleled by the recent development of modern-language teaching. This may also have been affected by the growing contacts of Englishmen with foreigners through travel as well as through cultural and political relations.

It is instructive to ask why these developments have not taken place before. An explanation may be found in the survival of the earlier traditions. To the elementary tradition, all these things were alien. They were suspected of interfering with the basic skills or, if admitted to the curriculum at all, they were treated in a jejune and unimaginative manner. In the preparatory tradition, however, they were firmly entrenched, but were taught in such a way as to make little appeal to children in the Midlands years. Formal French grammar, formal algebra and geometry and (very rarely) some elementary theoretical science figured in the programme of preparatory schools and of some primary schools which aligned themselves with the preparatory tradition. They were examined in the Common Entrance and other public tests, but in such a way that rote memory and factual reproduction were at a premium, while interest-based activity by the pupils themselves was a rarity. Consequently, adherents of the developmental tradition tended to align themselves here with those of the elementary pattern in one way, namely in a common suspicion of the studies themselves as unsuitable for young children. Needless to say, the backwash effects of the eleven-plus examination, with their encouragement to teachers to limit themselves more and more to the basic skills, reinforced this tendency to ignore the wider potentialities of language and mathematics. But

81

with the reduction in the harshness of secondary-school selection which has characterised recent years, the opportunity for widening the cognitive range of the curriculum has arisen, and with it an increasing realisation that subject-matter which was once associated with the preparatory tradition, and widely condemned on that account by 'progressives', could also be approached along impeccably developmental lines, giving due scope to the dramatic expansion in children's capacities and interests and enthusiasm for learning in the junior school.

One aspect of biological study deserves particular mention. The development of coherent principles of sex education has made fairly evident the advantages of giving the earliest factual information about animal and human reproduction at the primary stage, so that children are prepared for the consideration of social and emotional aspects of sex education when they themselves reach the age of puberty, which itself tends now to fall in some cases near or within the junior years. This type of instruction raises special problems, for some families in all social groups raise objections to sex education in schools, and some teachers attempt it in such an embarrassed way that they achieve more harm than good. Again, because of the high degree of self-reference which it involves, at least when children become more self-conscious in adolescence, sex instruction is inevitably linked with socialisation as well as instruction.

Similar considerations apply to the religious instruction which is required in junior schools, as elsewhere, by Sec. 25(2) of the Education Act, 1944. In denominational schools, especially those where an all-embracing parochial organisation bulks big in the children's world and where religious instruction is elaborately worked out in relation to particular dogmas, there is likely to be little cause for dispute within the primary school. It is in county schools, working rather erratically to an Agreed Syllabus, that this aspect of instruction causes dissension, as has been pointed out already in the case of infant schools. Here some teachers interpret their role in an unblushingly cynical way; some indulge in scarcely-veiled evangelism (in secondary schools they are usually called Holy Joes); some are fiercely indignant at being obliged, as part of their duties or for the presumed requisites of promotion, to give lip-service to creeds and ethical principles with which they strongly disagree; and still others make a conscientious attempt to introduce children, in ways appropriate to their age and interest, to paradigms of human experience whose significance, over the centuries, has at least given to English society a scale of values against which moral and ethical development can be fostered. As for the children in county junior schools, their receptivity is likely to be filtered, as in the case of the mass media discussed in Volume II, Chapter III, by their particular experience of Churches, Sunday Schools, and other adult-sponsored organisations.

The child of convinced humanist parents may begin to feel, before the junior-school years are over, one kind of disdain for the traditionalist teacher: the family of an enthusiastic minister or local preacher may develop a different kind of disdain for the time-server. Here, although some parallels can be drawn, the respective results of the three traditions are less clearly shown, for they are largely overlain by other influences.

They can however be traced in their impact on the physical and aesthetic aspects of the curriculum, with which the description of the instructional role is complete. Basically, the elementary and preparatory traditions viewed both in a rather formal and rigid way. In the former, the emphasis was on the minimum of accomplishments, often with a utilitarian stamp. In the latter, more was attempted, but it was at least partially intended to confer status on pupils through appropriate accomplishments, rather than to allow them to engage in activities which they enjoyed. (Often they did enjoy them, nevertheless.) Thus in the preparatory tradition there were more different games, more serious concern with art, and more instrumental music than in the elementary tradition. Little of this penetrated into maintained junior schools, however. They were more affected by the developmental trends which have come to emphasise free movement and dance, and creative expression in art, the crafts and music.

In any particular school, the implementation of the instructional role involves some balance between the various elements in the curriculum. This is again likely to be affected by the relative importance of the three traditions, and also by the social setting of the school. For example Musgrove (1961) has pointed out that parents in a school in a predominantly middle-class district, which already laid considerable emphasis on the basic skills, were anxious for still greater concentration on this aspect of the work, while those on a Corporation estate were more concerned about the extension of useful skills and religious education, the latter (it was a county school) being seen as a better basis for moral development than the parents themselves felt able to give. It may be that where the school has a mainly middle-class clientele and where the preparatory tradition still exercises a recognisable influence, particularly under the shadow of fierce competition for places in selective secondary schools, the combined outcome is that homes will provide a wide range of general knowledge and experience while the school concentrates on the success-bearing skills. A similar tendency may apply to middle-class children within less favoured environments, for Douglas (1964, p. 35) points out that middle-class children from physically unsatisfactory homes show a relative improvement in intelligence-test and attainment-test scores between the ages of eight and eleven, as though this feat is accomplished at the expense of something perceived as less important. On the other hand working-class children in an area where the instructional role undergoes a characteristic middle-class pattern of implementation are likely to be absorbed into the majority ethos, as Jackson and Marsden (1962, p. 76) and Douglas (op. cit., pp. 37–8) have indicated.

In this connection, it is important to consider some other aspects of Douglas's survey of a nation-wide sample (op. cit.). He found not only that there was an important residual effect of social class on attainment and intelligence test results when other factors were held constant, but also that (p. 46) this differentiation too increased between the ages of eight and eleven. Often this social-class influence coincided with a concentration of parental interest in their children's work, for this tends to be more usual in middle-class circles. It also appears (pp. 71–4) to have affected girls and boys rather differently, for the rate of progress in basic attainment was lowest among boys in the lower working class. In addition, the effect of parental interest over the whole sample seems to have been greater on girls than on boys. Here, as elsewhere, the girls appear to be the more home-based sex. How far these findings indicate the *relative* emphasis laid by middle-class children, and girls, on the basic skills remains a matter for conjecture.

It may be that where the developmental tradition is well established, social differences are less marked: this is a subject on which research could well be carried out. But even here there are initial variations which have to be taken into account. For example Brunt (1963) carried out an interesting study in a city district in which he indicated that middle-class children at the beginning of their junior-school life have a wider range of individual interests than working-class children, although this difference (unlike Douglas's difference in basic attainment) was reduced before the age of eleven. This result may reflect the earlier individuation in middle-class children noted by Bernstein (1958). So even in an interest-based curriculum differences can be encountered. At the same time, interests are not immutable. They can be fostered, and this may, within the developmental approach, be itself one of the most effective forms of instruction. A school has to work out for itself how this may be most effectively blended with attainment in the basic skills.

Most schools achieve some compromise between traditions and between social pressures, and in most cases the compromises bear sufficient resemblance to each other to ensure a rough homogeneity in junior-school education, so that when a child or a teacher moves from place to place, the social process in the new setting is not entirely unfamiliar. But there are some exceptions, when an extreme position is taken up or where circumstances are very unusual. One of the most difficult situations arises when there is a sizeable minority of non-English-speaking children. Then, as suggested in Chapter III, it is necessary to modify the formal structure and to institute specific instruction for the minority. Other minorities may also call for special arrangements.

In any case, instruction itself remains central to the functioning of the school. Whether it is derived from formal teaching, or from books or audio-visual media, or through self-teaching by programmed learning, it is implicit in the overt activities of the entire junior school, and impinges on all the other roles, which will be considered more briefly.

Socialisation is the second role. As in infant schools, it implies adjustment both to the school society and to the Great Society outside. This at once involves a difficulty, because it is often assumed that the values inside a school should be superior to those outside. Thus it often seems that junior schools are trying to adjust their pupils to two different value-systems simultaneously. One is the normal pattern which runs through much of society, that of continuous selection and classification, which constitutes the third role of primary schools themselves and which is generally accepted as necessary by the children, whether they are fortunate in the process or not. The other system, intended to be characteristic of the school and hence perhaps to influence society, stresses co-operation and mutual understanding and the common good and is likely to be officially blessed from the platform at Assembly. Both systems are genuinely fostered, and incidentally they show a partial correspondence to the two value-systems in the formal structure mentioned in Chapter III. For the competitive pattern is stressed in the sphere of academic attainment, while the co-operative pattern emerges more clearly in games. Status-holding is less easy to assign, because it is essentially co-operative, though it depends on superordination and subordination, but it tends to be associated with academic rather than athletic achievement.

It is interesting to see how individual schools reconcile the claims of the competitive and co-operative patterns. Sometimes one or other is soft-pedalled in response to the surrounding climate of opinion. At other times they are ingeniously combined in what may be termed, with apologies to Thorstein Veblen, 'conspicuous competitive co-operation'. For example Heather and Adrian, who are bright, good-looking, accustomed since the infant school to prominence and success, and certain of grammar-school places when the time comes, figure prominently in both value-systems. In the former, they bring a flush to each other's cheek by their prowess in mental arithmetic; but it is friendly rivalry, for they are well ahead of the field and there is room at the top for both of them. Moreover, largely because of their joint prowess, they are often deputed to take the lead in the co-operative activities too. They are entrusted with special functions on Sports Day or at the School Concert, and when a resplendent visitor from Nigeria arrives, it is they, jointly, who shepherd him round the school and entertain him in their confident oral English. In contrast, Janice and Bernard are out of the limelight both academically and socially, never thinking of a grammar-school place, and never chosen to carry out special functions for which their shy and stereotyped behaviour is a poor qualification.

From the point of view of socialisation, Heather and Adrian learn to do more than conform and compete. They are groomed for leading social roles. The school is their oyster: all this, and the grammar-school heaven too. No wonder that they grow confident, though until they enter secondary education they are relatively unaware of their advantages and so remain very nice children. Meanwhile Janice and Bernard learn the opposite social lesson, that they are not destined to be conspicuous either in competition or in co-operation, and that success in the one value-system seems to go with success in the other. In this way socialisation and classification are intimately bound up, while the value-systems of school and of society are integrated.

The actual process of socialisation involves also the maintenance of institutional behaviour through a system of discipline and order. This has in fact a dual function. On the one hand, as will be seen in the discussion of social cohesion and control, it is a necessary pre-requisite of the school as an institution. On the other, it presents a pattern of organisational behaviour which is intended to function as a prototype for the more elaborate patterns which will be encountered at the secondary stage and afterwards. Here it is important to appreciate that the actual pattern of discipline and order in a particular school, and the consequent direction and effectiveness of its socialising process, is the result of interaction between the social factors influencing the school's pupils, and the values held by its teachers, the latter being themselves related to their basic beliefs. Viewed from the standpoint of the three traditions, it seems probable that the elementary emphasis would be on enforced conformity to minimal rules and standards, and the preparatory emphasis, on the rapid absorption of attitudes and habits considered appropriate to selective secondary schools, while the developmental approach would be more concerned with adjusting the process of socialisation to the children's growing capacities for social and moral behaviour (Piaget, 1932) and with promoting children's experience of a wide range of social roles, as will be discussed in Chapter VII. Perhaps also the elementary tradition tends to regard the children as masses, the preparatory tradition to stress their function as competing individuals, and the developmental tradition to look upon them as individuals in an evolving democratic community.

The social values conveyed by the school will vary considerably according to which tendency is dominant. Of the three, it appears incontrovertible that the developmental approach, in which children work largely in groups and share in planning and responsibility for their work, is the most appropriate form of socialisation in a democratic society, provided that individuality is fostered too and that the degree of responsibility assigned to the children is not in excess of their development. If it were not already pre-empted for other purposes, the term 'guided democracy' might be used to epitomise the type of régime which is intended to lead towards a fuller democracy later on.

In circumstances when there is a marked discrepancy between school values and home values for some or all of the children, socialisation may come to include what anthropologists call acculturation, the bringing of values from outside to supersede those already regnant in a community. This can arise from cultural discontinuities between teachers and taught, whether these are related to social class, to urban-rural contrasts, or to differences between religious groups. The confrontation is likely to be more acute in the elementary than in the developmental tradition: in the preparatory tradition it is probably less likely to occur. With juniors any conflict of this kind may be slightly more developed than with infants, but much less than in secondary schools, for most parents and most children welcome rather than resent the efforts of primary schools towards socialisation for the wider society.[1]

Whether the values promulgated by the school are accepted in the local community or not, one point remains important to consider, namely how far the children between seven and eleven are capable of grasping and absorbing social attitudes. This is largely a cognitive question, and illustrates the interplay between socialisation and instruction. It has already been raised in relation to sex education and religious education. It applies also to social development in general. Although some American studies (Radke *et al.*, 1949; Foshay and Wann, 1954) suggest that the absorption of social attitudes can begin at an early age, there is little English evidence apart from the imprecise investigations carried out long ago by Wadmore (1921–2) and Macaulay and Watkins (1926). For the most part we are content to assume that the values disseminated in schools are dutifully absorbed, though in more cynical moments we may have doubts. We may tend to overlook the differential impact of socialisation, hinted by Macaulay and Watkins in their suggestion (op. cit., p. 33) that children in the more socially sheltered environments may find it easier than others to give lip-service to conventional values of service and unselfishness just because their circumstances make it easier for them to practise these values without excessive cost. Meanwhile we also work on the assumption that ideas are conveyed with particular effectiveness at times of communal solemnity such as

Assembly, or of collective and relatively agreeable activity such as Sports Days and Swimming Galas and school journeys, or even during school meals as advocated in the Report on *The Primary School* (1931):

> The midday meal, which is now taken by the pupils in some primary schools, should afford invaluable opportunities for training the children not only in hygienic habits, but also in manners and general social sense (p. 203).

Since this opinion was originally expressed, the mid-day meal has become much more regularly a feature of junior children's days and teachers have worked, with varying degrees of enthusiasm and success and in a wide variety of social contexts, to implement the habits and the manners and the general social sense. In this they have been aided by the School Meals Service, as indicated in Chapter VII, and henceforth there may be further ancillary assistance.

Another and more specific assumption about the cognitive aspects of junior-school socialisation is that social distance is at a minimum at this stage. As Edith Warr (1951, p. 105) puts it:

> . . . to young children, other people are significant as individuals, and their attitude is entirely personal. As they grow older they begin to generalize and human personality tends to become obscured by labels, and an individual becomes a communist, a socialist, a conservative, a German, a Jap, a Jew.

Left to themselves, children in the Midlands years are unlikely to discriminate against ethnic out-groups, partly for reasons of cognitive immaturity. But when they are strongly influenced by community attitudes and pressures, they may be just as prone to form stereotypes as the elders from whom they take them, and the more visible the minority-group is, the more readily it is stereotyped and the more easily the conventional response is learnt. Almost all schools follow a policy in socialisation which is opposed to stereotyping, but it requires skill and determination to implement it through what the Americans describe as 'intercultural education' (Kilpatrick and Van Til, 1947: Chs. 2 and 3 are on young children). This should be easiest to achieve in the developmental tradition, but that does not mean that it happens without effort.

It is not possible to describe socialisation adequately without referring to one further aspect. In an age of changing values, there is less certainty in society at large, and even in its subdivisions, than formerly about the social behaviour and attitudes which should be developed. At the same time it is generally agreed that children are harmed if this adult uncertainty is paraded too readily before them. For the most part, then, junior schools adhere to a set of values and conventional manners, partly derived from Christianity, which appear generally suitable as preparation for English society and indeed for something slightly superior to existing English society. These values are deeply embedded in English life, and the 'cake of custom' should not be too rudely broken. Some teachers, some children and some parents agree, especially in denominational schools, on much more than this: but this at least is generally common ground. Of course, these values are disputed, in some quarters, vehemently and coherently, but: *pas devant les enfants.*

Classification is patently a function of junior schools. Indeed, sometimes it appears to be *the* function which they exercise, and as Ross (1960, pp. 126–7) points out, it may encroach upon the others so much that

> . . . the children (learn) to regard work not connected with an examination as pointless.

If Parsons' theory, mentioned in Chapter I, namely that classification by achievement is a central process in primary schools, is upheld by observations in American elementary schools where selection for secondary education is conspicuously absent, it is even more likely to apply to English junior schools where the implications of achievement are so evident. Within junior schools this is the main, though not the only, aspect of classification.

From the first-year or transition class onwards, standardised testing of intelligence and of attainments in the basic skills takes place, and usually constitutes the basis of the formal structure itself. Record cards may also be assiduously maintained: some records may in fact be passed on from the infant school, though there are instances when these are viewed with some scepticism. Tests and record cards alike are carefully designed, and the former are creditably free from bias, but both are of limited value for prognosis. Now, as more and more local education authorities are abandoning the actual eleven-plus examination, various series of standardised tests and primary-school record cards are increasingly used as a principal basis for secondary-school selection, or for initial assessment within comprehensive schools. Where objections are raised to this type of classification of children, they depend not so much on the inefficiency of the actual test procedures as on the emphasis laid upon them and the sinister significance which they appear to have. Comparisons of junior schools with coke plants and egg-grading stations, with the implication that children are treated like commodities, are sentimental and far-fetched but they do embody a protest against over-emphasis on the apparently measurable and predictable aspects of the educative processes in general. More will be said about this in Chapter VI: here it is only necessary to add that protests of this kind have been raised, perhaps for different reasons, from both Left and Right in politics.

It seems reasonable to assume that the impact of classification on children will depend more on adult attitudes than on the classificatory process itself. This, too, will be further discussed in Chapter VI. However it is apparent that adults do differ in their attitudes. Martin (in Glass, 1954, Ch. 7) shows how parents' anxiety about secondary-school allocation varies, partly according to socio-economic status. Douglas (1964) shows too how influential *mothers'* aspirations and encouragement can be in respect of classification (pp. 21–2), how important parental encouragement appears to be in schools with an average (rather than a very good or very poor) record in secondary-school selection (p. 109) and how parents of juniors who are upwardly mobile in academic (and social) terms seem to allow and perhaps to encourage their children to absorb the social characteristics of the level in society towards which they are moving (p. 41).

Teachers, too, differ in their attitudes. Some vehemently assert the superiority of the co-operative value-system mentioned when discussing the socialising role. Others maintain that realism requires them to classify strenuously. It is almost certain that these teachers will adopt differing views on the value of streaming, and perhaps also on basic social philosophy, as indicated in Chapter III. In any case it is likely that streaming renders re-classification progressively more difficult as the children move through the junior school so that when the fourth-year climax is reached, the different streams are as it were playing in different leagues while the coaching-power is concentrated on the First Division. Some teachers' role-achievement (see Ch. VII) is centred in this area. Ross (1960, p. 127) reminds us that there are even extreme cases in which the 'scholarship teacher' is used, like some pedagogical locomotive, to go

> . . . back to the third year after the examination to bring on the next bunch of aspirants.

Presumably the third-year 'A' stream is implied.

Therefore, as Jackson and Marsden point out (1962, p. 85), it is necessary to become established early in the First Division, especially when this régime is strictly enforced. For not only is the teaching more strenuous, but the children invigorate each other with what has already been termed 'conspicuous competitive co-operation'. Teacher and peers alike keep the class right up on its toes as the contest approaches. Douglas (1964, p. 107) points out that teachers can themselves exercise an important residual influence in choosing children for the First Division and encouraging them within it. So, if they are impressed by the outward manifestations of behaviour appropriate to middle-class families—and it is hard not to be—then it seems all the more likely that working-class children who take on

90

the protective colouring of middle-class behaviour at the age of seven or eight or nine will improve their chances in the process of academic classification. This is more readily achieved when they are in a minority (Jackson and Marsden, 1962, pp. 76–7) or when they already belong to Bernstein's 'associative levels' of the middle class (1958, pp. 160–1) or to the 'sunken middle class' of which Jackson and Marsden (ibid., p. 53) have written. For these, entry or re-entry to middle-class educational processes is generally easier, especially if they draw up and ahead in the classificatory table during the junior-school period. To state this is not to approve of it: to deny it would be unrealistic: to combat it involves a complex reorientation of the classificatory process in which it is ideally desirable that the relative advantages enjoyed by middle-class children and their imitators should be reduced while their *absolute* development and progress should be maintained and even improved. But this involves social change beyond the limits of primary education itself. Even if it were achieved, academic classification would still inevitably take place; but it would be less obviously linked with status in society at large.

The effect of parental and teacher attitudes may be felt in other ways too. Douglas (1964, pp. 105–7) brings out the tendency for junior schools with a high reputation for successes in grammar-school selection to perpetuate their position presumably through attracting children of discerning and intelligent parents and also teachers who like to work with able children in an atmosphere of success. For other schools the process works in reverse, and not only in slum districts, for it is often small rural schools which fall most completely and continuously out of the First Division altogether. In neighbouring villages, one school may draw patrons from miles around while the other stagnates in isolation. Social factors work together to ensure a very different process of classification—and of the other roles too—in these contrasted schools.

Douglas (ibid., pp. 73–5) also suggests that teachers, especially women teachers, may unconsciously discriminate against boys rather than girls, especially if they are of lower-working-class origins, and may thus reinforce the girls' superiority in taking the good-pupil role and also their chances of success in secondary-school selection. If so, this constitutes another differential in the classificatory process, and one which could become more influential than it now is in areas in which, as already indicated, increasing weight is to be given to teachers' assessments in the procedure of secondary-school selection.

Because of the predominance of secondary-school selection and its dependence on basic abilities and skills, little attention has hitherto been paid to the classificatory significance of the rest of the junior-school curriculum. For in all aspects of instruction and of socialisation, children begin with an innate equipment fostered in the children's world during the early years, in different ways for different individuals. Achievement in these various fields begins to acquire some significance during the junior-school period, so that they may begin to affect children's role-complex and self-picture. Carole is good at art; Peter can act well; three or four children are quite accomplished recorder players. In such ways mild role-playing is begun. Much of it proves impermanent, but here and there it constitutes the beginning of an interest which, if encouraged at home and again in the secondary school, can influence the direction of a child's vocational aspiration.

Prowess in physical skills is in rather a different category because of the prominence of games in the alternative value-system of schools. Greater interest attaches to the taking of particular roles. It comes to be generally known that Fred is a fast-moving winger, that Maureen is a steady defence, and that Malcolm is safe as an opening bat. This is partly a consequence of the structure of the games themselves, which compels role-allocation. At first this may take place almost by chance. In Fred's case, for example, his first appearance on the wing may have taken place because the teacher put him there, or because he fancied it, or nobody else would go, or possibly because he was already used to playing there in scratch games in his own habitat. Once there, he tends to stay there by force of his own and everyone else's habit, unless he wants a change or proves useless. On the whole, however, he tends to adjust to his role, and to show the level of skill and the pattern of agility expected of him. So do Maureen and Malcolm, for expectation, as well as skill, ranks as a determinant of performance. Conversely Graham, habitually put in to bat last, accepts his role with resignation and obligingly spoons the ball into a fielder's hands, as everyone knows he will, even though he may have the potential neuro-muscular capacity for better things. In such ways physical skills are woven into a web of stereotypes which powerfully affect the children's conception of themselves. Moreover, since physical skill enjoys such prestige in the children's peer society, this set of stereotypes may become dominant. Incidentally it is more likely to do so under the influence of the elementary tradition, with its limited conception of physical education, or of the preparatory tradition, with its tendency to figure as the preamble to a games cult, than in the developmental tradition where modern approaches to physical education as 'moving and growing' are more strongly represented, and therefore performance in any one particular skill is less likely to be over-valued.

Just as in the infant school, classification takes place continuously in the day-to-day interactions in the classroom. Sex-typing, a topic mentioned in relation to family life in Volume II, Chapter III, is reinforced by the school as the two sexes draw apart. Meanwhile some children find their particular abilities more valued than others do. It is better to be good at arithmetic and fielding than at climbing roofs and skipping 273 times; at least, it is more appreciated by the teacher. The detailed classification is indeed often conveyed incidentally by the teacher's own verbal behaviour:

> Good girl, Dorothy! . . . Yes, Michael, we all know *you've* got the answer. Give somebody else a chance . . . Thank you, Paul, that's what I was waiting for . . . My word, boys! You're letting the girls beat you every time . . . All watch Gillian . . . Let's hear yours, Patrick . . . Now let's see, how are *you* getting on? . . . I thought so! Mary's nearly *finished* hers . . .

No doubt this is a travesty of the actual behaviour of any teacher, but it shows in concentrated form the type of classification which can take place. Some teachers resist it strongly; others feel unable to do what they might wish owing to the pressure of numbers and circumstances. Meanwhile, classification by achievement goes on. Leonard, sitting almost unnoticed in the middle of the room, is not mentioned at all.

This is partly because, as Talcott Parsons points out, the good-pupil role involves achievement in both instruction and socialisation. Those who achieve in both are praised; those who fall short in both are not. Those who achieve partially, for example in one value-category only (good at work, poor at games, rather unreliable in conduct) are given qualified approval. But those who are at, or just below, average in everything tend to be overlooked. They are not the teacher's most obvious priorities, so they tend to be left until the more conspicuous children have been dealt with, and since there are so many of those that they take more than all of the teacher's time, the residue can in an extreme case go from teacher to teacher and from year to year almost unnoticed and almost unclassified except in a negative sense.

The children themselves, in their peer society, promote and intensify role-allocation. Where they are in step with the teacher, as they usually are, roles in and out of the classroom tend to be parallel, and cement the relationship between the formal and informal social systems in the school.

Once a child's reputation is established, however casually, it tends to take root. For example Brian once or twice surprises the class by his detailed knowledge of some point of mechanical interest. Thereafter he is 'Professor', and well on the way to being his peers' official consultant. Similarly Trevor makes a couple of witty comments, at an age when wit is first coming to be appreciated, and from then onwards he is established as a clown. Thus when Trevor or Brian speaks in the classroom, the class and teacher know what to expect, and welcome it much more readily than an interjection from silly Marilyn or stolid Clifford. Indeed, there comes a stage when the learned response to Trevor's voice results in a laugh, and to Marilyn's a groan, even if they say exactly the same thing.

Moreover, prestige acquired in the informal social system becomes transferable to other roles. If a strong man is needed to move chairs, or a speaker to take a leading part in a Carol Service, there may be several possible candidates, but a quick exchange of glances after a teacher's request often results in the choice of a sociometric star, possibly already prominent in games: 'Have Stanley!' 'Have Sylvia.' Differentiation of roles is not yet very far developed: the popular boy or girl, even at the age of ten or eleven, is still expected to be good at most things.[2]

In the rare cases where teacher and class are at loggerheads, a different pattern may emerge. Then Brian and Trevor will exercise their skills at the teacher's expense. Stanley will be liable to organise rebellion, and Sylvia's speech may begin in embarrassment and end in giggles. Perhaps the situation is still more difficult when the class is divided, with some roles on the teacher's side and some against. But in any case the roles are basically the same: it is circumstances which alter their expression.

In classrooms where teaching is less didactic and the social climate more permissive, a different pattern may develop. For one thing, the classificatory impact of the teacher's tongue is different where children are working in groups or otherwise on projects and similar activities, and where the situation gives less prominence to individual children's remarks. For another, the group situation itself leads to a different and richer pattern of roles. Some of these are leader and some follower roles, so that it is still quite possible that the less prominent children may be reinforced in their mediocrity. However, as mentioned in the previous chapter, sociometric stars and isolates appear less readily in a more permissive social climate, so this may be a sign that roles are more flexibly distributed. Thus the developmental tradition may result in a modification, almost certainly an improvement, in classification. The aim should be to prevent it from being premature, rigid or complete, that is, to combat the tendency towards stereotyping. This involves maintaining, as suggested in the discussion of socialisation, a wide range of roles and ensuring, if necessary through active intervention, that all the children sample many of them and thus discover their strengths and weaknesses and those of their peers. Nobody can succeed, or fail, all the time. To learn this is itself a valuable piece of socialisation as well as a limit upon classification.

One last and rather different kind of classification takes the form of medical and dental examination. Begun in the infant school, it is continued at the junior stage and often succeeds in locating defects, sometimes quite serious, which were previously unsuspected. This may also apply to educational subnormality, though here official classification (ascertainment) by a qualified expert is more likely to follow a long period of classroom failure. As will be seen in Chapter V, recruitment to all kinds of special school is considerably accelerated between the ages of seven and eleven. Meanwhile, remedial treatment of a less drastic nature may be carried out within the normal junior-school pattern. School Medical and Dental Officers maintain the detailed records of children's physical conditions but these, as well as test results and other comments on educational progress and even on personality-development are often entered on some form of record card which epitomises, with rather varying reliability, the principal features of the classificatory process as it affects a particular child.

Welfare

The maintenance of records is itself some index of the role of the junior school as a welfare institution. But in general, as with infant schools, it is difficult to assert that the junior years are characterised by any particular features of the welfare role. Since the minimal age of criminal responsibility (ten, recently raised from eight) falls within these years, it is true that junior schools are involved in occasional contacts with the police, the magistrates and the probation service[3] which lie right outside the purview of infant schools. Since selection for secondary education takes place at the end of the junior years, it may perforce fall to junior-school staffs and particularly to Heads to explain to parents the workings of their local education authority's selection procedure. Apart from this, junior schools implement the general aspects of welfare as indicated in Chapter I, some facing bigger demands than others, and some carrying them out more willingly than others. This role, which is particularly associated with the developmental tradition, is often most prominent and most appreciated by parents in the very environments in which the other roles are least comprehended. Where a numerically disproportionate amount of attention is paid to remedial work. this too is strictly an aspect of welfare, especially as it is often concentrated in the very places where environmental handicaps are greatest.

Autonomy

Just because children attain, during the junior years, a stage of social development which permits greater autonomy in their corporate life, the junior school has a greater obligation to develop an autonomous culture. Parents are generally willing to allow a school to decide for itself how to develop, especially at present when so many of them can contrast their own schooldays under the continuing influence of the elementary tradition with the much more ambitious activities and trustful atmosphere which the developmental approach has brought into their children's schools. If autonomy is suspected of encroaching on instruction, especially in former strongholds of the preparatory tradition, there may be less readiness to accept it, and where it is feared for its consequence on children's values and beliefs, it may be actively resisted: but in general it appears to be welcomed.

Its actual implementation depends in part on the children's capacities for appreciating tradition. Unlike infants, juniors have a developing sense of corporate loyalty to what has become the central focus of their lives outside home, and can begin to appreciate its symbols. Simple uniform can be effective and, provided that it steers between the pretentious and the trivial[4] can stimulate a sense of belonging and help to submerge social differences. Other corporate expressions, such as a school song, are of more doubtful value and can lead to ridicule, not least in the Staff Room.

An autonomous culture also depends on the children's capacities for creativity. Plato has perhaps received too little recognition for his appreciation of the significance of movement and feeling in the education of young children. Because he was at pains to control these in the interests of social stability, he can be credited by implication with grasping their potential for autonomy also. It seems to me that the autonomous role of a junior school cannot be effectively carried out unless it is based on the arts. This has been demonstrated by teachers of genius such as A. L. Stone (1949) and Sybil Marshall (1963), the one working in a Birmingham slum and the other in an unpromising Cambridgeshire village. Their modest but confident chronicles of inspiring success give some indication of the immense potential for creativity that ordinary children can show. Stone used movement and dance as his principal medium: Mrs. Marshall started from visual art: but in both cases the flowering of their work can only be described as poetry in the widest sense. Others might reach a similar goal starting from music, or from the spoken or written word. In such a situation, social distance is reduced almost to vanishing-point, ascriptive influences and social pressures are almost forgotten, and every child can find some valued significance. Where the necessary leap of faith is taken, the consummation of the autonomous role involves not the supersession, but the transformation of the other roles too.

It is unfortunately true that teachers cannot all be Stones or Marshalls. Nevertheless they can be very effective disciples. This means of implementing the autonomous role requires to be frankly based on the developmental tradition, and involves a readiness to experiment in new methods, in team teaching, and in school-community collaboration. However it is also likely to embody the best aims of the other traditions too. Despite the sequel which may befall children from such schools at the secondary and later stages, it seems probable, to say the least, that some of the impressions left on children by a school with a vigorous autonomous culture will be permanent and will vindicate the claims of primary education to be a creative force in English society.

B. SOCIAL COHESION AND CONTROL

This aspect of social process may be considered in two parts, first as it affects a school in general and then also as it affects particular classes within it.

In the Junior School as a Whole

Like infant schools, junior schools can draw on a considerable reserve of psychological assets in the maintenance of their social cohesion. The generally favourable attitudes of parents, already noted in connection with the schools' social roles, combined with the children's own preference for a stable social framework and their tendency, reaching a peak in the middle junior years, to invest their social interest in the school itself, all work in favour of the school as a self-regulating system. The more effectively it discharges its roles, especially the socialising and autonomous roles, the more readily social cohesion will ensue.

The actual maintenance of cohesion and control depends, as was shown in Chapter I, on the establishment of norms including explicit rules, on the use of some form of rewards and punishments, and on the self-maintaining process which schools as institutions engender.

The establishment of school *norms* is closely linked with socialisation and perhaps with autonomy too. At least in part, it is within the control of the Head of a school; otherwise the school would be the resultant but not the determinant of social processes. In fact it is incumbent on a Head to select both the norms themselves and the means of establishing them. The choice is partially circumscribed by social factors such as the nature of the staff, the history of past social process in the school and the characteristics of the parents and children, as well as by the Head's previous experiences, but there is still some scope for the Head to put ideals and principles into practice. At first the translation of principles into norms may also entail social change, as indicated later in this chapter. At all times they depend on the skill and determination and good sense with which they are pursued; for if there is a serious mismanagement of policy the norms themselves can fall into disrepute. The loftier they are, the worse the consequences can be: *corruptio optimi pessima*.

There is also a danger that high-sounding principles may mask less desirable practices. Enthusiasm for 'activity' in the classroom may lead to easy-going underestimation of children's potential. A professed concern for the prospects of all the children may in practice be confined to securing grammar-school places for some of

97

H

them. Yet lofty pseudo-norms seem to be endemic in English education, and unfortunately some Heads, and some parents and local dignitaries too, seem to acquire an impenetrable obliviousness to the ways in which their principles are interpreted in practice. An adequate explanation of this tendency would require quite a thorough examination of English society itself. However, professed pseudo-norms of this transparent nature eventually deceive nobody who is in close contact with the school situation and, however much scope is allowed for their ritual maintenance, they serve in fact only to induce scepticism about the school and indeed about social institutions in general. At the opposite extreme, in the rare school with a really impressive range of autonomous activities conducted in a spirit of genuine sincerity and enthusiasm, these activities may themselves engender sufficient norms, in line with the Head's ideals, to enable the school to dispense with any others.

To some extent, norm-establishment must be related to the children's social background. Even if basic attitudes are more or less applicable in any place, their expression must vary. Urban middle-class modes of communication may do little to establish norms in slums or villages, even when the norms themselves would prove acceptable. Dahlke, in his interesting discussion of the 'functional' and 'normative' aspects of elementary schools in the U.S.A. (Dahlke, 1958, p. 253) points out that the institutional procedures necessary for the maintenance of any social institution may be more readily appreciated by middle-class than by working-class children, perhaps because of their earlier introduction to what Bernstein means by 'formal language', and to the thought-patterns which it facilitates. Again, children who belong to particular religious communities may be under some constraint to resist the norms prevailing in a school.

The Head's choice of norms may be affected by the educational tradition which is uppermost in his own attitudes. The elementary (and preparatory) emphasis was on a rather predetermined pattern of norms, coloured by the presumed requirements of acculturation, whereas the developmental approach requires that the children themselves should participate substantially in the evolution of norms. If the latter emphasis is predominant, it can be implemented more readily in a school with a vigorous autonomy of its own than in one which overstresses instruction and classification, both of which tend to require external criteria.

From the standpoint of the children, the school's official norms are usually associated with the good-pupil role. Since this tends to be a feminine rather than a masculine attribute, the norms themselves may tend to have a feminine emphasis, especially where the teachers are women. Little is known about the impact of this on boys between seven and eleven, though perhaps it implies that junior children, of both sexes, should have some experience of teachers of both sexes. Where alternative value-systems develop, for example those associated with work, play and order, or just pro-school and anti-school, then perhaps the systems which diverge most from the central norms come to be seen as 'masculine'. If so, they may involve a marked anomaly in the significance of men teachers in junior schools. Actually, the onset of this type of masculine rebellion is probably restrained by the incidence of transfer to secondary education, but in the U.S.A., where women teachers are more predominant in the elementary grades than in English junior schools and where incidentally less social emphasis is laid on transfer, boys in the later Midlands years are more likely to rebel against the essentially feminine régime which 'school' has hitherto implied (Blair and Burton, 1951, Ch. 2).

Formal *rules* require little further comment. As with infants, they must be perceived as fair and comprehensible. Where formal status-positions such as prefects and monitors are introduced, their holders can take some part in enforcing the observance of rules, but, as indicated in Chapter III, they are not generally ready to pass judgment on their peers. When allowed to do so, they sometimes show the good sense to decline.

Rewards and punishments are often determined on a whole-school basis rather than in separate classes. They are more explicit at the junior than at the infant level. Sometimes, indeed, a house or team system, with names based for example on colours or celebrities, is added to the formal structure as in secondary schools in order to foster social control through group loyalty. In such instances achievement and behaviour can be rewarded and punished within one framework, and the nice calculation of additions and subtractions can reach a level of complexity reminiscent of Anglo-Saxon law. But the value of this pattern of external, institutionalised motivation is open to question. More usually rewards, and particularly punishments, are regarded as an individual matter.

Punishments are more in evidence than rewards. In the elementary tradition, with its enormous material and psychological problems, the use of punishments in the first four standards was the rule rather than the exception, and corporal punishment was firmly established. It was freely practised, though local regulations ensured its limitation with some distinctions of age and sex, and it would be futile to say that it has vanished from junior schools. It was almost universally held, at one time, and was widely believed a decade ago, that some large junior classes could be kept in order by no other means, as Highfield and Pinsent showed in the survey mentioned in Chapter I (Highfield and Pinsent, 1952, Chs. 14–15, esp. pp. 279–80).[5] In this volume they traced the history and existing state of local education authorities' regulations about corporal punishment and found that in most cases juniors were aligned with secondary-school children for this purpose, and also that corporal punishment was confined to Head Teachers most conspicuously in small village schools with a familistic character, while the call for severe punishment at all levels was obviously at its highest in large industrial towns and cities. It is perhaps surprising to note that (p. 85) junior children were regarded collectively as more 'difficult' than those in infant, grammar or secondary modern schools and that nine-year-olds in large cities were actually regarded as including the largest proportion of 'really difficult' children—over 10 per cent. Perhaps it is a result of the incidence of really large classes (p. 84). In 1962, 18·6 per cent of all primary pupils were in classes exceeding the legal maximum of forty (*Statistics of Education in 1962*, Part I, Table 10, p. 40) and of these it is the older juniors who would be more likely to develop corporate resistance to disciplinary efforts by teachers. Perhaps in addition it epitomises the norm-conflict already mentioned between women teachers and boy pupils, though oddly enough Highfield and Pinsent did not differentiate between girls and boys in this part of their analysis. However, elsewhere in their survey they hint (p. 264) at the greater docility of girls and claim (p. 163) from their results that

> . . . even the more difficult girls as a group are more amenable to milder forms of correction than the difficult boys.

It is also suggested (p. 165) that girls of all ages were more open than boys to the countervailing effects of praise within the school's social system.

Another finding of some interest in Highfield and Pinsent's study referred to urban-rural differences. In general, as already indicated and as would be expected in the light of the general characteristics discussed in Volume II, Chapter III, rural children appeared less 'difficult'. But at the age of nine they were apparently equally hard to control, and at ten perhaps more so. Moreover, the smaller the school, the more marked this tendency was (p. 136). The authors suggested that heterogeneous teaching groups in very small rural schools added to the teachers' difficulties.[6]

Of course, corporal punishment is not the only deterrent used. Others are: deprivation of pleasures and privileges, deduction of points from teams and houses when they exist, the setting of extra work or of mechanical impositions, and the forcible movement of offenders from one part of the physical or social structure to another. Of these, the most effective are usually those which involve some element of social segregation, for this has the effect of lowering a child's status with his peers whereas corporal punishment manfully accepted may actually enhance it (as it certainly does at the secondary level, and as Borstal and prison may do among young delinquents). For the same reason, the procedure known in the North of England as 'shouting at' children may have the greatest effect of all. However, individuals differ widely in the response to punishment, as Highfield and Pinsent emphasise (ibid., p. 170) and so do communities. 'Shouting at', for example, may induce ribaldry in one place, a sense of deep insult in another, and surly indifference in a third, even though some individuals in each may wilt and weep under its impact.

The lengthy discussion of punishment, and its disproportionate treatment by Highfield and Pinsent in a study of *rewards* and punishments, is symptomatic of its predominance in the elementary tradition. In the preparatory tradition a similar emphasis is found, attributable according to some opinions to an inherited emphasis on original sin, but less obviously designed for the need for acculturation in the slums or for keeping down the Helots. But in the developmental outlook, punishment is viewed quite differently. It is regarded, at least ideally, as negative reinforcement in the psychological sense, and perhaps secondarily and regretfully as a means of rendering possible the implementation of something more positive. Reward, rather than punishment, is stressed by modern learning theory, and those 'progressivists' in education who derive their inspiration from John Dewey and his followers lay their principal emphasis on rewards that arise from satisfaction in the work itself rather than from any external motivation. Consequently, it has become usual for adherents of the developmental approach to seek not just to replace corporal punishment by some other form of restraint, but to work through a different social climate and a more interest-based curriculum. Thus, where the autonomous role is most fully stressed, rewards tend to be least artificial and punishments least necessary.

In the more usual junior schools, official rewards are not only fewer than official punishments. They are also different in character. According to Highfield and Pinsent (ibid., Ch. 6), the individualistic pattern of reward, typical of secondary and particularly of grammar schools, was already disappearing from junior (and infant) schools a decade ago. It could perhaps be said that the developmental tradition had made more headway in respect of rewards than of punishments. This is even true to some extent where a house or team system is in use, for in the light of an institutional procedure of this type teachers appear impelled, for considerations of self-esteem as well as of learning theory, to reward more than they punish. Stars and other indices of good conduct and good work are much more readily given than are the black marks reserved for punishments. When this balance is maintained, and when group cohesion is enlisted even on an artificial basis in the interests of social control, this pattern of reward and punishment can be reasonably effective within the limits of its social and philosophical assumptions.

It should be noted that all of these comments on rewards and punishments apply to the *official* system used in the school, the disciplinary counterpart of the formal structure itself. Informal procedures, such as those already discussed in relation to socialisation and classification, are often more potent psychologically in the reinforcement of knowledge and skills and attitudes. They are all the more potent for being unobtrusive and perhaps unconscious.

In Individual Classes

During the junior years, an important change takes place in the teacher-pupil relationship. From a nexus of almost sacred dependence, it moves over to something more akin to a feudal compact: 'We will be your class, and you shall be our teacher.' Therefore a teacher's pattern of role-achievement (see Ch. VII) with a class of any particular age-range will be affected by the stage of the children's social development. (When the age-range is wide, the pattern will perforce be more complex.) With seven-year-olds, much as with infants, the capable teacher is accepted and the incapable gives rise to diffuse and bewildered anarchy. With nine- or ten-year-olds there is something more like a formal test of efficiency. The children are basically full of goodwill towards a teacher, for they want to have a fitting object for their loyalty and identification, but for this very reason they often try a newcomer out, much as members of a golf club might try out a new professional. The teacher who survives this trial is gladly admitted as a signatory of the 'feudal compact'. The one who appears inefficient, self-conscious, irresolute, arbitrary or unfair will earn quite vehement and concerted resentment, in which case overt group hostility may ensue. In general, as may be inferred from what has already been said about social processes, it is the boys, especially those from working-class areas in large towns and cities, who show this tendency most markedly, apathy tending to replace hostility in the suburbs and villages and among girls in all types of environment. However the correlation between environment and behaviour is relatively low. An unacceptable teacher may encounter occasional intense and feline opposition from a group of rural middle-class Boadiceas, or may be unexpectedly encouraged by the touching if desperate attempts at loyalty shown by a handful of urban working-class boys.

It is against this background of changing social relations that norm-establishment in particular classes must be considered. At first norms will arise from an interaction of the teacher's intentions with the outlook of the majority of the pupils. Later, more import-ance will attach to the values projected into the social arena by the more prominent girls' and boys' groups within the class. As Evans (1962, p. 62) emphasises, there is some evidence in support of the hypothesis tested by Hallworth (1953) that a group's values are most clearly expressed by its 'leading crowd', as Coleman (1961) would call it. As indicated in the discussion of informal social relations, the various ecological components of a junior school's catchment area may inject rather different value-systems into the classroom, and in any particular case it appears[7] that the norms associated with the more vigorous and numerous groups, especially those with middle-class values acceptable to the school, will colour the norms of the class as a whole. Where the informal structure follows the normal pattern, the dominant norms will readily characterise the class as a whole and will become ingrained. In mixed classes, this will take place for the two sexes in parallel, with a certain amount of inter-action between the two.

Sometimes, however, the established norms are not accepted by the whole of a sex-group within a class. This is likely to happen when distinctive minorities appear in the informal social system. These may then take on some of the characteristics of social minorities in general, banding together closely. In certain circumstances, the norms of the class as a whole may be imposed on the minority by techniques of social control among the children themselves. Where the minority is out of step with the school's values as a whole, the majority works with the teacher to constrain them. This is apparently what is hoped for by those who claim that an adequate admixture of middle-class children in primary schools will exercise an uplifting effect on the rest (e.g. Willig, 1963, p. 153: see p. 63 above). But where the reverse applies, as it can, and the social deviants are in a majority, the minority may figure as immature and lacking in virility, especially in the case of boys, particularly because in such circumstances the majority norms are likely to embody increasingly marked opposition to teachers. Here the ten-year-old boy who defies the class norms and takes the good-pupil role may risk suspicion of betraying his associates, his habitat, and even his sex. Brusque methods may be used to bring him to heel, and to devalue his behaviour. Girls may occasionally be in a similar position, though this more often happens at the secondary stage. When it does occur in junior schools, other techniques of control, mainly verbal but equally effective, are employed to enforce conformity to the majority norms.[8]

These situations concern the relation of majorities to minorities. A less desirable outcome may ensue if the two factions are evenly balanced in numbers but hold sharply conflicting norms, a situation which may be described as a polarised cleavage. This is rare in junior schools, but can give rise to intensive group maintenance and exclusiveness and angling for the adherence of newcomers, the whole procedure being somewhat reminiscent of political activity in a marginal constituency.

Formal rules, rewards and punishments are more characteristic of the school as a whole than of individual classes, even though each teacher gives them an individual interpretation. In addition, teachers individually are the agents of the unofficial rewards and penalties already mentioned.

Much more important is the way in which the children's own social system tends to maintain itself within a class. Once the norms are established, the very continuity of the class symbolises something worth belonging to: children who move from their accustomed secondary group at the age of eight or nine can be quite desolate as a result. Within the framework of the class, the school's roles are discharged for its members and their own role-development and self-building takes place. While it remains the focus of their social experience, they have no desire to disrupt it; indeed they will make strenuous efforts to maintain it.

However, the social structure and articulation of a junior-school class becomes more particularised and developed as the children grow older. This, too, makes demands on the teacher. Ruth Nedelsky (1951–2) emphasises how a teacher in an American elementary school should set about promoting healthy social development in her class, and how failure to do so may induce conflicts among the children and an undesirable continuation of dependence on the teacher herself. She points out also that undue concentration on the basic-skill aspect of instruction may result in a rather defensive, babyish response from the class, while a failure to give sufficient guidance may produce feelings of bewilderment, lack of confidence and compensatory aggressiveness. The parallel with the famous experimental results on social climates among ten-year-old boys by Lippitt and White[9] is fairly close. They indicated broadly that what they called 'democratic leadership' was more effective than either autocratic control or leaderless *laissez-faire*; and general experience gives some support to this policy, which is in harmony with the developmental approach. However, in itself it may not be enough, for democratic leadership will not guarantee social cohesion unless adequate attention is given to the needs of individuals and minority groups within the class. The teacher's function here, in the class but not of it, promoting the social development of individuals and the cohesion of a social unit which will pass into other hands and eventually disintegrate when the children move out of primary education, calls for social insight and artistry of the highest quality.

Of course, in a situation such as a polarised cleavage, the needs of the different sections of the class thrust themselves into the teacher's gaze anyhow. Then the teacher's role-complex (see Ch. VII) may need at least temporary amendment, for social control must be to a considerable extent imposed and it may be necessary to extend the use of the official sanctions of reward and punishment. Much the same may be required in the face of sudden social change, such as the abolition of streaming or the merging of two existing classes or schools. Some teachers are more able than others to make this type of adaptation, while others, developing a 'born-rebel' role, are equipped to establish themselves in classes with deviant majorities. But in junior schools there is comparatively little demand for great deviation from the usual teacher roles.

One particular aspect of social control deserves a special comment. The two sexes have been treated so far as co-existent elements within a class, differing in their response and ignoring each other as much as they can, but still working more or less in harness. In the final year or so of junior-school life sex may begin, at least for some girls, to take on a new and bewildering significance. Here is it important for teachers to be aware of the possibility that rapid growth and developing breasts may symbolise a breakdown, reluctant at first, in the self-maintaining process within a class. Usually this implies little more than slightly withdrawn, slightly self-conscious behaviour by a few girls, a realisation that they need the company of older friends and that their classmates no longer hold the same interest for them as they formerly did. This realisation takes hold only after a period of fluctuation during which the accustomed immersion in the class and its doings is often as marked as ever, but is interspersed with days of unrest. With the falling age of puberty and the possibility of a readjustment of the age of transfer from junior to secondary schools, new and less cohesive forces may operate in future at this upper frontier of the Midlands of childhood.

C. SCHOOL CULTURE

School culture as a whole is closely related to all the social processes already described. Indeed, collectively they constitute that culture. But its full development is possible only when the autonomous role is adequately implemented. Whether in the school as a whole or in its various classes, the emergence of a satisfying we-feeling depends largely on the originality and distinctiveness of the particular objectives and values which are pursued. Once again it appears that a curriculum based on aesthetic activities and inspired by the developmental tradition is most apt for the building of a worthwhile culture. Incidentally, this helps to weld a school together. At Christmas and other times such as Sports Days, any school ceases to be a federation of little republics under a suzerain and becomes instead an entity. The formal structure becomes a servant rather than a master. In a school with an autonomous culture, this process can go further. Classes and teachers become more used to collaboration. Although classrooms retain their own particular characteristics and apparatus and ritual jokes, they interpenetrate as recent developments in the physical structure encourage them to do. Children then learn the value of working with those of different ages and experience as well as different sex and background, as in vertical grouping, while teachers benefit from team work and exchange of ideas and skills, a process which may be of particular support and value to a new or a relatively weak teacher, who requires some experience of acceptance before achieving an adequate role. A further advantage of this interdependent culture is that no one class can become too smug, too settled or exclusive, and therefore all can be ready to move on to secondary schools when the time comes.

D. SOCIAL CHANGE IN JUNIOR SCHOOLS

This aspect of social process in junior schools requires a brief concluding comment.

Intentional Change

Because of the increasing autonomy of the children's social relations as they grow older, the impact of a new régime is mediated less directly to the children than in infant schools. A new Head, or a new class teacher, needs to become established by the processes discussed in Chapter VII, that is by adjusting his role-commitments to the role-expectations of the school and community. In order to initiate policy changes, too, he must take into account the social structure of the staff and the social-psychological considerations involved in encouraging them to co-operate with him. Sometimes, indeed, as in the small village schools in Kent mentioned by Morris (1959, pp. 54–5) entrenched opposition from elderly and irreplaceable assistants can effectively curb the brisk reforms intended by a new Head. Usually, unlike Headmistresses of infant schools, the Heads of junior schools have a greater variety of staff to take into account: men as well as women, and a greater variety of qualifications and interests, so that there is a more complex problem of human relations.

On the other hand, if these characteristics are allowed for, there is more scope for social innovation and change than in infant schools. There is a greater range of possible strategies available for its implementation. Also, just because the children are socially more mature and can sustain a more intricate and responsible social organisation when they reach the upper end of the junior school, there is more scope for amending the formal structure by the introduction of new roles and status-positions such as prefects, and also for delegating aspects of responsibility within the curriculum and within the school's culture in general. However in one respect junior schools are more restricted in respect of social change than infant schools are, because of the demands of secondary-school selection.

A particular interest attaches to changes in social climate, for this is what happens when a school makes the transition from an 'elementary' to a 'developmental' pattern, and begins to allow full scope to the fulfilment of the autonomous role. For here, not only does it appear likely that staff and parents require convincing, but the children may also be sceptical at first. Where a rather punitive régime has flourished, the introduction of a more permissive climate may readily be mistaken for incompetence. (Waller, 1932, pp. 253–4) Temporarily, during the transition, it may be necessary to continue and even reinforce some use of overt rewards and punishments, which may involve for a Head the further dilemma that if he enforces the rewards and punishments, he may be branded as a hypocrite; if he does not, he may be regarded as a weakling. The successful transition from one régime to another depends on a series of shrewd judgments of policy. In junior schools, these have rarely been documented.

Neither have other studies of intentional change. However my own study of junior-school prefects (Blyth, 1958) was concerned largely with their introduction and the consequent impact on the school's informal social system. It was noticeable that a 'prefectless zone' emerged in both sexes in each class, as though some of the children were not ready to accept the advent of a new type of formal status. In the second year, when this status was no longer novel, resistance was apparently less. Again there is evidence from various studies and descriptions that when informal methods of instruction, based on groups embodying the children's own choices, are introduced into junior schools, this can assist in the reduction of social distance between streams and other formal divisions among the children.[10]

Unintentional Change

A number of studies of changing urban and rural environments have included incidental comments on the implications of such external social change for junior schools in these areas. Some of these are discussed in Volume II, Chapter IV. In addition, current research such as that by Stockton (p. 77 above) inevitably includes some reference to the impact of demographic and social change on a community—an overspill area in his case. On a somewhat wider canvas H. C. Dent (1944) gave a number of anecdotal but factual and uniquely interesting accounts of the interactions between rural schools and their urban guests during the great evacuation in the early part of the Second World War.

Clearly, if a junior school is to fulfil its social roles adequately, it must develop some mechanisms of adjustment to unexpected changes outside its own control, and it is important to find out more about how it can do so. Such information could be valuable to planning authorities as well as to the education service.

Secular Change and Junior Schools

For sociologists with a taste for the grand scale, it is perhaps more interesting to consider the long-term changes in primary schools which distinguish one generation from another. In a sense these can only be built up from the findings of particular 'sociographic' studies in individual schools and areas, but they can be significantly amplified by analysis of published statistics such as the 1962 figures on which I have drawn heavily throughout this book. Comparisons over a period of time indicate the major trends which are in progress, and could be used fruitfully in a study of junior-school education comparable to the work of Taylor (1963) on the secondary modern school.

In comparison with nursery and infant schools, junior schools are more complex and free-standing social organisations. They have also been more fully investigated. Yet when one considers the richness and variety of structure and process within these transitional institutions, in which over 95 per cent of English people spend a substantial part of four of their liveliest years, one is left with an impression of how relatively little, after all, we yet know about them.

V

A Note on Minority Schools

IN January 1962, some 99·95 per cent of the estimated total of children in England and Wales between the ages of five and ten inclusive[1] were in schools for which the Ministry of Education was responsible (*Statistics of Education in 1962*, Part I, Table 3, pp. 16–17). Since the population in this age-range as estimated for the mid-year by the General Register Office added up to 3,924,000 (ibid., Table 8, pp. 32–5), the balance of 0·05 per cent of children not in schools would on that basis have been about 2,000. Six categories of children could have contributed to that total:

1. Children assigned by Juvenile Courts to Approved Schools under the aegis of the Home Office.

2. Children who, after prolonged consideration of their case, have been ascertained as unsuitable for education at school and are the responsibility of the Ministry of Health and Local Health Authorities.

3. Children who, on medical grounds, are educated at home by visiting teachers.

4. Children who are legally required to attend school but for whom places are not available in maintained schools and whose parents do not wish them to attend independent schools.

5. Children whose parents have substantiated their right under Section 36 of the Education Act, 1944, to have their children educated 'otherwise' than at school (Baker, 1964).

6. Children whose parents evade their legal obligations.

Numbers are difficult to find for any of the last four categories, but figures are available for Approved Schools and to some extent for children catered for by Local Health Authorities. In the latter category, on 31st December, 1961, there were 12,534 children under sixteen in Junior Training Centres and a further 2,005 awaiting training, also 367 receiving training at home and 83 waiting to do so.[2] The statistics do not permit a breakdown within the 'under-16' range but on the assumption that the 5–10 group would be repre-sented *pro rata*, there must have been some 6,000 individuals within

109

that range. There were also 126 boys and 2 girls in Approved Schools in 1961.[3] Thus the total of children not in 'schools' obviously exceeds the 2,000 previously mentioned.

This is because the total of 3,924,000 is itself an estimate, though the other figures are based on actual returns. Such anomalies are inevitable whenever demographic prediction is undertaken; indeed, the official *Statistics* issued by the Ministry of Education sometimes show the apparent absurdity that there were more children of a particular age-range in school than in the country as a whole. For this reason there is a slight element of error in any percentages of the age-group such as those which follow, whereas the actual totals based on returns are accurate.

All the children aged 5–10, apart from this small total, were in schools. But (*Statistics of Education in 1962*, Part I, Table 3, pp. 16–17) only 93·73 per cent of the estimated total of 3,924,000 were in maintained primary or secondary[4] schools. The balance, which is accurately given (ibid., Table 8, pp. 32–5) as 243,840 and which corresponds to 6·22 per cent of the estimated total population aged 5–10, was distributed as follows:

NUMBERS OF PUPILS AGED 5–10 IN SCHOOLS OTHER THAN MAINTAINED PRIMARY SCHOOLS: 1ST JANUARY, 1962 (ENGLAND AND WALES)

Type of School	Number of Pupils	Percentage of Estimated Total Population, 5–10
Direct-grant and independent schools (excluding special schools, hospital schools and institutions)	217,434	5·54
All special schools other than hospital schools	23,910	0·61
All hospital schools	2,100	0·05
Maintained nursery schools	317[6]	0·01
Direct-grant institutions	79	0·01[*]
Totals	243,840	6·22

The schools in this table, except for the nursery schools already mentioned in Chapter II, and the direct-grant institutions which are numerically negligible, will be collectively described as *minority schools*.

Of these, the independent and direct-grant schools obviously constitute by far the largest category. They include three main subdivisions: direct-grant schools, independent schools recognised as efficient, and other registered independent schools whose premises satisfy the minimum requirements for health and safety. The first of these is really an anomaly, for (apart from the few direct-grant nursery schools mentioned in Chapter II) direct grant is not in fact made in respect of primary education. (Introduction, p. 12 above.) The grant is made to grammar schools (very rarely also to technical schools) but they are not precluded, as maintained schools are,[7] from continuing to conduct preparatory departments in which fees are paid. Despite their theoretical separateness, these are associated with the upper schools, especially their own respective upper schools, in two ways. First, they can share in some of the facilities available for older pupils. Second, the aim and tenor of education in the preparatory or 'lower' schools is such that the children are likely to be placed at an advantage, compared with those from maintained primary schools, when competing for places in the upper schools. Comparison of Tables 8 (pp. 32–5) and 23 (p. 53) of the 1962 *Statistics* shows that there were about 250 times as many children aged 5–10 in maintained primary schools as in the preparatory departments of direct-grant grammar schools, but that they secured only seven times as many free or reserved places as the children already in preparatory departments, while the share of residuary or fee-paying places falling to each group of pupils was almost identical. This is demonstrably disproportionate even in view of the relatively small number of primary-school pupils who compete for direct-grant school places, which is itself a fact of considerable social interest, and one which is often overlooked in social and political discussion about secondary-school selection.

Two other points should be mentioned about these 'lower' schools. One is that they are often invigorated by the very contact with the upper schools which has just been discussed, for the direct grant itself depends on the upper school's academic standing. The other is that, in common with the upper schools themselves, they often have a distinctive denominational character, and are usually single-sex, though some girls' schools admit boys in the lowest forms.

The other two types of independent school are accurately described by their designations. Those 'recognised as efficient' have been through the mill of Ministry inspection, for recognition is far from nominal, and many of them are extremely efficient by any criteria. Pride of place among them must go to the boys' preparatory schools, especially those who are members of the Incorporated Association of Preparatory Schools, and to the comparatively few girls' schools which follow a similar pattern. They usually cover an age-range from about seven or eight to twelve or thirteen. Some are day schools, but many are boarding schools. Some of the most famous are directly associated with the most distinguished of the independent secondary schools; Colet Court, for example, was established as the preparatory school for St. Paul's. Others, such as the Dragon School at Oxford, have built for themselves a reputation in their own right.

The next group of recognised schools is that of the junior departments of independent day grammar schools. They resemble the direct-grant lower schools in all respects except that they do not conclude their primary years with a selection procedure of quite the same kind. Beyond these again there are many other types, including some which combine an experimental approach to education with a high level of academic efficiency.

The 'other' independent schools cover a wider range still. Many of these are mixed schools. Some are very good but have not been anxious to secure recognition. Others are small local private schools of a type which has flourished for many years. Some are, literally, almost unrecognisable as schools. All of them will eventually have to seek recognition, for the survival of the 'other' category is rendered

GIRLS AGED 5–11 IN NON-MAINTAINED SCHOOLS OTHER THAN
SPECIAL SCHOOLS AND HOSPITAL SCHOOLS, 1ST JANUARY, 1962.
(ENGLAND AND WALES)

Type of School	Number of Girls, by Age[a]						
	5	6	7	8	9	10	11
Direct-grant schools							
Nursery	2	1					
Grammar—Lower[9]	991	1,180	1,468	1,741	2,041	2,099	622
Grammar—Upper[9]					5	226	5,245
	993	1,181	1,468	1,741	2,046	2,325	5,867
Independent schools recognised as efficient							
Nursery	9	1					
Primary	3,372	3,344	3,673	4,082	4,054	4,011	1,937
Secondary			1	12	87	510	2,642
Primary and Secondary	2,950	3,143	3,880	4,899	5,766	6,519	9,411
	6,331	6,488	7,554	8,993	9,907	11,040	13,990
Other independent schools							
Nursery	690	381	62	1			
Primary	6,607	6,250	5,826	5,183	4,870	4,237	1,849
Secondary	5	6	2	5	2	28	491
Primary and Secondary	2,388	2,332	2,466	2,808	2,992	3,281	40,94
	9,690	8,969	8,356	7,997	7,864	7,546	6,434
Totals	17,014	16,638	17,378	18,731	19,817	20,911	26,291

(Source: *Statistics of Education in 1962*, Part I, Table 8, pp. 32–5.)

possible only by the delay in implementing the provisions of Part III of the 1944 Education Act.

The official *Statistics* give further information about the numbers of children in the Midlands years who attend these types of school. Figures are given separately for boys and girls. In this case children aged eleven are also included in order to indicate something of the impact of the transfer to secondary education.

BOYS AGED 5–11 IN NON-MAINTAINED SCHOOLS OTHER THAN
SPECIAL SCHOOLS AND HOSPITAL SCHOOLS, 1ST JANUARY, 1962.
(ENGLAND AND WALES)

Type of School	Number of Boys, by Age*						
	5	6	7	8	9	10	11
Direct-grant schools							
Nursery	4	1					
Grammar—Lower	245	288	522	1,108	1,700	1,673	538
Grammar—Upper				7	25	408	5,237
	249	289	522	1,115	1,725	2,081	5,775
Independent schools recognised as efficient							
Nursery	9	9	1				
Primary	3,436	3,798	5,224	8,255	9,209	9,508	8,592
Secondary				20	144	363	1,773
Primary and Secondary	1,236	1,193	1,203	1,812	2,384	2,850	4,111
	4,681	5,000	6,428	10,087	11,737	12,721	14,476
Other independent schools							
Nursery	715	443	67	5			
Primary	7,672	7,249	6,900	5,439	4,890	4,524	2,499
Secondary	8	4	7	11	5	49	818
Primary and Secondary	2,006	1,928	1,934	1,979	2,124	2,351	2,882
	10,401	9,624	8,908	7,434	7,019	6,924	6,199
Totals	15,331	14,913	15,858	18,636	20,481	21,726	26,450

(Source: *Statistics of Education in 1962*, Part I, Table 8, pp. 32–5.)

These figures are quoted in full because, unlike those for maintained infant and junior schools, they indicate that there is a considerable variation from year-group to year-group within the Midlands span. The most obvious trend is one that might be expected, namely that the unrecognised schools cater more for the younger children, many of whom are transferred to recognised and direct-grant schools later. Indeed this is a sequence which can often be traced and which is, in some influential sectors of English society, regarded as normal

113

and even as unquestionable. A small 'pre-preparatory' school takes a few children, perhaps starting in the nursery years, until they reach the age of about seven or eight when they transfer to a preparatory school, or in the case of girls to the preparatory department of a day school, with the expectation of a further transition respectively to a public school or 'the big school' (see Vol. II, Ch. II, p. 34).

A few other points can be noted. For example, there is a slight upward curve in numbers in direct-grant and recognised schools at the age of ten, in the 'secondary' category, which presumably reflects the practice in some schools of transferring pupils to the upper school one year before the normal age of transfer, or, in the jargon of traditional girls' grammar schools, 'in the Lower Thirds', thereby establishing the confidence of the children from the preparatory department before they meet the invasion of 'scholarship children' or their equivalent. Conversely, in the boys' figures there is a continuation of large numbers in the 'primary recognised' category for two years outside the table (7,896 at 12; 3,472 at 13) owing to the age-distribution customary in preparatory schools. The sudden rise in 'primary-and-secondary' figures at eleven may indicate an escape route from the secondary modern school after 'failure' in secondary-school selection. It is also possible to detect the greater readiness of the leading girls' day schools, as distinct from the leading boys' schools, to admit very young pupils, for the numbers of girls aged five to eight in direct-grant schools, and of all ages in the recognised primary-and-secondary independent schools, are much greater than the corresponding figures for boys. Finally, it is apparent that the unrecognised schools, largely by virtue of their large component of small local schools, do not cater so markedly for the combined primary-and-secondary range, though they are so diverse that it is more difficult to generalise about them than about any other category.

If these figures are compared with the totals of boarders as shown in Table 7 (pp. 30–1) of the same *Statistics*, it is evident that the only category with a substantial proportion of boarders (about 45 per cent of the total) is that of boys' primary schools recognised as efficient, for these include the preparatory boarding schools. For girls, the recognised primary-and-secondary category includes most boarders, but even so, over the entire age-range, the percentage is only about twenty-three. It would therefore be quite incorrect to regard primary independent-school education as predominantly or even substantially boarding-school education: that is true only of its topmost echelons, and then only for boys.

Further information about some of these types of school is made available by organisations of independent schools themselves. For example, the *Public and Preparatory Schools Yearbook* (1964 edition) gives fairly full coverage to the boys' schools, especially the recognised schools. It lists over 500 as members of the Incorporated Association of Preparatory Schools, most of them in pleasant places and mainly in Southern England, as they always were, and also about forty choir schools which, educationally, are first cousins to the prep. schools. The *Girls' School Year Book* has a rather wider range of contents. Specific bodies such as the Girls' Public Day School Trust furnish information about their own schools, including preparatory departments. 'Progressive' schools, such as advertise in the *New Era*, have recently been the subject of an important sociological study by Professor Campbell Stewart of the University of Keele, whose forthcoming book will give authoritative information about them.

Denominational classifications cut across other lines of division. The Ministry of Education does not provide information about the denominational allegiance of independent and direct-grant schools, but the denominations themselves provide sets of figures, one of the most useful being the Newman Demographic Survey's data published in *Catholic Education: A Handbook, 1962–63*. Though these do not distinguish between primary and secondary pupils in respect of direct-grant or independent schools, they do give a breakdown by sex, type and religion (Catholic or non-Catholic). From this source (Tables 6–7, pp. 174–5) it appears likely that many parents, not all of them Catholic, take advantage of the opportunity to send their girls and small boys to Catholic independent schools, including convent schools, where an efficient primary education is given in a gentle and devoted atmosphere for comparatively low fees. They may make similar use of other denominational schools, but the data about these are less readily available.

The second group of minority schools is that of *special schools*. They may be divided according to their legal status (maintained or direct-grant), according to their organisation as day or boarding schools, or as mixed or single-sex schools, and most significantly according to the type or types of handicap for which they cater. The official *Statistics of Education in 1962*, Part I, Tables 7 (pp. 30–1), 26 (p. 55) and 27 (pp. 56–7) give the following figures for January

NUMBERS OF SPECIAL SCHOOLS. 1ST JANUARY, 1962.
(ENGLAND AND WALES)

Type of Special School	Number of Schools, by Sex-pattern				Number of Schools: Day or Boarding		
	Boys'	Girls'	Mixed	Total	Day	Boarding	Total
Maintained	105	44	475	624	405	219	624
Direct Grant	27	17	70	114	3	111	114
Totals	132	61	545	738	408	330	738

A Note on Minority Schools

1962, for special schools other than hospital schools in England and Wales. They cover the whole age-range up to the statutory leaving age of sixteen (Education Act, 1944, Sec. 38(1)).

The cross-tabulation is not carried further than this. As regards pupils, three times as many attended day as boarding schools, with little sex-difference. These schools included the following pupils within the primary age-range:

NUMBERS OF PUPILS UNDER 12 IN SPECIAL SCHOOLS,
1ST JANUARY, 1962. (ENGLAND AND WALES)

Category of Special School	Age of Pupils								Total 2–11
	2–4	5	6	7	8	9	10	11	
BOYS									
Blind	20	28	35	44	50	71	92	62	402
Partially Sighted	8	42	50	62	104	98	118	115	597
Deaf	193	120	127	116	138	126	125	134	1,079
Partially Hearing	27	26	23	52	76	80	94	95	473
Physically Handicapped	81	224	276	350	383	408	384	362	2,468
Delicate	28	151	362	529	748	693	698	646	3,855
Maladjusted	2	8	16	47	86	166	206	241	772
Educationally Sub-normal	18	109	240	664	1,260	1,796	2,360	2,855	9,302
Epileptic	0	2	15	19	36	33	45	58	208
Speech Defect	1	5	6	8	8	9	8	13	58
Totals	378	715	1,150	1,891	2,889	3,480	4,130	4,581	19,214
GIRLS									
Blind	24	21	31	32	48	60	66	58	340
Partially Sighted	3	22	37	45	60	63	80	75	385
Deaf	170	114	90	103	98	89	94	131	889
Partially Hearing	9	24	29	36	47	69	63	62	339
Physically Handicapped	72	176	228	234	274	296	255	271	1,806
Delicate	39	113	233	388	469	510	513	494	2,759
Maladjusted	8	3	7	14	30	44	48	47	201
Educationally Sub-normal	8	89	143	381	837	1,286	1,546	1,913	6,203
Epileptic	0	4	16	20	21	17	16	27	121
Speech Defect	1	2	7	5	2	2	5	3	27
Totals	334	568	821	1,258	1,886	2,436	2,686	3,081	13,070
Total girls and boys	712	1,283	1,971	3,149	4,775	5,916	6,816	7,662	32,284
As percentage of estimated total of age-group	0·04	0·19	0·31	0·48	0·73	0·92	1·05	1·16 (Boys: 0·55) (Girls: 0·42)	0·48

(Data derived from Table 8, pp. 32–5, and Table 28, p. 58, of
Statistics of Education in 1962, Part I.)

NOTE—It should not be assumed that these places are adequate to meet the demand.

From these figures it will be seen that the more overt physical handicaps appear to be diagnosed earlier than those of a more psychological nature. It is also evident that in every category of handicap, boys are over-represented in proportion to their numbers in the population as a whole, especially in the categories of psycho-

116

logical handicap and above all among the maladjusted. It is interesting to speculate how far social factors contribute to this male predominance.

Incidentally, almost exactly 50 per cent of the special-school population was aged under twelve, so that the remainder was concentrated in fewer years and the percentage per age-group continued to mount, actually reaching a peak at fourteen. No further breakdown is given to indicate what proportion of these pupils were in schools in the various administrative categories. However in Table 8 of the same *Statistics* it is shown that of the total of children under twelve in special schools, 2,596 boys and 1,854 girls were in direct-grant schools: about a seventh of the total. In *Catholic Education: A Handbook, 1962–63* (Table 7, p. 175) lists of Catholic special schools, pupils and teachers are given, with a breakdown by sex and religion but not by age.[10] Again, Table 27 (pp. 56–7) of the official 1962 *Statistics* indicates the distribution of day and boarding schools by type of defect, as well as by status, showing that day schools were predominant among maintained schools largely because the most numerous categories of pupil (such as E.S.N.) were mainly accommodated in day schools. This set of data does not, however, permit of any breakdown by age.

In the Ministry statistics, *hospital schools*, the third type of minority school, are sometimes reckoned as special schools and sometimes as a category of their own. The principal difference is, of course, that they normally retain children for much shorter periods, so that individuals included within hospital-school returns may quite usually proceed to other schools during the year, though some undergo long periods of hospitalisation. On 1st January 1962, according to Table 7 of the official *Statistics* there were 99 hospital schools in England and Wales, 85 mixed schools and 1 boys' being maintained schools, and 12 mixed and 1 boys', direct-grant schools. There were no girls' hospital schools. According to Table 8, the following pupils (all boarders) were in these schools:

PUPILS IN HOSPITAL SCHOOLS, BY AGE, 1ST JANUARY, 1962
(ENGLAND AND WALES)

	2	3	4	5	6	7	8	9	10	11	Total
BOYS											
In maintained schools	68	108	125	169	169	209	153	170	119	142	1,432
In direct-grant schools	24	26	34	43	46	48	41	37	39	34	372
GIRLS											
In maintained schools	86	70	75	126	144	127	118	104	103	116	1,069
In direct-grant schools	30	34	19	25	23	15	24	23	25	32	250
Total	208	238	253	363	382	399	336	334	286	324	3,123

It is noteworthy here that boys are again slightly over-represented, but that there is no consistent trend towards greater totals in the older age-groups, though totals in the pre-school years are noticeably lower. No further details are given, except that the Newman Demographic Survey, in the Catholic handbook already mentioned specifies that two hospital schools (irrespective of age-range) were Roman Catholic.

These, then, are the three principal categories of minority schools. To do justice to them would involve specialist knowledge and experience and would in any case require more space than can be given within the present volume. Since very little specifically sociological study has yet been directed towards minority schools as social institutions, there is really a need for specific investigation of all of them before anything definitive can be written. All that is possible at present is to indicate, in the broadest terms, the ways in which the schema of analysis of social structure and process outlined in Chapter I and applied to maintained primary schools in Chapters II–IV might yield a different picture if it were used to examine the minority schools.

Social Analysis of Minority Schools

Although adults in primary schools will be considered separately in Chapter VII, staffs in minority schools require a brief additional comment before the children's society is examined. As indicated in Chapter VII, the demographic character of independent-school staffs differs from that in maintained schools. They also tend to differ in background and training: indeed, until recently many of the men in the more traditional independent primary schools would have viewed the whole question of professional training with puzzled incredulity, although the women teachers, with their strong Froebelian emphasis, have been more favourably disposed to it. Together they have tended to represent an interaction between the preparatory and developmental traditions and, in a slightly status-conscious and formal fashion, they have at best maintained an impressive level of culture and devotion. At the same time, some independent schools have attracted staffs eager to stand in the forefront of the developmental advance.

In some independent schools, mostly in the non-recognised category, there appears an adult role not considered in Chapter VII, namely that of the *proprietor*, who runs a school as a profit-making concern. His influence is bound to require consideration in a sociological analysis. At the opposite pole, from the economic point of view, stand the teaching Orders (mainly Roman Catholic, but including some Anglican Orders too) whose members renounce individual rewards and career prospects under their vows of poverty and obedience. They constitute a recognisable part of the teaching strength in independent schools and are unexcelled in devotion to their pupils, although they tend to shelter some of them, particularly girls, rather closely.

Special-school and hospital-school staffs do not differ markedly in general characteristics from junior- and infant-school staffs, as will be shown in Chapter VII. Only teachers of blind, deaf and partially-hearing children are at present required to undertake further training (Dent, 1961, p. 135) though others often do. For all special-school work, special skills are needed, and also an attitude of professional commitment. For certain kinds of work, notably that in residential schools for the maladjusted, it is particularly important to consider what types of teacher personality are appropriate, especially because the emotional strains of living with maladjusted children are superimposed on, and interact with, those associated with close contact with a small number of other adults in a closed community. Occasionally, teachers opt for special-school work owing to psychological difficulties of their own, but this is something of which appointing committees are well aware.

Special schools also include among their adults a range of medically-qualified and nursing personnel not mentioned in Chapter VII, who are necessarily in much closer association with the teachers and children than in other schools. It is impossible to do justice, within the scope of the present chapter, to the roles and status of these members of the medical and nursing professions or of the psychologists who are in a sense intermediate between them and the teaching staff, but it is evident that this area of interaction between the teaching and medical professions, with its scope for conflicts of role and status and bureaucratic organisation, is a subject which deserves attention.

The *formal structure* of minority schools, as it affects the children, tends to be different in a number of ways from that of infant or junior schools, especially when the minority schools are also boarding schools. In that case the formal structure expands into the whole of the children's world, during term-time, and involves some annexation of the domestic to the educational institutions in society. In hospital schools, it is in fact subordinated to the still greater formality of medical institutions. These characteristics are often reflected in the actual architecture of minority schools. Residential preparatory and private schools, and special schools, are often in fact houses which symbolise their absorption of the domestic organisation, while special schools for various kinds of physical handicap, and hospital schools, usually have some specially-built accommodation in which easy and regular access to medical facilities such as physiotherapy is available. Meanwhile day special schools such as those for the educationally subnormal, which do not require these special medical facilities, do often look like junior or infant schools, sometimes intentionally so in order to minimise their separateness. In some day independent schools, on the other hand, the use of the domestic pattern of architecture to accommodate activities which, in infant and junior schools, would normally be carried on in buildings which are obviously schools, may have the incidental and sometimes deliberate effect of emphasising that these independent schools are different from 'ordinary' schools, and even that they share the outlook of families whose cultural standards are developed within their domestic institutions, rather than those of the rest of the population who need specific and recognisable educational institutions to civilise them.

The formal social structure, too, expresses differences between minority schools and others. For one thing, the age-structure is more flexible. Independent schools can choose when they transfer from one level to another, as has already been seen, while special schools are specifically exempted by Section 8(2) of the Education Act, 1944, from the obligation to organise separately into primary and secondary schools, even though there may be some informal division into junior and senior departments or sections. Again, the size of classes is much smaller, in many cases. Some independent schools are able to retain their support by offering small classes in return for high fees, while special schools are specifically required by Regulation[11] to keep their classes down, irrespective of age. The problem of streaming is less acute in minority schools, for in special and hospital schools numbers are sometimes so small and individual needs so varied that organisation has perforce to be based on individual programmes. Larger special schools, including E.S.N. schools, do sometimes make use of a flexible system of grouping by a combination of age and attainment, but this is different in its impact from junior-school streaming because the grouping does not itself apparently figure as a determinant of educational progress, or a result of social-class or other background influences. In many private schools too, numbers prevent subdivision within an age-group, or even within a combination of age-groups, but in some independent schools, where numbers permit, streaming by ability is entrenched even to the extent of including an 'express stream' modelled on the practice customary in direct-grant grammar schools: a good instance of the penetration of primary schools by secondary-school ideas within the preparatory tradition. Even so, this streaming is unlikely to have quite the same significance as in junior schools, because it is conducted within a more restricted socio-economic context.

Boarding schools of all kinds, and day special schools, have particular responsibilities towards newcomers which do not apply in infant and junior schools. The move away from home usually involves some specific catering for newcomers in a distinctive corner of the formal organisation. Indeed, special schools have an additional problem for they have to cater for children, often admitted at any point during the school year, who may find it doubly difficult to settle down, especially in residential schools, because their transfer to a special school symbolises and emphasises that they *are* handicapped.

Lastly, there is a contrast with infant and junior schools in the distribution of formal status-positions, especially in special and hospital schools, where the maintained-school pattern is scarcely applicable, and in experimental schools where the allocation of formal status may be rejected on principle. However, special schools may encourage alternative forms of status and role in order to minimise the tendency for their pupils to feel 'different', and may for the same reason make use of as much of the conventional status-apparatus as they can, while the leading independent schools often model their own status-positions deliberately on independent secondary schools, a form of anticipatory socialisation which again denotes the preparatory tradition but which may occasionally defeat its own purpose when boys who have been accustomed to command have suddenly to obey.[12]

To a sociologist, one of the most important questions about the formal structure of minority schools is that of their social composition. Since there is a tendency for some physical defects, and some psychological defects also, to be associated with social-class level, there may be an important correlation between socio-economic status and attendance at some kinds of special school. In hospital schools this is less likely, though it is never wise to be confident about such opinions until they have actually been put to the test. On the other hand independent schools, because of their dependence on fees, are likely to draw disproportionately from the upper socio-economic strata; indeed, the political case against them is based on this assumption, and on the correlative belief that they confer advantages on their pupils of such a nature that they are likely to retain their superior status because of their education. Incidental evidence from a number of sources supports these assumptions.[13] However it would be incorrect to say that independent schools cater exclusively for upper- and middle-class children, though some do; indeed a few of them afford some of the most convincing available evidence for the belief that there still is an upper class in England, and that our social geometry is still Euclidean enough to prevent the middle from coinciding with the top.

Semi-formal activities are more prominent in minority schools than elsewhere, particularly in boarding schools. In the traditional independent boys' schools, great stress is laid on organised games, since it is often assumed that they play a major part in character-building, though they are usually conducted in a milder social climate than at the secondary stage. Other semi-formal activities are numerous, and often combine high standards with a rather traditional range of content and a somewhat paternal type of organisation. One would not expect, for example, to find on the staff of a county junior school a retired major organising a rifle club, but in a preparatory school it would be quite possible, and he would produce some crack shots too. On the other hand, the more deviant of experimental independent schools have a quite different emphasis in semi-formal organisations among which the violin is more likely to appear than the rifle and the pupils themselves are more likely to take initiative in organisation, especially if the school caters for the secondary range also. Of course the violin is quite likely to appear in preparatory schools too; more so perhaps than in 'State' schools, and quite likely in the very same school as the rifle.

In special schools there is often an emphasis on activities which can help to counteract handicaps or help to compensate for them, especially in instances where the children feel excluded from the games and other pursuits which carry prestige in the children's world. Thus some of these activities are physical, often of an original type, while others cater for interests such as collecting and aesthetic pursuits. The latter are particularly important in hospital schools and in schools for the severely handicapped, where they are virtually a part of the treatment of the handicap itself. For example, self-esteem can be developed in E.S.N. children through successful participation in a swimming gala with primary schools, and stability can be fostered among the maladjusted through the use of the arts such as movement and painting, though in such cases the possibilities of the pupils' taking part in the actual organisation of the work are limited.

In boarding schools, whether independent or special (or both, for here they overlap) there is room for the development of branches of adult-sponsored organisations, another part of the children's world which is annexed by boarding schools. The Baden-Powell organisations are the most conspicuous among these, and their work among handicapped children has a particular significance because of its potential for promoting some solidarity of interest between other children and themselves. In some preparatory schools with an evangelical Christian emphasis, prominence is also given to branches of organisations such as the Crusaders' Union. In such ways the schools encourage (and sometimes compel) the development of a range of values all of which are compatible with the school's chosen purposes but which do give some scope for individual preferences.

The informal structure of minority schools is potentially very interesting, yet very little is known about it. Boarding schools, in particular, must develop an intensity of social interaction without parallel in day schools even at an age when schools in general are the focus of social life. Indications of this are given in autobiography and fiction about boarding schools, coloured in most cases by prejudices of one kind or another, but it has scarcely been investigated, and there is even a possibility that attempts at investigation might be regarded as a form of impiety. This is less likely to be the case in residential special schools; indeed the one example which I know of a scientific study of informal relations in an English boarding school was conducted in the residential school for E.S.N. pupils at Monyhull Hall, Birmingham, by Murray (1953). He confined his investigation to the choices made by boys in one 'home' including a number of boys of Midlands age, and found that they chose their friends almost entirely from their own sex and mainly from that 'home'. In addition he was able to trace some very interesting relationships between acceptance and stability of social contact on the one hand, and social behaviour on the other. A relatively low level of stability was associated with poor behaviour within the community: more extreme lack of social contact led to over-aggression or absconding.[14] This last point is possibly of wider interest for it calls attention to the possible significance of absconding or 'running away' as a form of withdrawing behaviour which can be contemplated as a desperate solution, when an individual's adjustment within the informal system of a boarding school becomes too great a problem to admit of any other. For the encroachment of the school on the children's world must polarise problems of adjustment. It is hardly necessary to add that this tendency is maximised in a residential school for those who are already maladjusted, or who have other handicaps likely to induce maladjustment. It is also probable that in boarding schools informal relations among the staff are more visible to the children than in day schools, and thus make a more direct impact on the relations between the children themselves, for in the Midlands years all teachers are to some extent models of adult behaviour with which the children identify themselves, and the very completeness with which these adults are exposed to the children's gaze may intensify this influence. If the provision of boarding schools by local education authorities is extended from the secondary to the primary age-range,[15] then these characteristic features of informal relations in boarding schools will no longer be confined to the minority schools.

In day schools, the patterns of informal relationships are likely to resemble more closely those which were discussed in Chapters II and III. One could conjecture that the same types of variation according to age and social climate would appear, though in special schools the modifications would be considerable. However in independent schools there is likely to be a different range of social backgrounds and in special schools a different impact of the formal organisation of the school on its informal system, so that in both cases the informal social system is probably subject to influences different from those which operate in junior and infant schools.

Yet at present all of this remains in the realm of speculation, and the invitation is open for research to be conducted in this unknown region.

The *social roles* of minority schools really require much more detailed consideration than is possible here, for it is in the distinctiveness of their roles that they find their *raison d'être*. Instruction, for example, must be the business of them all, since none of their pupils are 'unsuitable for education at school'. But the type of instruction varies widely. Independent schools vary within themselves from those which are the principal strongholds of the preparatory tradition and lean towards formal studies and Common Entrance, to those which discount specific teaching completely. Special schools have various kinds of emphasis: those concerned with cognitive handicap (the E.S.N. schools are the largest single category) emphasise some basic attainments and social competence, while the various types of physical handicap require specific instruction in skills such as Braille reading and lip-reading, and thus have to undertake *more* instruction in some ways than infant or junior schools. On the other hand, there may be difficulties in providing sufficient range of instruction because of the small numbers. At the secondary level this can result in stereotyping of children and allocation to a limited range of occupations: the effects of this can penetrate down into the Midlands range. This is less likely to apply to hospital schools because, although they may make great demands on the knowledge and versatility of their small staffs, the majority of their pupils are only in hospital for comparatively short periods.

There are similar variations in socialisation. Minority schools must vary widely both in the initial social awareness and attitudes of their pupils and in the range of socialisation which they regard as desirable. The leading independent schools often operate in a social environment quite unlike that of maintained schools and, intentionally or otherwise, tend to preserve its separateness. The means of socialisation may also be different. A manly sermon may still help to make small boys into little gentlemen, while the same sermon delivered in a voluntary primary school might expect little more than dutiful incomprehension. At the opposite pole, experimental schools sometimes deliberately foster attitudes of social nonconformity or at least let it be known that no objections will be raised if such attitudes develop. In special schools there is a closer approximation to the position in maintained schools except that part of the process of socialisation may consist of adjustment to the children's handicaps and perhaps preparation for return to a normal school. For E.S.N. schools, the problem of basic social competence is likely to influence socialisation as well as instruction, and in schools for the maladjusted, and in particular those which cater for autistic children, socialisation is almost the basic objective.

Classification is relatively easy to consider. Where there are handicaps, one of the principal dimensions of classification is concerned with keeping a check on the children's physical or psychological condition—or both, in some cases of multiple handicap. In independent schools the classificatory processes are likely to be more akin to those in maintained schools, except that the modes of classification probably range from the traditional patterns associated with the preparatory tradition, in which preparation for secondary education, often in specific schools, is paramount, to the more flexible procedures associated with the developmental tradition. Some progressive schools, indeed, claim to have eliminated classification altogether, though this can only be true of the more ostensible kinds of classification.

Welfare is one role in which independent schools stand in sharpest contrast with maintained schools. Although some ancillary services are extended to them (Education Act, 1944, Sec. 78) they are essentially an enclave in the welfare state, a reserve of choice which is open to parents who prefer freedom of choice, for reasons of conscience or of social advantage, to the acceptance of their share of educational provision within the maintained system. That is not to say that the welfare of individual children is neglected within independent schools: on the contrary, these schools are often at pains to emphasise that their pupils enjoy more individual care than would be possible in the large classes of infant and junior schools. However, this preferential solicitude is not what is usually meant by the welfare role.

Special schools, on the other hand, are in a sense its embodiment. Their growth during the nineteenth and twentieth centuries is almost an index of the extension of this role, and also of the developmental tradition itself. Moreover, circumstances virtually oblige special schools to devote a greater part of their time and energy to their welfare functions than would be usual in a junior or infant school. Indeed, where skilled treatment is required, for example among cerebral palsied or aphasic children, the role extends beyond the usual scope of welfare and the term 'therapy' might be used to denote an additional role in their case.

As for autonomy, the arguments in favour of this role for maintained primary schools apply with equal force to minority schools. Although their role-ascriptions may be more precise in other respects, they cannot function fully as social institutions unless their other roles are balanced by something which makes each school worth respecting in itself. Many of them achieve this, although for special schools it is particularly difficult. In one way it is also difficult for some independent schools, since they may depend for their support on parents who are suspicious both of the nature of 'autonomous' activities and of the proportion of time which they require, apparently at the expense of instruction.

A Note on Minority Schools

Social cohesion and control are necessary as properties of minority schools, just as they are necessary in other primary schools. However, their situations and functions necessitate a wide variety of policy. Two factors are involved, namely the mechanism by which norms, rules, and informal control are maintained, and the values on which these norms are based. The pattern of rewards and punishments reflects both. In the first case, the actual mechanism in independent schools is basically similar to that in maintained primary schools, with one important addition. Since they are independent, they can expel. On the other hand, they have to attract pupils. Therefore they are both freer and less free than maintained schools in their treatment of pupils. On the whole, they can count on the interested support of the parents who invest in them. This applies, incidentally, as much to schools which vaunt their abolition of formal sanctions as to those which proclaim the social necessity of maintaining them. The position of special schools is rather different. Here, too, parents are generally appreciative and ensure their support, though they tend still to think that some stigma attaches to children who attend schools catering for psychological difficulties: perhaps they feel that the stigma really attaches to the parents. Although expulsion is not possible, discreet transfer is sometimes necessary, and new admissions can be carefully sifted because of the limits on numbers. In some special schools the very nature of the situation renders less necessary the overt maintenance of social control, while in others it may be more than usually necessary. To take the extreme instances: orthopaedic cases stay put, whereas maladjusted children may at any moment erupt into diffuse activity.

In minority schools, as elsewhere, the actual system of informal control among the pupils themselves is the anchor on which the system of overt control depends. In independent schools, especially boarding schools, this may be deeply rooted in inherited lore, awe-inspiring maybe to the newcomer and rather insipid to the old hand, which the staffs of the schools tolerate with amused approval, reminding each other perhaps how much more barbed and virile it all was in their own schooldays, and for the rest taking it for granted that it can be manipulated easily enough by any teacher with maturity and a sense of humour. So it can; for the children perceive that basically most of them share the outlook of most of the staff on their education, and gain from their solicitude even when it is expressed in rather unctuous terms. While they may oppose ferociously or with schoolgirl disdain those who transgress the norm by showing undue dependence on the staff, they are also likely to ostracise those who reject school values too completely. Thus the good-pupil and fairly-good-pupil roles, together with their correlative norms, are generally approved and enforced by group pressure even though they permit a reasonable amount of self-assertion.

126

(This can be seen even in the youngest classes, where pert little people flourish but rapidly learn to observe norms acceptable to the school.)

Under these circumstances, as in most infant or junior schools, social control is maintained with comparative ease. Moreover, in particular independent schools the momentum of social control is assisted because their characteristics tend to intensify. Schools acquire reputations, which in this way become self-perpetuating. Parents tend to choose those schools which already appear to conform most closely to their expectations, and in this way the schools acquire a distinctive public which reinforces social control from outside. This may even be the case in relation to progressive schools with a libertarian régime, for some cohesion may be guaranteed externally even though it is not enforced internally.

In special schools there is a rather different situation, depending very much on the type of handicap for which they cater. E.S.N. and maladjusted children are often rather dependent on the staff, though occasionally erupting into clumsy rebellion. They find it difficult to develop a coherent peer organisation, though when they do succeed, social cohesion tends to improve, especially if their informal relations are taken into account in the actual programme of the school.[16] On the other hand children with physical handicaps are often anxious to prove their maturity by showing social responsibility especially towards their juniors, and it may be generally beneficial to allow them to evolve a society in which they develop complementary roles and discover that each of them can earn recognition for something. Of course in the case of multiple handicaps, or in schools catering for a diversity of handicap, the position is more complicated.

The schools' officially espoused values are the other major component affecting the procedures for social cohesion and control. They too are very diverse. In independent schools they can range from the preparatory to the developmental extreme. So they may in special schools, but there they may vary concurrently along a second continuum from a pastoral-religious to a professional-therapeutic orientation. As for the children's own values, which play an essential part in norm-establishment in minority schools as well as elsewhere, it is likely that there will be a fairly predictable homogeneity in most categories of independent school but that the situation in special and hospital schools is much more open to chance. Thus, in general, independent schools can expect a greater stability of mores and of basic social control.

It is in the light of these factors that actual rules, rewards and punishments are devised. In view of the factors working in favour of cohesion in most independent schools, it is not surprising that they can usually. operate a mild régime. Rules there must be, especially in a boarding school, because so many more facets of life are organised within the same social framework. But where punishments are concerned it is perhaps surprising that such an elaborate apparatus of lines and keeping-in and caning is apparently considered necessary. Perhaps it is a function of tradition, or of the deliberate elaboration of mores and folkways to emphasise the distinctiveness of the institution. Perhaps it is necessary to the authority-structure operating in this type of closed community. Perhaps it is itself an aspect of the preparatory approach, in that it leaves the children more ready for the régime which follows. However the smaller schools for young children, and the girls' schools generally, show less rigidity, while the progressive schools whittle away their punitive apparatus until in extreme cases such as A. S. Neill's Summerhill there are no rules, no rewards, no punishments. Elsewhere, as in junior and infant schools, rewards are less prominent than punishments, but praise is often generously and wisely distributed among those who excel in the good-pupil role.

In special schools the situation is different. Just because of the need to safeguard children with particular handicaps, extensive rules are often necessary, but they are rules for adults rather than for children. Actually there is sometimes a danger that the older children, being less self-assured and more school-based than most adolescents, may collaborate with adults so zealously in the enforcement of regulations in order to prove their own status that the under-twelves are unduly cosseted. The need for punishments, in the fragmented situation normal in schools for the physically handicapped, is generally less, and the call for rewards proportionately greater. Psychological handicaps however call for firmer and more explicit external control. In E.S.N. schools this may take the form of cogent direction. In schools for the maladjusted, actual punishment including corporal punishment may be meted out even by those who are on principle opposed to its use. This is particularly true in residential schools. In one of the very few empirical studies in this field Kellmer Pringle (1957) found in a representative sample of residential schools for the maladjusted (not confined to the Midlands age-range) that nine out of thirty-six schools admitted using it, however reluctantly. She observed that:

> ... maladjusted children because of their very maladjustment are much more likely to provoke or challenge the endurance of the staff; moreover hysterical outbursts may on occasions,, make a slap essential (p. 35).

and also stressed the great strain under which staffs of such schools inevitably work.[17]

The *culture-patterns* of minority schools have already been mentioned incidentally. Here again, the same considerations apply as in schools at large. It is through the fostering of a satisfying culture, based in part on the children's informal relations but also on the values promulgated by the school, that its autonomous role can be most effectively discharged. Here again this can be most impressively achieved when the activities of the school are in substantial measure related to creative work in the arts. This is true of a boys' preparatory school with an established academic reputation; it is also true of a school catering for children with a variety of handicaps.

Finally, *social change* constitutes an essential aspect of the sociological study of minority schools. The small-scale changes involved in substitutions among personnel affect them much as they affect other schools, though more intensely if they are small and isolated residential schools with a close community life. A monitor, a housemaster or a resident psychologist may take over his predecessor's functions without making a fundamental alteration in the social structure and processes of the school, but after a number of such changes the whole institution will begin to alter slowly. This process of change will be accelerated if a number of concurrent changes of personnel are all characterised by similar shifts of outlook. The replacement of a religious by a professional pattern of staff motivation in a special school affords an example of this; the penetration of a predominantly aristocratic preparatory school by the sons of successful business men, or of a private school which was formerly a middle-class preserve by the daughters of highly skilled workers, constitutes another. Less obvious, but also important, is the impact of new trends of professional orientation. For example, the pattern of instruction in an E.S.N. school may be reoriented through the advent of an enthusiast for modern dance or rural science; a development in hearing aids may result in a new approach to formal organisation in a school for the partially hearing; the gradual percolation of more 'developmental' methods of instruction may diversify and alter the roles and behaviour of children in an independent school.

In any case, over the years, these minority schools respond in some measure, like all other social institutions, to the major patterns of demographic, economic and social change in English society. If more children are ascertained as in need of special educational treatment, partly because methods of ascertainment are themselves improved, then the relative demand for special-school places will grow; but if it appears beneficial for more of these children such as the partially sighted to be accommodated in other schools where they can mix with other children, then to that extent the demand will fall. Similarly, if the increase of affluence enables more parents to pay school fees, and if the nature or quality of education in maintained primary schools declines, perhaps through shortage of

129

teachers, the number of independent schools for children of Midlands age may increase. On the other hand, if a higher proportion of the gross national product is allocated to maintained primary schools, the relative attraction of the independent schools may be greatly reduced.

It may seem a dubious procedure to group these three categories of minority schools—independent, special, and hospital—together in one chapter, since two of them depend on handicaps and the other on willingness and capacity to pay fees (except where this is undertaken by Local Education Authorities for other reasons). Yet the three are alike in that they absorb nearly all the children who do not attend maintained infant and junior schools. They are also similar in one other respect, for they exemplify the readiness of English society in its present phase to sanction the existence of particular educational institutions for particular purposes. This readiness is not unchallenged, even at the primary level, but it is there. Meanwhile, it is to be hoped that this sketchy application of the basic schema of analysis, used throughout this book, to the minority schools will indicate that they, too, are worthy of a fuller sociological description.

VI

From Primary Schools to Secondary Schools

PRIMARY education, as understood in England now, is a stage in its own right, but one which is in itself incomplete. In this way it exemplifies the developmental rather than the elementary or preparatory outlook. A sociological survey of its institutional aspects would therefore be incomplete without some comment on transfer from primary to secondary education[1] and indeed on the whole question of the relationship between primary and secondary education. In this chapter, the method of analysis of social structure and process hitherto employed will be set aside, and three aspects of this relationship between the two stages of school will be considered from the sociological point of view. The first of these is the most familiar, namely the actual allocation[2] of children to secondary schools. The other two, the transition from primary to secondary education and the continuing influence of primary schools within secondary schools, are also important though, largely because they are less controversial, they are also less often discussed.

A. ALLOCATION OF CHILDREN TO SECONDARY SCHOOLS

Any sociological account of English primary education which overlooked this issue would resemble a social history of the nineteen-forties which made no reference to the Second World War. Yet so much has already been written about it that it would be superfluous and even presumptuous to discuss it without presenting new data. Fortunately, the very thoroughness with which it has been studied has also led to the publication of adequate scholarly and accessible surveys of the subject. Probably the best sociological study of the historical determinants of selection for secondary education is given by Olive Banks (1955), while the most adequate general introduction to the various aspects of the problem is to be found in the survey made by the British Psychological Society and edited by Vernon (1957) under the title *Secondary School Selection*. All that is necessary for the present purpose, then, is to summarise the

131

sociological factors which bear upon secondary-school allocation, and the sociological consequences of the allocation itself. This will necessarily involve some reference to material already mentioned in previous chapters.

Sociological influences upon allocation

In theory, there are three main ways in which sociological influences affect allocation to secondary schools, namely through the provision of different types and proportions of secondary schools, through the nature of the allocation procedure itself, and through the response to it which is shown by children from different social backgrounds.

The first of these is largely a matter of local social history, and is too complicated to warrant analysis here. It has however resulted in a situation in which the proportion of selective-school places varies substantially from region to region (Douglas, 1964, Ch. IV) and from one local education authority to another (Ministry of Education List 61, 1959). This is likely to cause variations in intensity of pressure on selective-school places, wherever a selective pattern of allocation is practised. But this does not necessarily happen without qualification, because of three other factors. First, some areas may have a sizeable proportion of parents who habitually look towards independent and direct-grant schools, a point which will be further discussed in Volume II, Chapter IV. Again, there may be differences between places in demand for selective education of any kind, though these (Floud, Halsey and Martin, 1957, pp. 88-90) are often less marked than a simple sub-cultural theory of educational aspirations might suggest. Sometimes indeed it appears that the demand for secondary technical education exceeds that for the grammar-school curriculum, but there is little positive evidence about this.[3] Thirdly, the intensity of demand for selective education depends, not surprisingly, on the quality of the alternatives to selective schools. Bowyer (1961) was probably justified in assuming that there would be considerable pressure in a school characterised by a:

> ... combination of parents with high educational traditions and a residential area where the alternative to a grammar school was a school with a reputation for low standards of work and discipline (p. 269).

However, this consideration is probably less important than might appear at first sight, for whatever the alternatives may be, parents tend to believe that a grammar school's a grammar school, for a' that. Thus in general the proportion of selective-school places is an important determinant of pressure and anxiety within primary education, whatever mitigating factors there may be.

The actual allocation procedure has also received considerable attention. It is in fact the principal institutional form taken by the classificatory role of primary education as a whole. In any particular area it tends to give rise to an island of professionalism, symbolising the capacity of institutional education to stand out against political and other pressures but which is, partly for that reason, often made the scapegoat for resentments which are really directed against the selective principle itself. The characteristic English-arithmetic-intelligence pattern was originally devised as a safeguard of social justice against the advantages which appeared to accrue to middle-class children whose home background and primary education, in independent schools or the more favourably-situated elementary schools, had equipped them with initial advantages in the informational subjects and in general culture. However, the usual selection procedure (usual, that is, until very recently) has often itself become a target for criticism on ideological grounds, not only because of its inhibiting backwash effect on primary-school teaching but also because, after all, it proved less culture-free than had been expected. Informed criticism was directed less against the test procedures themselves than against their impact on children and schools and against the assumptions of educational predictability which were sometimes associated with it, and which could be interpreted by some left-wing opinion as an unjustifiable means of defending the practice of giving a limited education to working-class children and thus of preserving the existing structure of society. It would be interesting to trace in some detail the social mechanisms by which this scapegoating of the selection procedure took place locally and nationally, and the means by which the bureaucratic organisation (in Weber's sense) sought to justify its procedures.

In terms of socio-political action this is closely lined with the third main sociological influence on allocation, namely the different chances of selective places which accrue to different social groups. Although there is some evidence that rural children undergo some specific handicaps, being penalised by speed tests more than urban working-class children (Moreton and Butcher, 1963), the main controversy has centred round the difference in chances between middle-class and working-class children. On this at least, and for reasons which are themselves partly socio-political in character, there is a reasonable amount of research evidence. In one of the most important of these studies Floud, Halsey and Martin (1957) suggested that where, as in South-West Hertfordshire, prosperity was relatively high and middle-class patterns of aspiration comparatively widespread, children of working-class origin were admitted to grammar schools in about the same proportion as would have been expected from the social-class distribution of measured intelligence. There was in fact no 'discrimination' against working-class children except just possibly on the actual borderline of selection (pp. 56–7).

Interestingly enough, the same general pattern emerged in Middlesbrough, where working-class levels of prosperity and of educational aspiration were more variable. In the same piece of research they demonstrated (p. 45) that, owing to the differing distributions of measured intelligence in different social classes (as far as these could be defined), the working-class share of grammar-school places would tend to vary directly according to the number of places available. In other words, within the limits of their data it appeared that the more selective a school was, the greater the proportion of middle-class children it would be likely to admit even on the criterion of measured intelligence. If this is generally true, its social implications are of obvious importance.

So are those of Swift's (1964) study which suggests that, among middle-class families, there may be two types likely to gain selective-school places, one based on the usual concepts of middle-class culture and the other, found particularly in the lower middle-class, associated with a sense of frustration and a frankly utilitarian pursuit of formal qualifications. (See also supplementary bibliography.)

Hitherto, no reference has been made to variations in patterns of allocation. In fact, there is a growing trend towards modification of methods of allocation to secondary schools even where the selective pattern of allocation is maintained. These have been introduced partly as a result of the social pressures already discussed, and particularly in response to protests against the baleful practice of basing selection on a once-for-all examination, however efficient. Some critics of existing practices believed that a modified procedure would be more equitable. As between individuals, it probably is. It does not necessarily follow that it must lead to greater social equality. In a further study Floud and Halsey (1957) examined the situation in South-West Hertfordshire after intelligence testing had been eliminated from the selection procedure in the county. They found that the proportion of middle-class children entering grammar schools rose subsequently. In the light of findings like these it appears that intelligence tests, in spite of their limitations as predictive instruments, do appear to function in this context as guarantors of social equity.

Sometimes it is suggested that more weight should be given to estimates by teachers, and especially by Head Teachers. Here again there are likely to be many occasions when individual children are more equitably treated because their teachers claim that their test performance is unrepresentative. Yet Douglas (1964, pp. 73–4) has intimated how teachers' estimates, if widely employed, might favour middle-class children of both sexes and girls at all social levels, though Yates and Pidgeon (1957) working with rather different data, indicated that Head Teachers' assessments may sometimes be better predictors than intelligence tests, in terms of grammar-school success (which, however, embodies an element of self-fulfilling prophecy). Thus there is some variability in opinions about their value. In addition, however, the use of teachers' assessments must inevitably increase the importance of a school's classificatory role at the expense of the others. In suburbs and especially in villages, the social pressures on teachers could then be heavy (Vernon, 1957, pp. 55; 139).

Another modification of the usual procedures, introduced in Kent and elsewhere, involves using a series of tests over the whole junior-school range. This, though reducing the immediate impact of once-for-all selection, again throws considerable emphasis on schools' classificatory functions, as teachers observe the children's measured progress. There is as yet no evidence about its effect on social-class chances.

The extreme case of modification of allocation procedures, one which is not extensively established even in areas which have introduced fully comprehensive secondary education or have reorganised their secondary education on the Leicestershire plan, involves the abandonment of any form of selection. Allocation is then made by parental preference, or by zoning, or some other means. It would be rash, none the less, to assume that for that reason there can be no social-class influence on allocation. Evidence drawn from the U.S.A., where this is a normal situation, would indicate the contrary. There is a limit to the social changes which can be achieved by institutional reorganisation alone.

The social consequences of allocation

The social consequences of secondary-school allocation fall into three main categories, those relating to individual primary schools, those affecting individual secondary schools, and those which are of wider significance in society. Of these the second is not relevant to the present account, but some attention should be paid to the first and the last.

The effects on individual primary schools have been indicated in previous chapters. To a considerable extent they depend on local circumstances already mentioned: the supply of selective secondary-school places in the area, the nature of the local allocation process; and the degree of parental anxiety which is prevalent in the district (Martin, F. M. in Glass, 1954, Ch. 7). Of these, the first two differ widely, and the third less so, as has already been indicated. What does differ from place to place is the way in which parents express what anxiety they have, and the assumptions which they make about their roles and responsibilities in relation to those of teachers. All these differences would exist in some measure if selection did not take place, but the exigencies of selection intensify them.

However, some of the social backwash effects of allocation are intensified within primary schools themselves. The reasons for this will be broached in Chapter VII. Where groups of primary-school teachers internalise the middle-class educational norms and the assumptions usual within the preparatory tradition, aligning themselves with grammar-school expectations and in fact taking the grammar-school world as their 'reference group', then they will tend to generate pressures of their own. Conversely, where teachers adhere strongly to the developmental tradition, their pressures and preferences will be differently expressed. Where, as often happens, both patterns of attitude are to some extent represented in the same school, a further series of internal tensions can develop and can affect the relations of the teachers as a whole with parents and children alike. All of these pressures will have different consequences according to the local circumstances.

There is another issue too. Throughout the history of the elementary tradition, teachers have been bound to some external criterion, first the Revised Code, then 'the scholarship', and then 'the eleven-plus'. These have been hard taskmasters, but also convenient scapegoats. Without any demand of this sort, primary-school teachers will be free—indeed, are already becoming free—in a way that they have never been free before. That does not imply that they will know what to do with their freedom. Some will; a few may regret the lack of stimulus that the old grind provided (Vernon, 1957, p. 64); and a few others may secretly and even unconsciously regret the passing of a known framework with predictable demands.

Apart from Martin's pioneer study and Swift's (1964) interesting and scholarly investigation into parental influence on selection, both of which have already been mentioned, little empirical work has been conducted in this field. Most of the studies of children's anxiety (e.g. Sarnoff *et al.*, 1959; Bowyer, 1961) have taken some note of sub-cultural and local factors, but these could be more consistently and directly investigated. This is an area in which research could profitably be extended, especially during the years when patterns of allocation are themselves being modified.

Indeed, during the period of transition, the classificatory functions of primary schools will differ widely according to the degree of selection which persists in their areas. Even where maintained secondary schools are reorganised on a comprehensive basis, the retention of direct-grant or independent schools with a strong local tradition will tend to place some primary schools under heavy pressure to gear themselves to the entrance examinations of these non-maintained schools, as some already do. Where these are avowedly subject-examinations of the traditional 'preparatory' type, the primary schools most immediately affected may actually intensify a type of curriculum which the usual selection procedure was itself designed to supersede, one in which 'facts to be stored' are at a premium and the advantages enjoyed by middle-class children are greater than ever. This situation will possibly persist for some time, for it would be unrealistic to think that independent or direct-grant schools are about to disappear.

The wider, 'macrosociological' issues in secondary-school allocation are often discussed. They centre round concepts such as that of meritocracy and of the nature of social mobility in an industrial civilisation. These wider issues are concerned with the development of the whole of English society. Their specific relation to primary schools emerges in the need to maintain some balance between instruction, socialisation and classification there. For if classification is forced into a dominant position, resulting in emphasis on competitive values within the school's social system, then it not only distorts socialisation but also restricts instruction. This is of particular relevance to the immediate question of transfer to secondary schools, because grammar and modern schools alike tend to complain about the habits and attitudes with which their newcomers arrive. Grammar-school teachers often protest that children have been drilled in limited skills but lack persistence or imagination. In modern schools, the usual complaints are that the brighter children are inhibited by a sense of failure and simultaneously that the least able pupils have been sacrificed to the others and are carried forward like an overdraft into secondary education. Both complaints are exaggerated in a ritual manner, and probably derive in part from the cleavage between the two stages of education and from the consequent lack of communication, a point which will be discussed later. If so, then they will not be entirely eliminated even if selection for secondary education is abolished. But they will be amended, and perhaps reduced.

Throughout this discussion of allocation to secondary schools, no mention has been made of the corresponding processes at work outside the maintained schools. This is a question which cannot be adequately discussed here. It really has two aspects, one concerned with general allocation, which involves some measure of sifting by competitive (and often slightly old-fashioned) examination, and the other related to admission to particular schools, which is in some cases effected by personal contact and which always has also some financial connotation. Partly for this reason, this is a matter which has never received so much attention as has been directed at allocation to maintained schools. However, it is relevant to the maintained schools themselves, both through the impact of selection for direct-grant and independent schools which has already been mentioned, and through the decisions confronting local education authorities who exercise an option over places in independent schools.

B. THE ACTUAL TRANSITION
FROM PRIMARY TO SECONDARY SCHOOL

Just as pre-literate societies have their rites of passage from childhood to adolescence, so the transition from primary to secondary education fulfils a somewhat similar function in English society, marking the end of the Midlands years. Even in view of Tanner's data (1961, Ch. 7) on the falling age of puberty, however, this transition still does not quite coincide with the psychological onset of adolescence. At any rate among boys, the transition is usually effected before big noses and pubic hair begin to appear; some of them continue to wear short trousers for a while. Nevertheless, the transition itself carries and is intended to carry a considerable individual and social significance which is more far-reaching than the transition from infant to junior school discussed previously.

First there is a change of formal and informal institutional setting. At the very least, Blank Street Junior Mixed School is left and Blank County Secondary School is entered. This may only be up one more flight of stone steps in the same building, but it is different. The eleven-year-old who goes there finds a big and seemingly brusque world of leather jackets and swinging hips, with a vociferousness and bravado quite unlike the noisy but purposive small-scale community downstairs. Here the quality of the peer society is different, and to adults it seems much cruder and more assertive. Meanwhile, for others the comparable step may be from the uniformed, jolly sobriety of a suburban primary school to the equally uniformed but more sophisticated atmosphere of the secondary school across the road. Here, too, the quality of the peer society is different, though adults may perceive it as less threatening than its downtown counterpart. For other children again, the change may be more marked, especially when they are translated from the one type of primary school to the other type of secondary school. For example, after six years in a three-decker building that always seems to reek of stale cabbage and papier-mâché, they may suddenly find themselves wearing uniform for the first time and going to an educational palace whose modernity and grace positively demands a high tone of behaviour, and gets it. For an unfortunate few, the change to secondary education may have an opposite significance.

The change in formal structure is at once noticeable too. Instead of one class teacher, there will usually be (except for the retarded) a form master or mistress and perhaps a house tutor with specific responsibilities but also a range of teachers who figure as subject specialists. Even where the class-teacher system has been modified within the junior school, for example through team teaching or partial specialisation, the contrast in the secondary school is still marked. After the newcomer has begun to understand the purpose of the form teacher or house tutor, he or she has still to become accustomed to finding, for instance, that the teacher who takes history thinks of the pupil as a history pupil and may be unaware of his prowess in French or his failures in mathematics. The subject range itself increases too. In addition to the familiar primary-school subjects there are exciting new developments; Latin perhaps, or metalwork, mechanical drawing, or general science in a real laboratory. Physical education is taken by a specialist in full regalia, usually in a gymnasium. Most important of all to some children, games may be different, with perhaps an awe-inspiring initiation into rugby-football or hockey.

Simultaneously, the hierarchy of formal positions among pupils (Head Boy and Girl, prefects, teams, etc.) becomes clear, with varying degrees of dignity ranging in large grammar schools up to senior pupils who look like men and women and wield authority which, initially at least, appears impressive. In due course, too, the whole fabric of semi-formal organisations and societies becomes apparent, and there is usually a chance of joining some of them.

In fact, what the individual boy or girl has to do is to learn the many new roles of a secondary-school pupil, with no previous experience except that of the simpler roles of primary-school pupils, and to plunge into it at once. What is more, the new role-complex is not just that of a secondary-school pupil, but of a *first-year* pupil. Having reached the pinnacle of importance in the junior school he must like Sisyphus begin to climb all over again. From being a prefect in 4A, he may suddenly become a nobody in 1C. No wonder he (and more particularly, she) finds it prudent to start by pursuing the good-pupil role as it is perceived in the new context.

A considerable number of schools now make a deliberate effort to let their newcomers down gently, instead of adopting the procedure sometimes described with a complacent affectation of realism as 'breaking them in' (Jackson and Marsden, 1962, p. 95). Some schools in some areas go much further in order to effect a liaison of this type. One example is to be found in the part of South Shropshire in which C. F. Smith has conducted the research already mentioned in Chapter III. Here, the staff of a secondary modern school in a small town had frequently observed that the children from small village schools made less progress, when estimated in terms of their measured abilities, than did the children from the town itself. Being concerned about this discrepancy, the staff introduced the plan of bringing the village children into the secondary school for actual lessons one day a week in their last primary-school term, so that the children could become acquainted with the school, and its teachers with their teachers. The outcome of this experiment appears highly successful, and its initiation incidentally prompted C. F. Smith to embark on his own research: a happy instance of the way in which an atmosphere of adaptability in educational practice is conducive, as it should be, to the pursuit of more rigorous research which can in its turn more effectively guide future practice. Doubtless a number of similar instances could be found in various parts of the country. In the absence of such positive association between primary and secondary schools, or of more than a perfunctory initiation, the presence of an elder sibling or a neighbour who can act as a (usually very temporary) guide is a tremendous advantage to the individual child, for it not only obviates the worst shock of the transition, but also provides a ready-made source of initial prestige among the other novices. This simple social process has frequently been described in novels about boarding schools, where the arrival of a newcomer such as Harry Verney in Vachell's *The Hill* (1909) is conventionally regarded as a legitimate occasion for a touch of manly sentimentality, sometimes offset by laconical humour.

In addition to the actual change of institution, there may in some cases be other concomitant changes which reinforce the difference between primary and secondary schools. First there is the question of sheer size and complexity of organisation. In an extreme case, it is possible for a child from a two-teacher school to move into a comprehensive school with over two thousand pupils. In any secondary school, the proneness of first-term pupils to go to the wrong room, and to forget to take books and apparatus with them, is a byword among the staff, and makes demands both on the teachers' patience and on the children's resilience. Not that it is necessary for the school itself to *be* small—in any case, discussion of the appropriate size for secondary schools raises another whole series of questions—but it is necessary that the initial impact of the school's size should be taken into account and that, at least for first-year pupils, the organisation should be broken down into more comprehensible units.

Where there is a change of location that, too, can be sociologically important. For a country child the move to secondary education may involve the move to a town and a journey in a school bus too. Teachers and others in villages often deplore the outcome of this transition, claiming that it results in a coarsening of the children and an alienation from the village way of life. There is something true and regrettable in this, but it is implicit in the basic dilemma of rural primary education discussed in Volume II, Ch. IV. Faced as they are with the common experience of this change in environment, the eleven-year-olds from the village have an obvious incentive to intensify their peer relations in order to give each other group supportiveness, so that the private world of the school bus, or the compartment in a train (where it is permitted to survive), affords an ideal environment for this intensification and also a compelling pressure on the newcomers to learn from the old hands. This twice-daily enforced contact provides an almost inescapable pattern of answers to the uncertainties of adjustment arising from the move to the town, while the presence of older pupils in the same vehicle stamps the collective behaviour with the authority of greater experience and maturity. To the outside observer, there is something depressingly monotonous about the mutual cap-stealing and horse-play, the pulling of girls' hair and snatching of their possessions which some developing lassies half-enjoy, and especially perhaps about the uncertain role-relations between the children and the bus conductor. There is something equally dismal about the rapidity with which the newcomers one by one, take to the behaviour pattern which they had first encountered with wary disdain. But for them, in their situation, this is an essential piece of social learning, while on the other hand it is necessary to remember the regularity with which they eventually outgrow it and, when they reach the senior part of the school, take their turn in deprecating and controlling it.

Occasionally, individual villages develop a particularly adverse reputation for work, or conduct, or both. Then, each of its children feels some obligation to sustain the equivocal stereotype of the village. In such cases, something of the same atmosphere has often prevailed in the primary school itself. I myself have visited village schools in which this was obviously the case, and in which toughness was as much at a premium as in any slum school, though this is more characteristic of all-age than of junior schools.[4] But when this reputation is set in contrast with that of nearby rivals, as well as of the town where the secondary school itself is located, then the experience of transfer to secondary education can lead to identification of the secondary-pupil role with the bad-pupil role, and this can result in a new self-picture.

It is not only in the countryside that entry to secondary schools involves a change of location. Many cities and towns have found it possible to build new secondary schools in the relatively clean and pleasant conditions prevailing in their outskirts, while some of the primary schools, already entrenched in solid Board School buildings, seem fated to stay where they are almost until the economic millenium. Pupils from some of these, and from the less reputable primary schools on housing estates may, like those from the 'bad' villages, be manoeuvred into the bad-pupil role, especially in predominantly middle-class grammar schools (Jackson and Marsden, 1962, pp. 88–9; 240 et seq.).

However, it is greatly to the credit of local education authorities that they have largely succeeded in placing even one stage of education in new, attractive and well-situated buildings. Administrative and historical circumstances may render it inevitable that secondary, rather than primary, schools should benefit from this initiative, though it is slightly ironical that pre-adolescent children, who seem to plump for the country whenever they have the chance (see Vol. II, Ch. III) should often be educated for six or more years in the maze of streets where they already live, while adolescents, who are progressively drawn like moths to the bright lights of the town centre, should be removed for their formal education to the edge of the countryside. On the other hand, proximity to rural surroundings may perhaps do something to counteract the urbanised values of the adolescent society. But whatever the principles on which it may be based, this administrative development does imply that eleven-year-olds from inner districts have to learn to travel, usually by bus or more dangerously by cycle, to a distant if pleasant place, just when they are being confronted with all the other exciting novelties of the first-year secondary pupil's role-complex.

Here and there, where former pupil-teacher centres were deliberately built near railway termini and have since developed into grammar schools, the journey is in the opposite direction, but it still constitutes a significant new experience.

In addition to changes in institutional organisation, in size and in location, the transfer to secondary education may involve changes in school ethos and educational climate, for example from 'free' to 'formal', or the reverse. For entrants to selective schools, in particular, it may imply a much more instruction-centred pattern and a brusque change in aims and methods of socialisation, which may in some cases reinforce the social-class problem outlined by Jackson and Marsden, especially since the selective-school pattern is itself at present more generally built in to the educational expectations of middle-class than of working-class parents.

Transfer from independent primary to independent secondary schools is in two ways different, but requires some mention here. It sometimes means, especially for boys of high socio-economic status, a move from one *boarding* school to another, and it then takes place at the age of thirteen instead of eleven. The other differences—structure, size, location, social climate—all apply also, but in a somewhat different way. It is necessary to pass the Common Entrance examination, or to satisfy the particular requirements of a particular day school, but the whole process is more gentlemanly and less bureaucratic than within the maintained system. In many cases, the same road has been trodden by father or brother. Indeed, a boy is often 'put down' by a father for 'his' school as early as practicable after birth.[5] Within this framework, role-expectations are much better defined, and in the closing terms of life at a preparatory school, the socialising role in the preparatory tradition shows itself efficiently and humanely in the extent to which Headmasters and their wives, masters, the matron and her staff consciously prepare individual boys for academic and domestic life at the particular school or schools at which, with their parents' approval, they are aiming. Often there is no lack of specific communication from beyond the Rubicon: 'Charles is at R . . . now and *he* says you never have to . . .' There could scarcely be a greater contrast to the bewilderment of the primary school child with ignorant parents who is the first in the family to enjoy any kind of real secondary education. Then again, the boy who had some struggle to remain manly when he first left home at the age of eight looks amazed, when he is thirteen, at any suggestion that he might find difficulty in joining a boarding-house at 'his public school'. In fact, on arrival he may find that his seniors make it their business to dismantle some of the confidence built up in the preparatory school, and in any case he too must play Sisyphus and start climbing again. But such is the power of the social organisation within many independent secondary schools that this temporary loss of status is generally accepted as a necessary step towards the subsequent attainment of a still higher status. In the preparatory tradition, it has usually been thought worth while to be a fag for the time being, if this implied that some day you would have fags of your own, not only in school, but perhaps afterwards too (Wilkinson, 1962, p. 321).

Transfer has such different connotations in maintained and independent schools respectively that its significance must be further intensified for children who are transferred, at eleven or any other age, from the one system to the other as well as from one stage to another. It is not possible here to elaborate the problems inherent in a double transfer of this kind, but this is another consideration which must be borne in mind in the framing of public policy, and especially if there should be official encouragement of the practice of sending children to maintained primary schools but to independent secondary schools.

The total effect of the impact of transition to secondary education must vary from child to child according to their respective qualities of personality. Some remain apparently phlegmatic and unmoved; some welcome the new situation with almost disconcerting enthusiasm; some few develop symptoms of school phobia (Chazan, 1962, p. 210) and of general regression or anti-social behaviour. The last are the problems. They over-adjust their psychological reactions to the inferior sociological status which the new school accords them. It is as though the identity which had been built up in the primary school had been impaired.

Sometimes it can be quickly rebuilt. Even the discovery that teachers and children in the new school know and use a child's name may help considerably. This incidentally suggests that the practice of using boys' Christian names in primary schools and then abruptly using surnames in the secondary schools is worse than a piece of illogicality. Those secondary schools in which boys are quite un-officially called by Christian names, at least in their first year, have something to commend them. The converse practice of calling primary-school boys by their surnames may flatter the boys' masculinity but is otherwise faintly ridiculous. In an independent school transferring at thirteen, it is possibly more justifiable.

In view of the ramifications of the impact of the change of schools on individual children, it is strange that so few case-studies of transfer have been made, all the more so in view of the intensive investigations that have been conducted into the next major transfer, that from secondary school to work. There are probably three main reasons for this relative neglect. First, as already intimated, the selective aspect of transfer has predominated so greatly that others have been overshadowed. Secondly, there are few people whose own institutional roles permit them to keep in close touch with children both in their last year at a primary school and in their first year at a secondary school.[6] Thirdly, the problem has less immediate social relevance than the school-work transition, so that there has been less incentive to finance specific investigations in this field.

At present, indeed, partly as an aftermath of the Hadow re-organisation which is still incomplete,[7] there is some tendency to chop everything in two at eleven-plus. Not only teaching staffs (Taylor, 1963, p. 219) but to some extent administrators and inspectors too have their eyes increasingly focused either above or below the line. It is only recently, and largely for emergency admini-strative reasons, that some training colleges have introduced courses to prepare students for work with children between the ages of nine and thirteen. Meanwhile relatively few local education authorities, such as the West Riding of Yorkshire, have reconsidered their age of transfer, and even they cannot legally make changes until after the passage of the Education Act, 1964, one of whose clauses has facilitated amendment of the age-limits laid down in the Education Acts of 1944 and 1948.

Irrespective of these legal and administrative considerations, it is deplorable that so little opportunity is normally encouraged for teachers in primary and secondary schools to understand and appreciate each others' work. Even within professional organisations, this does not always take place. It is an outcome of trends in social and professional history, some of which are discussed in Volume II, Chapter II; but it is deplorable none the less. All too often, primary and secondary teachers live in mutual suspicion rather than mutual respect. Whereas the transfer to a new type of school is and should be an important and exciting river to cross in the course of growing up, it can only be so if the teachers themselves are accustomed to move back and forth across the waters at each stage of transfer: at five, at seven, at eleven, or whenever it comes. Rites of passage in preliterate societies are, after all, carried out before the faces of the elders of the tribe, rather than in a gap between two groups of elders facing in opposite directions.

C. THE ABIDING SOCIAL INFLUENCE OF PRIMARY SCHOOLS WITHIN SECONDARY SCHOOLS

It is worth while to penetrate a little way inside secondary education, in order to see how the children learn their new role-complex and how far they are influenced by their earlier experiences; to find, in fact, in what ways their primary-school experience continues to be influential. Even in respect of attainments, less is known about this than might be expected, though it is often noticeable how some skills such as italic handwriting continue to reveal the past. From the sociological point of view, however, it is more important to consider the ways in which patterns of social grouping, and norms of behaviour and of motivation may be carried forward.

It has often been reported (e.g. Richardson, J. E., in Fleming, 1951) that during the first year of secondary-school life children from different primary schools begin by adhering to their former friends but gradually launch out into new affiliations. My own investigations in secondary modern and comprehensive schools indicate some ways in which this may happen (Blyth, 1961). My results suggested that there were often three phases rather than two: an initial period of hesitation in the company of known associates, a period of experimentation with new acquaintances; and a period of consolidation in which the initial pattern was in part reconstituted. I pursued this social process a little further and came to two tentative conclusions, first, that it was really a two-fold development based on neighbourhood groups and reinforced by primary-school attendance, and, second, that the combined effect of these two social features proved more durable than had generally been realised. I found that, of the children whose close friends in their own neighbourhoods had accompanied them to the secondary modern schools, between a quarter and a half were still closely connected at the age of fourteen, and that those who had attended predominately middle-class schools, perhaps finding themselves a minority in their new environment (Himmelweit *et al.*, 1952, p. 166) were especially prone to cling together. This was in fact almost more true at the end of the third school year than at the end of the first. One boys' modern school in a middle-class area showed this development with a particular clarity. There the children from one primary school renowned for its eleven-plus successes (who must, therefore, have occupied rather a lowly place in their primary school's esteem by going to a modern school at all) formed at once a recognisable and

145

reliable nucleus in each of the first-year classes and, nine terms later, had retained such a permanent impetus from their junior-school years that they had drawn together again and almost all gained promotion from stream to stream, while many of their coevals from other schools had remained stationary or were actively preparing to leave. An opposite type of minority situation is indicated by an observation of Jackson and Marsden (1962, p. 241) about children from predominantly working-class primary schools as they move through the grammar schools:

> We were talking about schools and they said that the grammar school wasn't much different from their old school, but for us it was completely different. You can't imagine.

But there is one important difference between the two types of minority. The children from middle-class primary schools who go to the modern school may feel consciously different from their class mates but they do feel a sense of affinity with their teachers, whereas children from schools like 'Railway Street' (Jackson and Marsden loc. cit.), feel that teachers and classmates alike belong to an alien world. Nevertheless, both minorities exemplify in their different ways what may be called the *reinforcement effect* of primary schools in relation to habitat and social class.

In view of my initial results, I carried out a more intensive study in the eight first-year classes in a comprehensive school. In addition to a sociometric survey at the beginning and end of the year, I attempted to predict the way in which the informal structure would develop, and finally secured the help of the staff in assigning reputational scores to the individual children, and also the children's assistance through the writing of an informal guided essay about 'Our Class', to indicate how it had developed during their first year in a secondary school. My predictions of developments in sociometric affiliations were significant beyond the ·001 level, though in some individual instances the outcome did not concur with my expectations. In general, the final sociometric test revealed that the original primary-school friendships had gradually been superseded as in my previous observations, but in detail there were variations on which the data from the essays shed further light. It would be tedious to report the findings extensively, but they enabled me to formulate some principles of social development in the first year of secondary-school life which may be of general interest.[8]

As in primary schools, the general distinction between groups and gangs appeared valid. The groups, mainly but not entirely based on neighbourhoods and often closely associated with primary schools, were relatively permanent, though some of them underwent considerable change during the year. Meanwhile, both girls and boys banded together loosely in gangs for playing-field warfare and other transient concerns. They mostly restricted these gangs to their own sex, but boys occasionally combined with girls in some chasing game.

Within each class, social processes operated which were similar to those described in junior schools in Chapter IV. Norms were established, some running parallel with the aims of the school and some diverging from them. For the first half of the year, the children appeared to be re-establishing something of the social and even physical pattern which they had known in their primary schools, often choosing as desk-partners members of their previous classes. Only after that did new, specifically secondary-school influences begin to exercise an effect. For example, it was about the middle of the second term that, according to my informants, the collective interest of each sex in the other began to influence the norms of behaviour:

> As the year went on, girls spoke to boys as they had not enough curridge before.

Some, however, obviously regretted this development.

It was, however, in the original pattern of norm-establishment that the influence of primary schools was most evident. It happened in a very straightforward way. For example, boys from one housing-estate primary school who had played jovially together in its justly famous football and cricket teams found themselves together in force in two of the eight classes. In each case, another similar school was also well represented. Immediately, the boys in those two classes became renowned for their games simply because their recruits from those two primary schools arrived with a ready-made norm of values which was likely to be admired by the rest. As the year went on, these boys' sociometric status rose steadily, and the sporting values in the two classes became still more conspicuous, almost on the pattern described for American adolescents by Coleman (1961). In another stream, a more middle-class group of girls from another school jumped into the vacant norm-arena and planted their own Girl-Guide-and-netball pattern. In yet another, the bottom stream, a generally lethargic tone was established through the virtual transplantation of the entire lower end of the 'B' stream from a nearby school. All this may seem very obvious, but it has rarely been actually traced in practice. What is more, these norms appeared rather more durable than the sociometric patterns, since each class tended to preserve those values which were identified, irrespective of personnel, with its corporate existence. To this there was one exception, justifiably described by one of its members in these terms:

> Our class is what you might call a peculiar class.

and here, in the absence of any norm-setting group, there was little sign of coherence or of a stable value-system. For the rest, the children gradually came to feel more confident in their big new school and their initially deferential good-pupil attitudes faded. To quote another informant:

> . . . when we came to the scool we were always well behaved but now we have seemed to detereated.

Meanwhile, it is interesting to notice what happened to the children who were not members of one of the larger primary-school contingents. Deprived of the group supportiveness which others readily enjoyed, they soon found it necessary either to band together in a coalition or more usually to attach themselves to one of the existing groups. Sometimes they tried more than one until they were satisfied. Occasionally they got into bad company and their descent from stream to stream, into disrepute and even before the Juvenile Courts, could be traced and even predicted with lugubrious accuracy. Others completed an ascent in the reverse direction. One or two entire groups that started with a particular reputation carried out a collective ascent or descent, as though they had not found their true level at first.

These are a few general conclusions from my study, which indicate some of the ways in which primary schools can continue to exercise social influence within secondary schools, as new social processes become established there. Similar ground has been covered in other researches, including some which are unpublished, but there is a need for further investigation. For example, it would be useful to take some of the conclusions which I have derived from my own study, and to subject them to more rigorous empirical examination in a number of differing secondary schools.

In general, there appear to be two important tendencies here. One, already mentioned in Chapter IV, is for primary-school classes to develop their own persistent norms and to assimilate to them minority children whose background might suggest that they would develop contrasted values. The other is for a secondary-school class to perpetuate those norms which are first established. Since this initial norm-formation may often result from the projection into secondary schools of values originally developed in particular primary schools, it may result in a curious proliferation of the effects of differences between primary schools. This may well defy attempts to eliminate it by organisational means, and may thus set a limit to the capacity of secondary schools to effect social integration. Or rather, it may require the development of a strong autonomous culture within secondary schools if it is to be overcome.

VII

Adults in Primary Schools

HOWEVER much understanding and genuine affection there may be between adults and children in primary schools, there is inevitably a considerable social distance between them. Although the adults are aware that their pupils will in their turn become adults, and are at pains to encourage their growth according to the developmental tradition, primary schools are essentially two-tier institutions. In one sense, this makes for stability. Children in the Midlands years are not likely to be perceived as threatening the adult status of the other generation, as adolescents sometimes are. The end of their colonial status is not imminent. Their interaction with adults is relatively patterned, and both generations prefer it that way.

Within this two-tier structure, on the adult level the school is a relatively permanent society. For the children, it is a focus of life and growth: for the adults, the scene of an occupation and perhaps of a career. As the career patterns of teachers alter, especially for the younger women (N.U.T., 1963, p. 10) individual schools are less permanent societies than they once were, even for adults, but there is still a qualitative difference between a school's significance for its adult members and its significance for the children, which is essentially that of a transitional community (Curle, 1947–8).

Most of the adults in primary schools are teachers, though they do not exceed the combined total of others by a great margin. The rest constitute what Willard Waller (1932) calls the 'fringe personnel'; the secretary, caretaker, school meals staff, and others more peripheral to the school's basic functions, all of whom will be discussed in the final section of this chapter. Because they are peripheral and the teachers central to the school's purposes, and also because more information is available about teachers, it is the teachers who will be considered first.

A. TEACHING PERSONNEL

Primary-school teachers are a sizeable occupational group. In January 1962, there were in all 141,016 full-time teachers in maintained primary schools, and a further 946 in maintained nursery

149

schools in England and Wales,[1] as compared with 137,768 in maintained secondary schools of all types (*Statistics of Education in 1962*, Part I, Table 7, pp. 30–1). To complete the tally of teachers actually engaged in the full-time education of Midlands children it is necessary also to estimate the numbers of teachers in independent and direct-grant schools who are occupied with the under-twelves, and also to incorporate a proportion of special-school teachers. 24,837 teachers in direct-grant, recognised independent and other independent schools, including 345 in nursery schools, were working in schools in which at least some of the pupils were in the primary age-range (ibid., Table 21, p. 51),[2] as compared with 12,305 who were definitely working in secondary schools in the same categories. But both here and in the maintained schools a number of teachers—6,404 of the 141,016 and no fewer than 12,744 of the 24,837—were employed in schools with both primary and secondary pupils. It is quite impossible to ascertain what proportion of their time these teachers spent with children in the Midlands years, for some probably devoted all their days to them, some spent none, and others divided their time in various ways between the age-ranges. The only permissible conjecture is that just under 150,000 teachers confined their attention to primary-school children, while a further 20,000 or slightly fewer spent a part of their time in primary-school work and might therefore be regarded as the equivalent of just under 10,000 full-time teachers of primary-age children. In the case of special-school teachers there is still more difficulty in finding which teachers teach the younger pupils, since there is no statutory division between primary and secondary levels in special schools (Education Act, 1944, Sec. 8(2)).[3] However, on the assumption that approximately half of the special school teaching force is at work with the under-twelves, then (*Statistics of Education in* 1962, Part I, Table 26, p. 55) about a further 3,000 teachers could be added. If these are combined with the other totals (under 150,000 and under 10,000) it is possible to postulate an overall total of some 160,000 teachers who were in the early part of 1962 teaching children in primary schools or their equivalent.

A description of primary-school teachers' social significance involves also an estimate of the numbers of pupils for whom they are responsible. The actual numbers of pupils are easier to compute (ibid., Table 8, pp. 32–5) since the numbers per age-group in all-age schools are given. A difficulty arises in the case of eleven-year-olds who are in all-age schools and special schools, for if they are all allocated either to the primary or to the secondary category, a bias in the distribution is probable. The nearest estimate which can reasonably be made is to divide them in the same ratio as the eleven-year-old children who were in separate primary and secondary schools, i.e. 2:1 in favour of the secondary schools. On this basis, the total number of pupils of primary age, excluding nursery, approved-school and institutional pupils and those accommodated in secondary schools, was (to the nearest thousand) 4,149,000 on 1st January, 1962. If this total is divided by the roughly estimated total of 160,000 teachers, it appears that the overall staffing ratio for all types of teachers of primary-age children early in 1962 was about 1:26. For secondary schools, where at least in the maintained schools a more generous minimum class size (thirty, as against forty) is allowed, together with further provision in respect of pupils over fifteen, a comparable figure would be about 1:19. If 'full-time equivalents of part-time teachers' were also included, the two corresponding ratios would be slightly lower, though still more hypothetical in their significance.

The only value of such overall ratios is to emphasise the contrast in staffing between primary and secondary education. In fact, largely for historical reasons, the teaching personnel is distributed over primary education in a distinctly uneven fashion. First, there is the obvious disparity between the schools which have emerged respectively from the preparatory and elementary traditions. Any shrewd parent is aware of this, and the official statistics show it baldly (ibid., Table 7, pp. 30–1):

STAFFING RATIOS (ENGLAND AND WALES)

	Pupils per Full-time Teacher	Pupils per Teacher (with full-time equivalents of part-time teachers taken into account)	Average size of class
Maintained schools			
Nursery	22·1	22·1	—
Infants	30·3	29·4	33·9
Junior-with-infants	28·0	27·3	30·1
Junior-without-infants	30·6	29·8	34·4
All-age	26·6	25·7	30·7
All Maintained Primary	29·3	28·5	32·3⁴
Direct-grant schools			
Nursery	18·0	18·0	—
Independent schools recognised as efficient			
Nursery	14·8	13·7	—
Primary	14·3	12·6	—
Primary and Secondary	16·6	14·5	—
Other independent schools			
Nursery	16·8	13·6	—
Primary	18·3	15·4	—
Primary and Secondary	18·3	15·1	—

Adults in Primary Schools

But in addition, within the 'maintained' group, there is a sharp discrepancy between primary and secondary schools, which clearly accounts for almost all of the overall difference already noted:

STAFFING RATIOS (ENGLAND AND WALES)

	Pupils per Full-time Teacher	Pupils per Teacher (with full-time equivalents of part-time teachers taken into account)	Average size of class
All Maintained Primary	29·3	28·5	32·3
All Maintained Secondary	20·6	19·7	29·0

The next striking unevenness in the distribution of teachers in primary schools is the discrepancy between the sexes. The official statistics for January 1962, (ibid., Tables 16, p. 47 and 21, p. 51) yield the following information:

FULL-TIME TEACHERS, JANUARY, 1962
(ENGLAND AND WALES)

	Men	Women
A. *Maintained Schools*		
Nursery	0	946
Infants	44	31,727
Junior-with-infants	14,934	43,845
Junior-without-infants	17,518	26,544
All-age	2,379	4,025
Total in maintained primary schools	34,875 (24·57%)	107,087 (75·43%)'
B. *Other Schools*		
Direct-grant Schools		
Nursery	0	39
Lower Schools of Grammar Schools	149	589
Independent schools recognised as efficient		
Nursery	0	25
Primary	3,286	2,895
Primary and Secondary	2,905	5,623
Other independent schools		
Nursery	3	317
Primary	727	4,102
Primary and Secondary	1,237	2,979
Total in schools listed under 'B'	8,307 (33·39%)'	16,596 (66·61%)'
Overall total: (A and B)	43,182 (25·88%)	123,656 (74·12%)

152

Only once in this table, namely, in 'primary independent schools recognised as efficient', does the number of men teachers exceed the number of women, presumably because this category includes most of the boys' preparatory schools. By contrast, 57·63 per cent of teachers in maintained secondary schools (excluding all-age schools) and 56·92 per cent of teachers in all types of exclusively secondary schools, were men. Yet so ingrained is the assumption that young children are taught by women, and very young children entirely by women, that the fewness of men in these figures is unlikely to occasion surprise. Indeed, some people may be intrigued to find so many, especially since they include a handful at the infant and even the nursery level.

In the original tables there is another interesting piece of information. Maintained primary schools other than nursery schools are subdivided into boys', girls', and mixed, and the sex-distribution of teachers in these three categories was as follows (ibid., Table 16, p. 47):

FULL-TIME TEACHERS IN MAINTAINED SCHOOLS
(ENGLAND AND WALES), JANUARY, 1962

		Boys	Girls	Mixed
Infants	Men	0	0	44
	Women	18	20	31,689
Junior-with-infants	Men	15	2	14,917
	Women	27	646	43,172
Junior-without-infants	Men	1,742	4	15,772
	Women	696	2,072	23,776
All-age	Men	515	0	1,864
	Women	147	655	3,223

From this it is immediately apparent that the cross-sex relationship between teachers and pupils, as well as the age-relationship, is important. As children move from the infant to the junior stage, it is no longer so necessary for them all to be taught by women. An infusion of male blood is apparently considered suitable in boys' schools' though only to the extent of two-thirds of the total teaching strength. But in the case of separate girls' schools, there is nothing anomalous in perpetuating the exclusively feminine atmosphere until the age of eleven, interrupted only, it seems, by six brave men.

In the case of independent schools, the statistics are rather less useful because there is no separate classification for teachers of infants. However, it is clear from the following data that the position is substantially similar, except that there was a rather lower proportion of women in the boys' schools (and that thirteen men were in girls' schools).

Adults in Primary Schools

		Boys	Girls	Mixed
Direct-grant grammar schools				
Lower Schools	Men	149	0	0
	Women	84	501	4
(NOTE. All direct-grant *nursery* schools were mixed and staffed exclusively by women)				
Independent schools recognised as efficient				
Nursery	Men	0	0	0
	Women	0	0	25
Primary	Men	3,166	4	116
	Women	947	410	1,538
Primary and Secondary	Men	2,562	58	285
	Women	176	4,522	925
Other independent schools				
Nursery	Men	0	0	3
	Women	2	1	314
Primary	Men	470	9	248
	Women	360	115	3,627
Primary and Secondary	Men	750	24	463
	Women	214	761	2,004

The preponderance of women teachers in primary schools is, at least within the maintained schools, a long-established phenomenon. In fact, before 1939 and after 1945 it was still more marked, though around 1957 it was slightly lower than in 1962, as shown in the following composite table:

NUMBERS OF TEACHERS OF CHILDREN OF PRIMARY-SCHOOL
AGE IN MAINTAINED SCHOOLS, 1938, 1947 AND 1957–62
(ENGLAND AND WALES)

Year	Total Men	Total Women	Percentage of total that were male	Source of Data
1938	14,845	88,968[a]	14·31	*Education in 1938,*[1] p. 111
1947	16,071	85,632	15·81	*Education in 1947,*[1] p. 112
1957	38,869	111,667	25·82	*Education in 1957,*[1] p. 107
1958	37,723	110,761	25·39	*Education in 1958,*[1] p. 150
1959	36,391	108,059	25·20	*Education in 1959,*[1] p. 144
1960	35,368	106,819	24·89	*Education in 1960,*[1] p. 166–7
1961[b]	36,157	105,762	25·48	*Statistics of Education*[1] in 1961, Part I, Table 33, p. 75
1962	34,875	107,087	24·57	(See p. 152 above)

The slight recent fluctuations in total numbers can be regarded as due to the relative demand for teachers in primary and secondary schools respectively as the consequences of changes in the birth-rate have made themselves felt, except in 1961 where there is an anomaly owing to the different method of collating the data.

There are no comparable data for direct-grant and independent schools over the same period, but it is unlikely that the proportion of women teachers was substantially lower at any time than it was in 1962.

The next main differential within the teaching force relates to size and location of school. Data on this subject are available for maintained schools only. It is interesting to notice, within this range, the relative probability of teaching in various *sizes* of school for different *types* of school. The following data are taken from Table 11 (pp. 41–2) of *Statistics of Education, 1962*, Part I, with percentages added to the original data.

SIZES OF SCHOOLS OR DEPARTMENTS (ENGLAND AND WALES)
JANUARY, 1962

Type of School (excluding nursery schools See Ch. VI)	Less than 25	26–50	51–100	101–200	201–300	301–400	401–600	601–1000[10]
Infant	85	212	793	2,403	1,621	337	49	2
(Urban[11]	20	125	645	2,190	1,510	307	42	2)
Percent	1·55	3·85	14·42	43·67	29·46	6·13	0·89	0·03
Junior-with-infants	1,290	2,758	2,563	2,243	1,728	986	492	35
(Urban[11]	44	185	496	1,219	1,354	843	433	32)
Percent	10·67	22·80	21·18	18·55	14·29	8·15	4·07	0·29
Junior-without-infants	5	40	218	1,085	1,470	1,235	715	51
(Urban[11]	3	14	141	923	1,352	1,153	658	49)
Percent	0·10	0·83	4·52	22·51	30·51	25·63	14·84	1·06
All-age	18	46	101	201	222	115	67	5
(Urban[11]	0	4	25	132	174	101	56	5)
Percent	2·32	5·94	13·03	25·93	28·65	14·84	8·64	0·65
Percentage of all maintained Primary Schools and Departments in each category:								
Urban[11]	0·47	2·30	9·18	31·35	30·84	16·89	8·35	0·62 = 100·00
Rural	14·87	30·47	26·44	16·40	7·27	3·00	1·50	0·05 = 100·00
Percentages of Schools and Departments in each category classified as:								
Urban[11]	4·79	10·74	35·55	75·25	87·10	89·93	89·89	94·62
Rural	95·21	89·26	64·45	24·75	12·90	10·07	10·11	5·38
Totals	100·00	100·00	100·00	100·00	100·00	100·00	100·00	100·00

The relevance of these data to the position of adults in primary schools is that it indicates the various probable numbers of colleagues that a teacher might expect in different schools. The most striking point is that (combining the first two categories) there were 4,434 schools, 19·9 per cent of the total number of all maintained primary-schools (catering of course for a much lower percentage of the children) in which, at any one time, there were probably only two

155

full-time teachers. Since (ibid.) only 35 secondary schools had fewer than 100 pupils, and only 325 a number between 100 and 250, it is clear that the small school is usually a primary school. The N.U.T. Report (N.U.T., 1963) gives some confirmation of the percentage already indicated, for it showed (Table 3, p. 8) that 19 per cent of all primary schools in the sample were still one- or two-teacher schools. Of the 4,434 primary schools mentioned already, 91·14 per cent were in rural areas, and in view of the previous data, the teachers were likely to be women. In some cases, especially in Church schools, men might appear, but the predominant influence must be feminine.

From the adults' point of view, some 9,000 teachers have only one full-time colleague, and some have none at all. Further information on this point appears in *Statistics of Education in 1962*, Part I, Table 10 (p. 40), from which the following data are derived:

NUMBERS IN SMALL PRIMARY AND SECONDARY SCHOOLS
(ENGLAND AND WALES)

Category	Schools	Pupils
One-teacher schools	950	17,118
Two-teacher schools	3,953	153,146
Totals	4,903	170,264

In this case the number of pupils is given, but unfortunately there is no differentiation between primary and secondary schools. The combined figures represent 16·86 per cent of all maintained primary and secondary schools, and 2·44 per cent of pupils in this total of schools. Comparison with the N.U.T. figures again shows that the bulk of the small schools are primary.

Incidentally, these figures have not altered greatly in recent years. In 1952 the totals were 5,422 and 196,962; in 1957 4,946 and 177,018, so that the closure of small schools has actually for a number of reasons been decelerated. Certainly the demise of the small school has not proceeded at a headlong pace.[12]

One remaining piece of information about primary-school teaching staffs can be derived from the official statistics, namely the pattern of qualification of the teachers. Of the 35,852[13] men teaching in maintained primary schools (including nursery and all-age schools) there were on 31st March, 1962 (ibid., Table 33):

71 first-class honours graduates
740 second-class honours graduates
1,840 other graduates
—
2,651 graduates in all, constituting 7·4% of all men teachers in maintained primary schools[14]

156

while for the 106,026[13] women teachers in maintained primary schools there were on the same date:

58 first-class honours graduates
847 second-class honours graduates
1,707 other graduates
——
2,612 graduates in all, constituting 2·5% of all women teachers in maintained primary schools[14].

The N.U.T. survey found much the same (N.U.T., 1963, Table 6, p. 9):

Category of teacher (sexes combined)	Percentage of all teachers, full-time and part-time
Graduates with training	3
Graduates without training	1
Graduate equivalents	1
Other qualified	89
Unqualified	6
Total	100

and further corroborates the Ministry's figures by commenting in more detail: (ibid.),

Of all unqualified teachers, 90 per cent are women; but little more than 50 per cent of the graduates or graduate equivalents are women.

It is perhaps surprising to note the number of first-class honours graduates in both sexes: they include nearly twenty scientists (ibid.).

In independent primary schools, the pattern in 1962 was rather different (ibid., Table 22, p. 52).

FULL-TIME TEACHERS IN INDEPENDENT SCHOOLS,[15]
(ENGLAND AND WALES), 31ST MARCH, 1962

	Graduates		Non-Graduates	
	Men	Women	Men	Women
Independent schools recognised as efficient				
Nursery	0	2	0	23
Primary	1601	351	1685	2544
Primary and Secondary	2335	2389	570	3234
Totals	3936	2742	2255	5801
Other independent schools				
Nursery	0	20	3	297
Primary	226	278	501	3824
Primary and Secondary	539	587	698	2392
Totals	765	885	1202	6513

In the case of independent schools, the class of degree is not specified in the statistics, but it is possible to calculate the percentage of men and women graduates as a whole. These are:

PERCENTAGE OF GRADUATES AMONG FULL-TIME
TEACHERS IN INDEPENDENT SCHOOLS,
31ST MARCH, 1962

	Men	Women
Recognised schools (Nursery; Primary; Primary-and-Secondary)	63·57	47·28
Recognised schools (Nursery and Primary only	48·72	39·63
Other schools (Nursery, Primary, Primary-and-Secondary)	63·65	13·58
Other schools (Nursery and Primary only)	30·96	6·74

Thus in the independent sector, graduates are quite usual in primary schools, especially in the recognised schools, though among men teachers the percentage of graduates is a hair's breadth higher in the non-recognised schools. When the primary-and-secondary category is eliminated, the graduate percentages fall, but still remain higher than in the maintained schools. In fact, the lowest of all the independent-school figures, that for women graduates in the non-recognised schools (6·74 per cent) nearly reaches the *highest* figure in the maintained schools (Men: 7·4 per cent). The explanation is probably twofold. In the independent schools, the staffing ratio is much more favourable, as has already been indicated, though salaries may be less so. Again, most of the independent schools derive from the preparatory tradition within which education has been much more closely associated with the possession of a degree, the mediaeval mark of a teacher, than in the elementary tradition with its emphasis on 'training'.

Special schools are in this respect closely aligned with primary schools. The figures for graduates show (ibid., Table 32, p. 72) that 8·1 per cent of men and 7·0 per cent of women teachers in special schools on 31st March, 1962, were graduates. There is no reason to suppose that these graduates were confined either to the secondary or to the primary age-range.

In secondary schools in general, however, there is a clear contrast with primary schools. Table 32 shows that even in secondary modern schools, with the lowest graduate proportion of any kind of secondary school, there were 20·2 per cent of graduates among the men and 13·0 per cent among the women,[16] while in maintained grammar schools there were 81·5 per cent and 72·7 per cent respectively. For men, the percentages in direct-grant and recognised

158

independent schools were still higher (81·7 per cent; 85·7 per cent respectively—ibid., Table 22, p. 52) but for women they are somewhat lower (58·5 per cent and 61·5 per cent respectively—ibid.), presumably because this included teachers of primary-age children who are predominantly women non-graduates, often with a three-year Froebel certificate.

If the graduate is symbolic of the traditional grammar/public school tradition and conception of education, then it is clear that the independent schools, primary as well as secondary, and especially the men who teach in them, look in general towards this tradition in the determination of their staffing. Whatever the reasons for this, it is likely that the independent schools' 'reference group', and their main professional orientation, will also be found in the grammar-school and public-school area and the teachers in independent primary schools will tend to consider themselves schoolmasters and (to a slightly less extent) schoolmistresses in the same sense as those in grammar and public schools. It is unlikely that they would align themselves professionally with the overwhelmingly non-graduate teaching force of the maintained primary schools: indeed, the pattern of membership of teachers' professional organisations bears this out. The leading independent primary schools have few members of the N.U.T. or the N.A.S. on their staffs. Subject-associations could provide a common ground for meeting or at least for co-existence, though it is instructive to notice that one of the best of these, the Geographical Association, which has members in all types of school, nevertheless has a Primary Schools Section and a Public and Preparatory Schools Section, indicating clearly where the preparatory schools regard themselves as belonging.

Of course, the graduates are not the only distinctive subdivision of primary-school teachers. Within the remainder, in the maintained schools, some are two-year-trained, some emergency-trained, some hold Froebel or specialist (graduate-equivalent) qualifications; increasingly from now on some will hold three-year qualifications from non-specialist colleges, while some are still unqualified, including those waiting for admission to college. The professional divisions caused by this diversity can be easily imagined. The only reason why graduates have been singled out for special consideration is that they alone figure in the official statistics. Even the N.U.T. Report (N.U.T., 1963) in the table already quoted (p. 157 above) gives no subdivision of the large category of 'other qualified'.

For systematic attempts have been made to collect data about primary-school teachers as a whole, apart from the official statistics. The best-known supplementary study was carried out in 1955 under the auspices of the Nuffield Foundation and under the direction of Mrs. J. E. Floud, by W. Scott and R. S. Schenk at the University of London Institute of Education. This was an ambitious enquiry into the teaching profession as a whole, based on a nation-wide sample. An important interim report by Floud and Scott has been published in the symposium *Education, Economy and Society* (Halsey, Floud and Anderson, eds. 1961, Ch. 37) and from this it is possible to derive some additional information about the specific character-istics of teachers in maintained primary schools. It is clear from this report that (p. 540) manual workers' families are more likely to produce primary-school teachers, especially women, than teachers in other types of school, though (ibid., p. 542) there is some fluctua-tion in these proportions. Taylor (1963, p. 209) envisages that the line of division between primary-school teachers and those in secondary modern schools, hitherto their closest parallel, may be widened through the patterns of training which may emerge in the future, especially if universities tend to cater for modern-school teachers and training colleges for primary-school teachers. This may however be countered if training colleges or their successors develop degree courses of their own as intimated in the Robbins Report,[17] and especially if the line between primary and secondary age-levels is re-drawn. In any case there is no reason to think that primary-school work makes less demands than secondary-school work on teachers' abilities, even academic abilities. As the rigorous study of education and its cognate disciplines develops, this should become more apparent. Some able students recognise this already and devote themselves to work in primary schools in spite of financial and other discouragements.

Taylor also (ibid., p. 218) points out that modern-school teachers differ from primary- and grammar-school teachers in their role-experience:

> To an increasing extent . . . the Secondary Modern School is the school to which the Secondary Modern school teacher managed to avoid being allocated at the age of eleven,

whereas primary-school and grammar-school teachers will them-selves have been pupils in primary and grammar schools. In fact, these two categories cannot be so readily bracketed together. For one thing, the whole accumulated sediment of grammar school and of college or university training has been deposited above the initial primary-school detritus, thereby powerfully affecting the teacher's outlook, while in any case the ten years or so which divides a primary-teacher from his or her own primary-school days sees nowadays a large measure of radical change in primary-school teaching, so that schoolday memories can be a handicap as much as an advantage. In any case, in view of the prevalence of streaming in primary schools hitherto, most teachers will have been 'A' stream pupils, for whom contact with 'C' stream pupils or even with un-streamed classes may involve something of that social distance and brusqueness of culture-contact which Taylor (ibid.) indicates as characteristic of the newly-fledged teacher in the modern school.

It would be unrealistic to attempt a survey of primary-school teachers, however brief, without some reference to salaries. Here, it would be generally true to say that certified teachers in maintained primary schools reached their relative apogee in the salary scales of 1945, since when they have tended to lose ground steadily in comparison with all secondary-school teachers and with all graduates, for the Burnham scales have been consistently amended to include a larger proportion of graded and special-responsibility posts in secondary than in primary schools, a larger recognition of qualifications beyond the basic certification (these are most often found in secondary schools) and a weighting of Heads' salaries according to the numbers of pupils over thirteen and especially in the sixth form (see Taylor, op. cit., Appendix IV). Alexander (1961) showed that in 1961 33 per cent of primary-school teachers, 45 per cent of modern-school teachers, and 74 per cent of grammar-school teachers were in receipt of allowances above the basic scale. This has been the cause of much resentment, especially since it reacts unfavourably on public estimation of the needs of primary-school pupils as well as on the quality of their teachers, but it is difficult to see how all the conflicting claims involved can be resolved other than by a large increase in total expenditure on salaries.

Finally, it is worth while to enquire whether primary-school teachers express a distinctive pattern of personality or of social attitudes. There is little information on this subject, but a thesis by Butcher (1959) throws some light on it. In the course of an experiment in attitude-measurement he found within a relatively small sample of serving teachers that in political affiliation, primary-school teachers were slightly more likely to support the Conservative Party than would be expected from the sample as a whole (p. 49). Women primary teachers were (p. 47) more likely than men to be Conservatives, as likely to be Liberals, and less likely to support Labour. In religious affiliation, primary teachers appeared more likely than others to be Anglicans or Roman Catholics, and less likely to be Nonconformists or of no religious persuasion (ibid., p. 49). However, since few of these differences were significant, and since age-trends were obviously (p. 48) of considerable importance, they can hardly be cited in support of Vaizey's remark (1962, p. 85) that:

> Teachers have become a conservative force. None so ready as they to leap to attention for God Save the Queen; none so quick to criticize trade unions; none who enjoy the Young Conservative tennis parties more than the young primary-school teachers.

In any case, Butcher's study was carried out in 1958. It seems at least possible that subsequent developments may have effected some modification.

Butcher also found (ibid., pp. 78, 80) that primary-school teachers were significantly more likely than grammar-school teachers to be 'naturalist' rather than 'idealist' and 'tender-minded' rather than 'tough-minded' in general social attitudes. This is probably a more important type of finding, in addition to its significance. Steele (1958, p. 2) also found that training-college students wishing to train for infant-school work were much more 'progressive' in outlook than those intending to train for work with juniors, thus obliquely reinforcing Butcher's finding and suggesting that there may be a continuum of attitudes from infant-school to grammar-school teachers, though this cannot be assumed without further investigation.

As for personality, most teachers and trainers of teachers could hazard a guess about the types of people best suited to juniors and infants. Ross (1960) summarises them thus (pp. 78–9):

> A balanced person of even temperament is needed; one who can influence as potently as she [*sic*] can command. The voice should be pitched in a comfortable register, for the children will imitate what they hear, and must be encouraged to use their voices in the way least likely to interfere with those around them. Her individuality and positive qualities should be made manifest, but rather in her lively interests and sense of humour.

but Evans (1962, p. 126) points out how little is actually known about the personal qualities associated with success in teaching particular age-groups.

With this general picture of the teaching personnel in primary schools in mind, it is possible now to focus again on primary schools as social institutions and to consider the formal and informal social relations to be found among the teaching staff.

B. FORMAL AND INFORMAL RELATIONS AMONG THE TEACHING STAFF

Formal relationships among teachers in primary schools are relatively simple. In the very smallest units, the one- or two-teacher schools, they are rudimentary, but as the size increases, bureaucratisation of the formal structure becomes more likely, especially in those schools in which there is a large combined junior and infant population. One dichotomy is almost universal, that between the Head Teacher[18] and the rest, though this should not be regarded as necessarily implying great social distance. Next, there may be a Deputy Head, who enjoys (if indeed that is the appropriate verb) an intermediate status between the Head and the rest of the staff, one which is mainly dependent on the personal qualities of its holder rather than on precedent or parallel. The position of the Deputy Head may be further complicated in a mixed school because Head and Deputy are often of opposite sex. In that case, the task of acting as spokesman for one sex may devolve upon the Deputy Head. In a junior-with-infants school, she may also be the spokesman for the infants' staff and perhaps for the infants themselves. When a junior school is adjacent to an infant school, the Infants' Headmistress may exercise a similar function but on a basis of equality. Then her relationship to the Head of the junior school often needs to be carefully worked out in practice: precedent and personality will exercise an important influence, though the administrative relationship may be ill-defined.

The effective conduct of a primary school depends in part on the way in which these status-holders conduct their relations with the rest of the staff. Unbending autocracy is not likely to enlist their co-operation in the building of a democratic atmosphere for the children, although some Heads who would never dictate to a child seem ready to issue mandates to their staff. On the other hand, it is equally fruitless to conceal the realities of power behind a façade of *bonhomie* and of formal but ineffective staff meetings. It is essential that a Head should give the wise but unobtrusive leadership advocated by Ross (1960, p. 81) under which each member of staff is assured of consideration, support and respect. An occasional night out together, if genuinely enjoyed, can act as a powerful social cement, while emphasising that the adults in the school are none the less adult because of their prolonged immersion in the world of childhood.

Among the remaining members of staff, the formal structure is much more indeterminate than in a secondary school. This is largely a by-product of the formal structure among the children, whose age-grading and streaming—still the usual practice—is distributed through the school on a class-teacher basis. Some concession is usually made to the totally unmusical among teachers, and to the absolute non-starters[19] in physical education; but for the rest, the teachers are simply Teachers. This universality may earn them some disdain in an age of increasing specialisation, for as Wilson (1962) points out, the teacher's role is 'diffuse', in Talcott Parsons' sense, and thus commands less awe than is normally accorded to, for example, the polymer expert in a technical college who, in terms of technical expertise and division of labour, stands at the opposite pole within the teaching profession. Primary-school teachers in their turn sometimes adopt a defensive stance, claiming that any fool can teach a subject, but that it takes the real man or woman, tried in the fires of the old-fashioned training college, or even 'thrown in the deep end' among a crowd of fifty young thugs, to be able to teach anything that comes to hand.

Whatever the merits of these arguments and counter-arguments, it is certainly true that status-differentiation among primary-school staffs is difficult. Graded posts are ill-adapted to a class-teacher system, apart from functions such as that of librarian, though sometimes a member of staff can advise a whole school on one subject-area[20] and if team-teaching becomes widespread, the team-leader may more readily qualify. In addition, graded posts are grudgingly assigned to primary education in general, as any casual observer can gather by listening to primary teachers at a professional conference.[21] In fact, teachers in primary schools might be pardoned for thinking that the merits of excellent class teaching are blandly ignored in a salary structure which was designed for secondary schools and imposed on primary schools, a procedure which itself reinforces the impression that primary schools are considered less important. This impression may be reinforced by the difference in nominal maximum class size between primary and secondary schools: forty in the former,[22] thirty in the latter, as though the importance of a teacher and the difficulty of his task could be calculated from the average cubic capacity of his pupils.

Thus, the salary structure in primary schools is ill-adapted to their status-pattern. Therefore, a further articulation of formal status often appears irrespective of pecuniary satisfactions. This applies in the case of the actual distribution of teachers, and especially in those schools which bow down before 'the scholarship class'. The parental demand for selective secondary education builds up the formal status of those teachers who are the apparent arbiters of their children's fortunes. Even when the devoted labours of an infants' teacher have laid the foundations for attainment in the basic skills, it is the teacher who is directly responsible for the final icing of the cake who is likely to gain the credit. This is indeed a case of 'unto every one that hath shall be given', for the teacher who collects large numbers of scholarship scalps also often wins the approval of the Head Teacher, these being the outward and visible signs of success for the school. From this position of trust and esteem, that teacher can often exercise effective influence on the general functioning of the school. For good measure, too, the work of the 'scholarship teacher' is with the ablest and most responsible children in the school, those who are most likely to identify themselves with its formal aims, and who are in any case at a stage of development at which they have mastered basic literacy and numeracy but have not outgrown the eagerness, sincerity and charm of their earlier years. Thus, many coincident satisfactions are concentrated in the top 'A' stream, and to a less extent in other classes which are either 'top' (4B, 4C) or 'A' (3A, 2A, 1A) though not both at once. There is no need to point out where, under such a régime, the positions of lowest status are to be found.

Another type of semi-official status derived from a particular social satisfaction arises through participation in games and athletics. To coach a team provides status, even for the teacher of 1c, partly because it earns another sort of approval for the school. More than that, it brings a teacher into contact with other schools and is often also thought to draw him before the attention of Authority. It will be noticed that teachers of infants cannot achieve either the 'scholarship' or the 'coach' pattern of status. Work with the reception class is recognised as specifically important, but is not status-linked in the same way. So infant and nursery teachers must seek their pattern of achievement through superlative performance of their daily task; and many find it there. In their case, and others, there can also be a deep satisfaction in seeing the individual children develop and in feeling some sense of partnership with the majority of parents, though this carries with it the possible danger of undue emotional involvement and ego-identification.

Mention has already been made of Wilson's (1962) discussion of the diffuseness of the teacher's role. It is interesting to note that he also regards this diffuseness as more typical of feminine than of masculine roles in society. For this reason, perhaps, men in primary schools are often more uneasy in their situation than women. The familistic nature of the formal structure accommodates them less readily. Wilson (ibid., p. 28) considers the appropriateness of the three-generation family as a model for the formal structure of a school, the Head figuring as grandparent, the teacher as parent, and the children of course as children. This model is imperfect but in three ways it is useful. First, it gives some support to the attitude of affectionate interest shown by teachers in children. Second, it indicates the possibility of an alliance between alternate 'generations', in which a Head, one stage removed from the heat of the classroom, takes a more detached and less critical view of children than do the class teachers. Third, it throws into relief the anomaly of the elderly class teacher serving under a young Head, and of the man assistant who, to extend the analogy, seems to have married into the family rather than being one of its sons.

A perception of this basic anomaly may be one of the factors which predispose men teachers in primary schools to discontent. In this connection it is noteworthy that Rudd and Wiseman (1962, p. 285) in their study of teachers' sources of dissatisfaction, found that among teachers with five years' service, men teachers in junior schools showed greater dissatisfaction than any other category, even on issues other than salaries. It may be that social forces, including the explicit opinions of their women colleagues with their evident contentment and comparative lack of ambition, conspire to undermine the male connotation of their work, though there is one strong sociological argument in their favour, namely that without models of male identification in the later Midlands years, boys' development would lack direction. So the claims and counter-claims are staked: it takes a woman to understand the Junior Child: it takes a man to handle the Junior Boy. But in addition the men appear to take as their reference group the secondary-school teachers, and especially the grammar-school teachers, whose role is more specific and thus more 'masculine', and who in any case appear to be more adequately rewarded by society for their pains. Women in primary schools seem less discontented, partly because of their rather different life-goals, partly because they may have genuine misgivings, supplemented by hearsay or unfortunate experience, about their capacity to handle the older secondary children, especially the boys, but also partly because the diffuse feminine role of the primary-school teacher is more congenial to them.

These considerations all apply specifically to men assistants. Heads, in their grandpaternal role, find less frustration and anomaly. Since men assistants become men Heads (except when these are recruited from secondary schools, as quite often happens) they are likely to seek means of qualifying for this promotion, and partly for this reason it is becoming more usual for them to build up their formal qualifications. Max Weber might have said that primary schools were thus becoming more bureaucratic; Talcott Parsons might have added that this trend was itself more 'masculine' too.

The N.U.T. report (N.U.T., 1963) gives additional support to these observations. It shows (Table 9, p. 10) that far more men than women left posts because of promotion (50 per cent, as against 10 per cent, of the total), the balance being largely accounted for by the 33 per cent of women who left because of 'marriage or maternity'.

Few attempts have been made to study the formal structure of primary school staffs empirically; the difficulties would be formidable, and it would be almost impossible to divorce formal from *informal* relations. About the latter, however, some general descriptive observations can be hazarded.[23] First, there is the ubiquitous importance of age. Friendships between older and younger teachers do develop, with their attendant virtues and dangers, but in general the interests of different generations at different stages of their life-cycles ensure that the predominant pattern is one of association between coevals. With the present increase in the percentage of married women in primary schools, there is perhaps a tendency for a new line of division to develop between single and married members of staffs, because of the preoccupation of the married women with the daily problems of their homes and families. Another line of division is associated with different patterns of training, especially in those junior schools in which the predominant 'two-year-trained' pattern is modified by some veterans of the post-war emergency training scheme, by an increasing number of three-year college-trained teachers, and by graduates. When combined with age-status, these differences in professional preparation may correspond to social divisions and differential experience and may polarise divisions between the older, more formally-trained teachers and their younger colleagues whose own training was less rigorous but laid more stress on children's activities. When this occurs, the age-grading of the staff may reinforce the vehemence with which each party expresses its views. If the two sections are also divided, as may sometimes happen, on general religious and political questions, then there will be a tendency for those individuals who share most of the views of one faction but not all to approximate their views more and more to those of the faction which they prefer. This tendency is perhaps easiest to observe in newcomers, who align themselves in due course, just as new children do in similar circumstances.

After age, the other basically important dimension of division on a staff is sex. It does not affect the nursery or infant school but in the junior school, as has already been suggested, it plays an important part. G. W. Target's novel *The Teachers*,[24] set in a London junior school, is probably a caricature of actual schools, but by concentrating on the sexual aspect of staff relations the author brings into the open its potential significance. The very fact that men and women of different ages are present in the community is bound to engender social relations and even tensions which are foreign to infant schools. Then again, the pervading 'feminine' pattern in the formal structure, which has already been discussed, can react through the unease of the men teachers upon the harmony of the informal social system. At its most innocuous, this can be dispelled by that perennial chaffing and wit in which some teachers seem able to indulge even after an exhausting day's teaching; but it is not always as easy as that.

The greatest danger arising from developments in informal staff relations is that they may react adversely on the children. By being over-possessive in order to compensate for dissatisfaction elsewhere, by using children's attainments or conduct as prestige-symbols, or by appearing to invite children to make comments about other members of staff, teachers can unwittingly cause much trouble. A disharmonious staff will cause a factious and insecure spirit among the children, who are the first to sense it when the stability which they have the right to expect in a school is missing. It is conventional to assume, in the wake of psycho-analysis, that the main danger of such developments emanates from frustrated unmarried middle-aged teachers, but there are others who are also vulnerable: shy, immature girls straight from College, whose attraction to primary-school work is partly influenced by its comparative insulation from adult affairs; married women whose husbands show indifference or infidelity; childless wives in their thirties; men who suffer from a sense of inferiority and gain reassurance from their obvious command over young children; and status-seekers of any age and both sexes who use children as pawns in order to assert themselves.

Any of these can, for different reasons, seek from the children an immoderate degree of emotional satisfaction, to counterbalance their basic dissatisfaction with their colleagues or the world outside; but in aggregate their numbers must be small. Primary-school staffs are after all generally mature and sane people, whose informal relations promote rather than impede the functioning of the school and the discharge of its roles.

C. TEACHERS' ROLES IN PRIMARY SCHOOLS

Systematic study of teachers' roles, as distinct from the roles of schools, is still in its infancy in England.[25] It might be possible to derive some information about them from means such as those devised by Gross (1958). This would involve asking teachers, pupils, parents, teachers' 'superordinates' such as administrators and inspectors, and the general public, for opinions about what a teacher does (role-performance), what he is expected to do (role-expectation), who is involved in the discharge of a particular role (role-set: Merton, 1957b), what range of different roles are involved in a particular teacher's task (role-complex), and perhaps also the relation between role and status. In the absence of a study along such lines, it is necessary to depend on general theoretical considerations, and it is not surprising that Parsons' brilliant analysis of school classes and of teachers' roles within them (Halsey, Floud and Anderson, 1961, Ch. 31) has been followed by a series of thoughtful English observations on the same subject, notably those by Wilson (1962) and Floud (1962). Although these are not specifically restricted to primary-school teachers, it may be worth while to consider, in the light of their observations, what particular roles primary-school teachers may be said to discharge. They are of course related to the roles of schools, but not identical with them. It may be useful to consider first the roles which are generally ascribed to all, or most, primary-school teachers, and subsequently to look at patterns and procedures of role-*achievement*.

Ascribed Roles

First, a teacher is expected to be an *instructor*. When compared with a secondary-school teacher, a member of a primary-school staff is looked upon as purveying instruction at a somewhat humble level. Only in the nursery years is this genuinely set aside. As Musgrove (1961) has suggested, the three R's and moral training still bulk largely among the layman's expectations. Yet in another sense 'teacher' is vaguely expected to know everything: her word is law.

The second role is that of *socialiser*. It can be subdivided into three parts: *parent-substitute*, *organiser*, and *value-bearer*. Parsons, in the article already mentioned, points out that an essential part of the adjustment of young children to the adult world is achieved through meeting, each year, some new adult who has charge of the class. During that year, that particular adult takes over some of the nodality of a parent, but by handing over in turn to another adult ensures that the children gradually learn to distinguish the role of the protective adult from the personalities of their parents, and thus make an essential adjustment to the objective world. As they grow older, the formation of peer groups facilitates this progress, and the parent-substitute role involves some capacity for wise self-effacement as the children mature. As they pass from the infant to the junior school, it becomes advantageous that children shall be brought into contact with men as well as women, a point which has been noted already, and which is also stressed by Ross (1960, p. 80). In circumstances such as those of small village schools, where the annual exchange of parent-substitute is impracticable, it is necessary to develop a new quality of interaction between teacher and child, at the very least, in order to keep pace with increasing maturity.

The organiser aspect of the socialising role is concerned with the development of social behaviour among children on a scale unthinkable to any parent except the Old Woman who Lived in a Shoe. It is also a limiting factor in the general effectiveness of a teacher. As Herbart put it,

> . . . no lesson can be given in which the holding of the reins of government by a firm yet gentle hand can be dispensed with.[26]

This is at any rate true of the sort of teaching in which lessons are given, a sort which cannot be entirely eliminated, and of which Herbart himself was one of the gentlest and firmest of exponents. In itself, however, it is only a precondition of socialisation, and must be supplemented by the gradual and purposive development of co-operative activity under the 'democratic leadership' of the teacher, a role which, as is shown by the often-quoted Lippitt and White experiments (e.g. Cartwright and Zander, 1960, Ch. 28) is much preferred by the children themselves to any form of sentimental abdication of direction on the teacher's part.[27]

In traditional schools, this organiser role has received more than its due share of attention, for its effective discharge has often been regarded as the quintessential index of teaching efficiency. The 'good disciplinarian' and the good teacher have been too readily equated, while the 'bad disciplinarian' has almost provoked Macduff's outburst to Malcolm:

> Fit to govern?
> No, not to live . . .[28]

This role has been closely bound up with questions of prestige and personal adequacy in general, and has in fact been symptomatic of the exposed and insecure status of teachers in society. With the emergence of new attitudes, the organiser role is losing much of its specific significance, and the extension of team teaching may pluralise the role and thereby reduce its critical significance for individuals, though it must remain collectively a prerequisite for other forms of role-fulfilment.

The third aspect of the socialising role has already been termed the 'value-bearer' role. This rather clumsy expression appears less objectionable than 'inculturator', which is a possible alternative. In brief, it involves the transmission to children of the dominant mores and folkways of English society. Through it they learn not to put their knives into their mouths, and to respect the possessions and feelings of others, and many other behaviour patterns ranging in importance between these two. They are also introduced to the aesthetic and spiritual heritage of the nation, insofar as it exists and is suitable for them. In order to discharge this role, a teacher must first acquire the necessary equipment, which consists of nothing less than full adult stature. This is more difficult than it once was, because the rapidity of social change has rendered it necessary for a teacher not only to exemplify the comparatively definite values of a static society, but also to be aware of the nature and extent of change in the mores and folkways of English society. The task of an elderly teacher in an infant school is perhaps the most difficult in this respect, for all her pupils will have grown up entirely in a world which she has some difficulty in understanding. To remain 'young at heart' is not enough: she must also remain young in mind, and that is more difficult. It is a challenge to training colleges, or their successors, to consider what elements in their curriculum are best equipped to develop in students a capacity to be aware of social change and to keep abreast of it.

One example of the changes which may occur is reflected in Mrs. Floud's distinction (1962) between the 'cultural missionary' and the 'cultural crusader' role-patterns. Both are concerned with value-bearing, but the former is a role-complex appropriate to an age of poverty and to an environment of slums, while the latter is more needed in an age of affluence and an environment of Subtopia. Much educational discussion assumes that the former is still the prime necessity, and where slums and deprived subcultures survive, so it is, *pace* the cult of working-class solidarity. But increasingly the growth of mediocrity in a mass society presents the greater challenge to the teacher as socialiser.

The *classifier* role is closely linked to the third role of the school itself. For teachers, as for schools, the academic aspect is more evident than the rest, and in particular its dramatic climax at the end of primary education. Social and athletic classification is carried on much more unconsciously, even by those who are overtly opposed to selection as such. It enters into every part of the interaction process in which teachers are involved, and eventuates in that implicit rank-order from the 'good pupil' to the 'bad pupil' in which attainment and behaviour are almost inextricably combined. Douglas (1964, pp. 19, 73–5, 107) indicates the ways in which teachers, influenced perhaps by unconscious sex or class bias, evaluate juniors, with increasing effect as they grow older.

Of the *welfare-worker* role there is little to be said that has not already been mentioned. It is much more characteristic of a Head than of a class teacher, though many class teachers do develop it through a close and sympathetic study of the home circumstances of their pupils.

This leaves one of the school's roles, the autonomous role, without any correlative teacher role. The diagram indicates this.

School's Role	Teacher's Role
1. Instruction	Instructor
2. Socialisation	Parent-substitute
	Organiser
	Value-Bearer
3. Classification	Classifier
4. Welfare	Welfare Worker
5. Autonomy	?

However, there is no one teacher role which fills the gap. All those which have already been mentioned can play their part. But there is one additional role which will help immensely in all five of the school's tasks including its obligation to develop autonomy. It is that of *charismatic leader*, to use the term introduced by Max Weber. It implies both a quality of moral integrity and a type of personal magnetism such as is associated with a great religious leader. Few teachers possess this, and some democrats would think it preferable that there should be none; but the public associates this role with teachers, however humble. When it is found, this quality is often taken as evidence that the teacher is 'born, not made', though as Grambs (1952, p. 535) and Evans (1962, pp. 117–18) point out, it is more likely that this particular teacher has been fortunate in encountering a series of experiential situations through which he or she has developed a capacity for influencing children. It is through handling younger children since the days when, as an elder sister, she took her younger siblings and a couple of neighbours' children to the park, that many a successful teacher has acquired her insights into the needs and ways of children. Theoretical study in a Training College or a University Department of Education can enable a young teacher to reflect on this personal experience and to extend

171

and interpret it; but first comes the experience, which enables her to know, as it seems by instinct, what to do to gain and hold the attention of a class, what stories to tell, what jokes to make, when to be friendly and when to be firm, and how to gain, apparently without effort, the allegiance of her 2B who assert with vociferous unanimity that she is 'smashing'. A school with a few of these on the staff is well placed for developing its autonomous role effectively.

It is evident that a certain amount of conflict and indeterminacy is associated with each of these roles, even when they are considered simply and separately. However, there are in practice four further complications which it is important to consider. First, each of these roles is related to what Merton (1957) calls a 'role-set', a series of people who are involved in the discharge of a role. He chose teaching as his prototype in the article in which he expounded his theory, as though it were a particularly good example to take. Secondly, the combination of the various roles into a role-complex may involve some conflict between them. Thirdly, there are the many implications of the diffuseness of the teachers' roles, a point which has already been mentioned. Fourthly, as Brookover stresses (1955a, Part IV: 1955b) a teacher in any particular situation has to adjust his own role-expectations to those of his school. Each of these complications deserves some attention.

The role-set problem can be illustrated by taking the classificatory role and examining the people who comprise the corresponding role-set. If a teacher is too strict, he may earn the criticism of parents and Head, and may even attract the attention of local busybodies. If he is too slack, in their eyes, he may encounter opposition from exactly the same quarters. If he spends his time on organising school visits and thus becomes informally friendly with his pupils, he may be criticised for reducing the social distance between adults and children in general. If he tries to equip his pupils to use their reason in everyday affairs, as far as their maturity permits, he may find himself accused of being a latter-day Socrates, corrupting the youth without regard for the susceptibilities of their parents. If he errs in the opposite direction and encourages obedience to Authority, there will be no lack of voices accusing him of being a tame conformist and a humble pillar of the Establishment. All of these criticisms may be in some sense justified. The important point for a discussion of the teacher's roles is that the role-set is so extensive. There are so many interested parties all of whom feel qualified to say something about what the teacher does. They would be much less likely to pronounce an opinion about a lawyer, or a doctor, or a member of any profession which has preserved its homogeneity and *arcana* from mediaeval times.

If this is true of the role-set conflicts which arise in respect of teachers' particular roles, it is still more true of their role-complex as a whole. To take one instance again, it is difficult to maintain simultaneously the attitudes appropriate to a parent-substitute and to a classifier. Provided that all the categories into which the children are allocated are of equal esteem, there need be no conflict. But if everybody wants to be centre-forward, most people have to be disappointed. Much the same applies in actual classroom procedures. The teacher teaches impartially: nobody would expect to in primary schools the kind of absurdity reported to the Taunton Commission whereby fee-payers in some endowed schools received more teaching than the free scholars. But some children make more progress and are more responsive than others, and some neat, bright-eyed, eager ones may suggest themselves to teachers as potential grammar-school or even University material while they are still in the infant or even the nursery school, so that some teachers may feel it incumbent on them to give these children every chance, while others may feel it important to devote more attention to those who start with a handicap. There could be some justification for either procedure, according to the basic socio-political views held by a teacher, but in either case there is a role-conflict to be resolved, one that cannot be sidestepped by claiming that each child should be enabled to develop at a hypothetical 'natural' rate. This role-conflict is rendered more complicated because the very act of assuming that the children who look bright will be bright, or that the boy who slips first into the centre-forward position will be a good centre-forward, itself weights the scales in favour of the individuals who are selected. It is an instance of a self-fulfilling prophecy; and if it is consistently carried out, it involves the subordination of the parent-substitute role, according to which all pupils are uniquely significant, to the classifier role, which involves a continuous ranking and comparison between them.

Such conflicts within the role-complex are perhaps exacerbated by the diffuseness of the teacher's roles. There is no clear precedent, no body of case-law or jealously-guarded protocol which governs individual cases. There could not be, unless teaching were again to become the preserve of what Wilson (ibid., p. 15) calls the 'literati', the conservers of a static culture rather than the promoters of dynamic adjustment to change. Of all teachers, those in primary schools are most characterised by role-diffuseness, and for this reason their role-complex is particularly highly charged with what Wilson (ibid., p. 25) following Parsons, terms 'affectivity', or emotional involvement: a sense of commitment to the total welfare of the children. The parent-substitute role is the most clear-cut instance of this, but it applies also to the others. Primary-school teachers' work can never, by definition, be complete, nor can it be discharged with even that degree of detachment which a doctor or a trained social worker is expected to display. Thus the emotional demands of the work are great, though the rewards are also great. Yet at the same time there is an element in the role-complex which demands from the teacher a quality of resilience, a refusal to take self or role with hyper-conscientious seriousness. The successful discharge of this diffuse, affectively-charged role-complex thus demands a knife-edge balance between detachment and involvement.

The remaining problem associated with a teacher's role-complex is that his or her role-expectations may differ from those of the school and community in which they are to be put to the test. This is a problem of role-ascription, for different detailed views of teachers' roles are held in different parts of society. But its solution is more closely related to role-achievement, and will be considered in that context.

One special comment is necessary about the specific role-complex of Heads as distinct from other teachers. Within it, the particular roles are differently combined. That of charismatic leader is in heavy demand. The Head is also the ultimate socialiser within the school, and to large extent the ultimate classifier too. As instructor, however, he or she may be less prominent, although efficiency in the instructor-role may have been an important factor in securing promotion to a Headship. Most Heads deeply regret the diminution of this role, which is in any case less marked than in secondary schools: indeed, in small primary schools the 'teaching Head' is still the rule rather than the exception. As welfare worker, however, the Head occupies a central position not only in the school, but in the case of many maintained primary schools, in the district too.

Achieved Roles and Procedures

In Talcott Parsons' (1952) terminology, the roles hitherto discussed are ascribed, that is, they belong to the general properties of the teacher-status in society. But in a particular school, each particular teacher also has a range of *achieved* roles which stem from his or her personal contribution. These are the characteristics associated with Miss Brown, which come sharply to light when Miss Brown leaves and her colleagues declare that nobody could take her place. Any average teacher could assume her ascribed roles; her achieved roles are the part that she takes with her.

Role-achievement takes time. It starts from the situation already mentioned, when a new member of staff brings an array of role-assumptions and role-expectations to confront those of the school. There is never a perfect fit. For one thing, there will be genuine differences of interpretation of the basic role-complex, varying from the superficial level ('But Mr. Smith always let us come out to sharpen our pencils') to the fundamental ('We don't believe in these modern methods here'). In addition, as in any other social institution there is always a probationary period in which the newcomer is

174

tested, and this is especially important in a school where sub-consciously the children are probing the adequacy of the newcomer as a social focus within their class, one who can fulfil the social needs characteristic of their general stage of development. A new teacher is also, of course, tested as a suitable member of the staff community. During this testing period, a newcomer is normally expected both to conform reasonably closely to the *externa* of behaviour demanded by the mores and folkways of the school, and to demonstrate a capacity for mature social behaviour and adjust-ment in general. The demands of institutional behaviour require that a new teacher shall do as Rome does, at least at first, and this in turn involves perceiving what Rome does in fact do.

It is when this initial phase has been passed that role-achievement begins. Each of the basic roles can now be discharged in a character-istically personal way. The instruction and socialisation within Miss Brown's class are different from those in other classes, and her charismatic leadership is quite distinctive. As time goes on, and her institutional position is grounded in some continuity of successful experience and social acceptance, she is able to develop other roles too. She may become the recognised source of sympathy or good humour in the school as a whole, or the acknowledged expert in handling the reception class, or the focus of opposition to the régime of an autocratic Head: these are at least some of the achieved roles that teachers can develop. But first they have to prove them-selves through their ascribed roles.

In this, they are aided both by their professional training and, as previously mentioned, by falling back on the traditional folklore of the teaching profession with its fund of *ad hoc* (and often con-flicting) precepts.[29] From this matrix of ideas emerges the day-to-day programme which they conduct, and which also constitutes the mechanism of social cohesion and control in the school insofar as it depends on the teachers. This is not the place to discuss these procedures in detail, for they in fact constitute the whole programme of primary education in practice. But one aspect of this social control is particularly important sociologically, namely the way in which a teacher can interact with and make use of the informal social system among the children.

In one sense, a teacher can never be a part of the children's society. He or she is an adult, armed with legal authority, and enjoined with the duty of conducting the class's business for which a teacher is also responsible. The initial, mandatory control, based on simple and efficient organisation, is a precondition of all that follows. The capacity of a teacher to communicate effectively with the whole class is important in any aspect of the work. But beyond this, it is possible and necessary to take the children's own social system into account.

For example, the informal leaders in the class can be given a recognised but not excessive part to play. This is less possible with infants, where pleasure in collective movement and activity usually depends on direct stimulus by a teacher, but in the junior school there is increasing scope for division into groups and teams in which there is a place for leadership of a simple and straightforward character. Concurrently, it is possible to distribute positive roles appropriate to individual children, such as keeper of the nature or geography table, or news or weather reporter, or ink or milk monitor; and these can circulate.[30] There is much to be said for having a fairly large number of these, simple at first and rather more responsible as the children grow older, so that after two or three exchanges of role everybody has a positive stake in the class's activities, and the emerging leaders a more important position than the rest. All of this is facilitated if, at all levels from the middle infant years upwards, the practice of working in groups of various kinds is fostered and if the children assume an increasing, though not excessive, share of responsibility for its conduct. A teacher who makes use of individuals and groups in this way is thereby combining the ascribed instructor and socialiser roles effectively and also establishing an achieved role in that particular class, because his or her pattern of organisation is specific to the teacher and the class. Evans (1962, Ch. 6) reviewed a number of empirical studies of group organisation, including one by Wilkie (1955) in a junior school, and pointed out that there was a slight indication that attainment and adjustment were both improved by this pattern of role-fulfilment by teachers, though the evidence was too tenuous to warrant a firmer claim. Studies such as those of Gardner (1942) and Bradburn (1960) point to a similar result in infant schools, perhaps with more assurance, insofar as the circumstances are comparable. In all these cases it seems reasonable to assert that the more a teacher withdraws from a pose of confrontation with a class, and the more he or she becomes an adviser and observer, the more readily it will be possible to see the teaching situation from the children's side of the 'fence', and the more quickly a collective we-feeling and a pattern of role-achievement will be developed. This is, in a sense, the sociological justification for informal methods of teaching; but if it is developed in a school where it is alien to the general role-expectations, role-achievement along informal lines may take a little longer to establish. Incidentally, as suggested in Chapter IV, a teacher's role-achievement may be accelerated where team-teaching and similar procedures operate to break down professional exposure and isolation.

One other aspect of role-achievement deserves mention. Since it does take time, there is an apparent advantage to teachers and schools if teachers are prepared to stay in one school until their achieved roles mature. This is particularly true in primary schools, where stability is of crucial importance. Thus in the folklore of education, the praiseworthy primary-school teacher is Miss Steady, twenty years an assistant at Nether Slocombe Infants' before she took the plunge and was appointed Head at Over Slocombe C.E., where she remained until her retirement, a memorable occasion when she was presented with a token of appreciation from the Vicar and the Managers and heard a tribute to her services from the County's Chief Inspector who came over for the afternoon. However, with the increasing bureaucratisation of the teaching profession it is, as Wilson (1962, pp. 29–30) points out, not the good and faithful servant who stays in one or two places but the lively young teacher who jumps about gaining 'varied experience in different types of school' who attracts the attention of appointing committees when Headships, College lectureships, advisory and administrative posts become vacant. This is inevitable; but the result is that able and ambitious teachers are virtually obliged to follow a career-pattern similar to that of municipal treasurers or company executives if they are to aspire to those positions of eminence from which they can eventually praise their former colleagues for remaining loyal to the traditional concept of role-achievement. There are in fact two conflicting patterns of role-achievement with similar starting-points, and the contradictions between them remain unresolved. For an individual teacher, the choice between them is partly determined by the pattern of initial qualification and early performance of ascribed roles, but also partly through interaction with the role-complex associated with personal and domestic circumstances. It would be informative to investigate this problem thoroughly, as Berger (1959) has done in the case of nursery-school teachers in a French *département*. Indeed, this is only one of the many sociological issues related to primary-school teachers, of whose importance we are only now becoming aware.

D. OTHER ADULTS IN PRIMARY SCHOOLS: THE 'FRINGE PERSONNEL'

Adults other than teachers obviously occupy a less focal position in primary schools, and largely for that reason have attracted less attention in research and description. Their functions will be considered in more general terms.

First, there are those adults who approximate most nearly to the teacher's role. One of these categories of adult is peculiar to nursery schools and classes but is within that context very important. It is that of *nursery assistant*. Girls and young women in this capacity are often trained in a College course which includes some practical work in day nurseries as well as in nursery schools or classes, in addition to theoretical study, and which leads to an examination conducted by the National Nursery Examination Board. Others are trained in shorter courses. They are not entitled to be in charge of a school or class, according to Schools Regulations,[31] but they may work with a qualified nursery teacher and in practice form a team with her. Although they are distinct in status from qualified teachers, they are closely associated with them in function and share, at a humbler level, the same pattern of professional expertise and commitment that is characteristic of trained nursery teachers. To the children, they all represent the same pattern of adult stability, tempered perhaps in the case of the assistants by a youthfulness which makes them seem merely old, as distinct from the teachers who may appear positively ancient. Their lower age and status may impel the teachers to adopt various attitudes towards the nursery assistants: motherly, superior, dictatorial, envious, or just friendly, according to the sort of people they are, while the assistants view their technical superiors with a corresponding range of attitudes. Although they cannot develop into teachers without a new type of training, these assistants are professional people with in most cases a qualification, which is more than can be said for uncertificated teachers in other schools.

Table 8 (p. 9) in the recent N.U.T. survey of nursery education (N.U.T., 1964) indicates the proportion of assistants to teachers in nursery schools, and Table 30 (p. 18) gives similar information for nursery classes. The following composite table summarises the two:

STAFFING IN NURSERY SCHOOLS AND CLASSES
N.U.T. SAMPLE[32]

Category	All nursery schools		Nursery schools for full-time pupils only		All nursery classes		Nursery classes for full-time pupils only	
	%	Average per school	%	Average per school	%	Average per class	%	Average per class
Qualified teachers	28	2·0	28	1·9	17	0·6	17	0·5
Trained nursery assistants								
(a) at college for nursery education	18	1·2	17	1·2	17	0·5	17	0·5
(b) at courses	19	1·3	18	1·3	36	1·2	37	1·3
Assistants in training	27	1·9	27	1·9	17	0·6	15	0·5
Untrained assistants	8	0·6	10	0·7	13	0·4	14	0·5
	100	7·0	100	7·0	100	3·3	100	3·3

As the Report indicates (N.U.T., 1964, pp. 5, 17) these average figures conceal some instances of very inadequate staffing.

Another type of 'near-teacher', and perhaps of 'near-adult' too, is the *student teacher*. In one sense, this category overlaps with the previous, since, as is shown in the preceding table, a considerable number of trainee nursery assistants are to be found in nursery schools and classes. In infant and junior schools, however, students are almost all from three-year training-college courses, the minority being drawn from specialist colleges or from one-year postgraduate courses in University Departments of Education. So numerous are these students now that in many schools, especially in urban areas, some are present in every term. To some extent, inevitably, they are a burden, but in the long run the recruitment of staff depends on schools' willingness to accept them, and in the (frequent) event of staff absence they are very useful. In addition, they and their tutors may bring new ideas to an otherwise rather isolated community.

The students' status is basically anomalous. They are teachers, yet they are taught. Where they are sensibly accepted by the staff, the children accept them too, sometimes as a welcome and attractive change. Whatever may happen at other times, they almost always rally to a student when a tutor or examiner comes in. For a woman student, the girls become helpful and the boys chivalrous: for a man, both are helpful. The novelty of being able for once to look after the teacher rarely fails to make its appeal. Though the relations between children, teacher, student and tutor can be complex, in general they constitute quite a pleasant initiation for all but the weakest of fledgling teachers.

The other adults in primary schools are more evidently non-teachers. They may be divided into three categories: those who work full-time in one school, those who do part-time work in connection with one school, and those who divide their attention between several schools.

Of the full-time ancillary staff in primary schools, the most universal is the *caretaker*. Almost every school has one, and because of his job-pattern he is often a more permanent figure than many of the teachers, especially if he has a house on or near the premises. His functions are nominally simple: to maintain the heating, to ensure a reasonable standard of cleanliness and tidiness, to keep the premises in good condition and (sometimes most difficult of all) to guard against burglars. In some schools he (the role is a male one) may almost merge the school premises with his household, so that his wife also becomes informally involved in the school and its social processes. In a large school, the caretaker may have a status similar to that of an N.C.O., with a staff of cleaners under his partial control. Since some caretakers have in fact been N.C.O.'s in their earlier days, these afford an interesting example of role-continuity.

In addition to his formal functions, a caretaker often assumes a series of informal roles. In virtue of his long tenure, he is well equipped to achieve these additional roles: indeed, the ascriptive element in the caretaker's role-structure is perhaps less evident than that of any other adult in the primary-school world. He is essentially Bill, or Mr. Long, rather than 'the caretaker'—as soon, that is, as he ceases to be 'the new caretaker'. Frequently he succeeds in establishing a direct and distinctive relationship with the Head, and may even try to take a newly-appointed or a young Head under his wing. By reminding his Head that a certain pipe is still leaking, or that something will have to be done quickly about the floor in the Hall, he builds up his status as a man of practical common sense and observation. Sometimes he misjudges his Head, but usually they establish an effective *modus vivendi*. A pattern of relations is also developed between the caretaker and other members of staff, which can involve some reflection of the school's structure and functions. For example, since formal teaching tends to leave less 'mess' of various kinds about in the classroom than is found after informal activities, it may be just those teachers who are most enterprising in their teaching who are viewed with the greatest scepticism by the caretaker.

Meanwhile, he also conducts informal relations with the children, usually on a basis of mutual bantering, but on the clear understanding that Bill will tolerate no nonsense. His background and experience often predispose him to a more authoritarian outlook than is prevalent among teachers, especially women teachers, and while in an infant school he often assumes a paternal manner, in a junior school he may come to regard himself almost as the mainstay of the school's system of social cohesion and control:

> Wouldn't stand for it if *I* was a teacher. Never happened when I was a boy that age. Caught a couple of the little so-and-so's on the roof myself the other afternoon—they won't be up there again in a hurry, not if *I*'m about, they won't.

Although there has been no research into the sociology of school caretakers, either at primary or at secondary level, it seems quite likely that the typical caretaker's authority-pattern enables him to feel more confident in his dealings with older boys than with older girls, to whose sallies he is not quite sure how to respond, though they never 'go too far' with him. Of course some caretakers, like some teachers, fail to establish rapport with children at all, so that they reject him and tease him mercilessly; but usually his achieved roles are positive and effective ones.

Next, among the full-time ancillary staff, comes the *secretary*, whose role is as characteristically feminine as the caretaker's is masculine. Until recently she was a rarity in primary schools,[33] and still she is often part-time, so it may seem illogical to group her with the full-time personnel. But the role is a *potentially* full-time one, and it is generally recognised that secretarial assistance is defective until it is full-time. Some aspects of her role parallel that of the caretaker. She can mother the Head, organise the office, and achieve a role as an anchor in the community: 'I really don't know how we could manage without Mrs. Ford.' But in other ways there are inevitable differences. She does not live on the premises. She is much more likely to leave after a relatively short time. Moreover, being by status a clerical worker earning a salary and not a wage, she is more likely than he to align herself with the teaching staff.

Informally, she can aspire to quite a range of achieved roles. She may become a cipher, echoing the Head's intentions, as her ascribed role implies; conversely, she may establish an ascendancy over the Head at the expense of the staff. She may be accepted in the Staff Room, or excluded from it, according to the pattern of personal relationships which becomes established. For example, if she unobtrusively assists in relieving the teachers' own clerical burdens and allows them to use the office equipment occasionally, and if she helps to maintain the general tone and efficiency of the school, she can be a very acceptable figure. This is in practice closely related to the type of relationship which she develops with the children. If she is cold and formal, protecting the Head from their encroachments, the children will tend to regard her as hostile and may gain the staff's sympathy for their attitude. On the other hand, the staff may feel antagonistic if she begins to usurp the parent-substitute role herself. This she is well placed to do, for if a child is to be taken home ill or in distress for some other reason, it is often the secretary who makes the arrangements, and it is to her that they first bring the worries which are the business of the Head rather than of the class teacher. When this happens, it is not surprising if the teachers note the contrast between her task of consoling, or even of admonishing, a solitary child in trouble with theirs of discharging their entire role-complex in company with forty or more energetic youngsters. Yet if they regard her role as relatively simple, they are not altogether correct; indeed, one pattern of adjustment which some secretaries evolve is that of emphasising the confusions within their role-complex and of stressing to staff and visitors alike that they are rushed off their feet in an impossible attempt to please everybody.

The third full-time adult member of a primary-school community is virtually confined to boarding schools and a few day special schools, but is of crucial significance when she does appear. She is the *matron*. In a boys' preparatory school of the traditional pattern, she often shares with the Headmaster's wife and perhaps with the housekeeper the entire responsibility for the domestic side of the school, and is also expected to be intimately concerned in the social activities of the community. Her medical skill is only one part of her necessary qualifications. She has another role as an organiser, and a more diffuse one which requires her to display just those feminine qualities which are appropriate to a woman who bears authority in an otherwise masculine society.[34] She must be open to understanding of the occasional regressions and transgressions of small boys entirely away from home, but her understanding must be offset by a firm determination to develop masculine behaviour in the boys and by an effective defence against wily appeals to her indulgence. Brisk, alert and strict, Matron in such a context is typically a blend of the professional nurse with the vigorous maiden aunt, and her role-achievement is to be worked out within that framework. Sometimes she has an assistant, with whom another pattern of relationships must be evolved; but she usually maintains a certain social distance between herself and the teaching staff. In the (less numerous) girls' preparatory boarding schools, her role is rather different. She may be a little more indulgent, perhaps, but no less insistent on vigorous routine. Here her position is essentially that of a professional woman who, like the staff, is engaged in sustaining a rather masculine structure in a totally feminine community, but who is still insulated from the staff by her different training and different pattern of ascribed roles. Like a school secretary, she may achieve a dominant informal role which may in a boarding school pervade the whole establishment; but more often she is in fact rather isolated.

In a special school, a matron has quite a different role-structure. Here she is essentially a nursing sister, concentrating on the medical aspects which are inevitably more in evidence. For that very reason, the ascriptive elements in her work are more prominent and her role-complex in general more defined. If she has nursing assistants, this allows further articulation within the same general pattern rather than extension outside it.

Especially in boarding schools of various kinds there is often also, as already mentioned, an *assistant matron* with a role-complex somewhat similar to that of the matron but also with a particular role-relationship to establish between the matron and herself.

Boarding schools often have other full-time employees who have less direct contact with the staff and children. They include *housekeeper*, *cook*, *maid* and perhaps *odd job man*. Sometimes their separation from the children is deliberately maintained, and preferred by them, partly because they do not wish to be asked, in return for a fixed remuneration, to undertake diffuse and unlimited tasks. But it is perhaps unfortunate that the children at an impressionable age see this obvious instance of contrast between the specificity of wage-earning roles and the diffuseness of salaried roles among the teaching staff, especially since their own families are in many cases socially identified with the latter. It may convey a distorted series of ideas about the nature of service to the community.

In a nursery school, on the other hand, a cook has quite a different type of function, in virtue of which she is almost a member of the staff herself. The familistic structure of the nursery-school community almost demands this, and in many cases gives considerable opportunity for interaction between cook and children. It is obvious that, under such circumstances, social harmony depends considerably on amicable relations between the cook and the teachers and assistants. Thus in practice a nursery-school cook is distinct in function from the other employees of the School Meals Service, who are to be considered next.

The second main category of 'fringe personnel' comprises those who, while not in full-time employment in a school, still come into close contact with the children of one particular establishment. One group of these is the *canteen assistants*, often referred to as 'dinner ladies', who spend a part of their day in serving school meals and, in those junior and infant schools which are fortunate enough to have their own kitchens, in preparing them too. It is at 'dinnertime' that they meet the children and the staff. Eating, like learning, must be conducted in an orderly atmosphere, and since the school is charged with training in table behaviour as a part of its socialising role, the 'dinner ladies' are a part of the authority-structure of the school. Sometimes they have to ensure orderly procedure at the hatch, even if the actual distribution of food is carried out by the children through that remarkably brisk and effective method known as 'family service'. More frequently, they have to dispense dishes, often of indeterminate temperature, from containers brought from a central kitchen. These functions bring them into contact with the Head and staff, but since the relationship is rather ill-defined, its outcome varies. However, since the 'dinner ladies' are themselves often local parents, they can provide a useful bridge of interaction with the community. Incidentally, it often happens that their own children are among the most dependable pupils, as though they are determined to support Mum in her declaration of loyalty to the school and its purposes. In fact, it is equally likely that work as a 'dinner lady' is a social role that appeals particularly to women who are already, for various reasons, predisposed to identify themselves with the school's aims.

The *canteen supervisor*, or some role with a similar title, is to be found especially in schools which are fortunate enough to have meals prepared on the premises. She is in charge of the 'dinner ladies' and may appear at the meal time in their company, but she is professionally trained and this gives her status among them and with the teaching staff. Her role in respect of the teachers is ill-defined, but in her own realm of the School Meals Service she is quite clear about her status and functions and her relation with her superordinates and subordinates.

Cleaners resemble 'dinner ladies' in their general alignment with the formal purposes of the school, though their functions can lead to minor disagreements about the use of rooms outside school hours. As with the caretaker, cleaners' attitudes towards staff members may be coloured by the way in which particular classrooms are left at the end of the day, even when this results from the type of work which is done. Also, if they find a young teacher to mother, or an older one in whom to confide, or anyone prepared to listen, some cleaners extend their roles in unofficial directions. With the caretaker, too, their relations may be of various patterns. There is no protocol: much depends on his tact. Occasionally, for example in small rural schools (Marshall, 1963) a single cleaner combines her role with that of caretaker and achieves a central position in the informal structure, taking a sequence of Heads under her wing; but that is exceptional.

Sometimes cleaners are in a strong bargaining position owing to their scarcity at the price, and a shortage can give rise to problems, but for the most part they are favourably disposed to the Head and staff, and many of them are impressively devoted to the community. Like the 'dinner ladies', too, the cleaners may play themselves into an informal achieved role, especially by dint of their outside knowledge of some of the children. This often leads them to side with the school against its more disreputable clients:

A terrible home, that!

though the same detailed knowledge can sometimes lead them to a particular understanding of parents:

As if Mrs. Hudson hadn't got enough trouble already!

These aphorisms are exchanged by the cleaners among themselves, but are at times passed on to the staff.

In general, cleaners have a variety of possible identifications, with the teachers (especially perhaps the married women) and with the parents, the actual pattern in any particular instance being determined by many factors.

Traffic wardens—'lollipop men' or 'lollipop ladies' as the children sometimes call them—constitute another and more marginal role in this second category. Unlike the previous two, the warden can be either a man or a woman, as the adaptable nickname suggests, but the role itself is essentially a protective one and thus is in a sense 'feminine', while the specificity and authority associated with it are 'masculine'. It can lead to a close link with particular children as they hold the warden's hand before crossing the road, and as they trot across while this modern St. Christopher defies, with outstretched 'lollipop', the advancing Jaguar. Yet however close may be this identification with the children, the warden is not effectively associated with the other adults in the school.

Finally, there is a category of adults who are concerned with several schools. Among these the *senior members of the School Medical and Dental Services* have a well-defined role and status, which often raises them above even the Head by virtue of their training and of their professional associations. The *junior members* of the same services have less august but equally well-defined roles, and they co-operate with the teachers on a formal basis unless they are personal friends. The roles of both groups are in a sense oriented to the hospital ward and the clinic rather than to the school. Thus in their dealings with the children they have a specific rather than a diffuse role-commitment, even in the case of members of the Child Guidance Service whose actual contacts with children are extremely informal, involving for example the transference of far more aggression than a class teacher could possibly countenance if his basic role-complex is to be sustained. Doctors, incidentally, try to cultivate a 'medical-inspection manner' analogous to the bedside manner but they often have to be quick and almost brusque in order to get through their case-load. An exception to the general formality of the School Medical Service is that the *school nurse*, acting as an unofficial Health Visitor, may often forge an informal link between school and home.

Probation Officers and *Education Welfare Officers* are other social workers of middle-range professional status who collaborate fairly closely with schools; rather more informally, in practice, than in the case of the medical profession with its high level of bureaucratisation. In any area, according to its sociological structure, they are likely to have much more contact with some schools than with others, simply because delinquency and truancy and care-and-protection cases tend to be concentrated in particular districts and even in particular streets.

Beyond these again there are other categories of adults whose business brings them into primary schools from time to time. They include *managers, local councillors, administrators, inspectors,*[35] *advisers*, and *tutors* of various categories of students whose professional training includes practical work in primary schools. If the school is to be regarded as a self-contained institution, then all of these are to some extent invaders and their visits are liable to cause some initial *froideur*, exacerbated in some cases by the poised suavity and assurance of their bearing. But all of them can, and many do, achieve a very amicable relation with particular schools, calling in to give help and appreciation from time to time, when they can and less often than most of them would wish, and gaining in their turn both in ideas and in satisfaction at the sight of a happily-functioning community of nursery, infant or junior children. The creation of such an amicable relationship depends, however, on understanding on both sides, and requires more than a forced joke over a cup of tea or even a glass of sherry before it can be established.

One group of adults which is of some importance to the school never meets the children and rarely the staff, though the caretaker at least is involved. This comprises the *evening organisations* which use the premises. It can happen in County schools, but is more usual in voluntary schools whose premises are then virtually an extension of the Church. There are problems on both sides. Infant chairs and tables and desks (there are still plenty) are a poor environment in which to study the Modern Novel or to organise a card canvass or to run a Bible Study group, while it is far from ideal if the infant school day has to begin amid the scarcely-tidied remains of a whist drive or a dance. Even when the school is used in evenings for educational purposes such as a play centre, a youth club or an evening institute, there is room for friction, all the more regrettable because it is generated between fellow-members of ostensibly the same profession. Yet here, as elsewhere, amicable relations can be established through the diplomacy of the key individuals.

Lastly, some mention should be made of those adults who have no particular business in primary schools but who come as visitors. These include those adults who should in fact have vitally important business there: the *parents*. Increasingly they are welcome, and when Parent-Teacher Associations are established, they acquire a positive though rather indeterminate status in the formal organisation of the school itself. This is matched by the readiness of the school to go out and observe the community, a point which will be examined more fully in Volume II, Chapter IV. Some parents, of course, come to tell the school what to do, others feel insecure and assume that the best defence is attack, and others become inarticulate and uncertain, as Jackson and Marsden (1962) have suggested, when faced with the necessity of discussing children's progress and prospects with the staff. But all this is changing quite rapidly in many places. The hesitancy of parents can be dispelled by a carefully-planned programme intended to promote communication between home and school. Increasingly, as in the U.S.A., it may become usual for parents to make regular visits and to take part in school work; fathers making apparatus for the nursery classes, mothers accompanying expeditions, grandparents giving information about their own schooldays, while visitors from overseas, often with black faces, pass unobtrusively but appreciatively through the school, stopping to admire the pottery or the dancing. Indeed, in places it has for some time been an established practice.

A Comment on Plowden

THE publication of the two-volume Plowden Report on *Children and their Primary Schools*[1] in January 1967, some eighteen months after the first appearance of the present book, is one of those events which, at least for the time being, captured the attention of the nation. It has already become so familiar, and has appeared in so many excellent summaries, that it is now legitimate to assume some general acquaintance with its principal characteristics and proposals. What I shall attempt, in this re-written conclusion, is an evaluation of this latest Report of the Central Advisory Council for Education (England) in the light of the sociological approach which I outlined when this book was first published. Inevitably, this will involve an element of personal judgment.[2]

To avoid confusion, references to the Report will be made thus: (I, 13) for Volume I, Chapter 13. Where it is necessary to refer to either volume of *English Primary Education*, the following style will be used: (EPE II, 3) for Volume II, Chapter 3 of my own book.

General Comments

Any sociologist must surely be rather gratified by the nature and content of the Plowden Report, not least because one of its two volumes is entirely devoted to 'Research and Surveys'. Many of the issues neglected or by-passed in earlier official literature have taken a prominent place in this monumental study,[3] whose very scale is itself an encouraging indication of the importance which primary education has come to assume in the thinking of politicians and administrators. What is more, the generally favourable reception given to the Report suggests that, whatever reservations they may have in practice, few influential sections of opinion will oppose it on principle.

The first general point to be evaluated is the content of the Report. It presents a compelling logical sequence of thought leading from the children themselves, through their environment, to the structure and processes of primary education, to the adults in the schools and the buildings in which they work, and finally to the inescapable economic and legal considerations. This sequence is both child-centred, reflecting the developmental tradition, and socially oriented. It is only after reconsideration that we notice the omission of any section explicitly devoted to the historical determinants of the present situation. Sociology and education are bereft of a dimension when the past is overlooked or treated only incidentally. A report intended to mark a great radical step forward would surely have lost nothing by making a brief survey of the journey that we have already travelled. It was done in 1931 and 1933: why not now?

Apart from this, it would indeed be difficult to specify a major omission in the subject-matter. It would be somewhat easier to question the balance of the Report. The scanty treatment of independent schools, the only 'minority schools' that the Council[4] regarded as falling within their terms of reference, is not altogether surprising, for the 1944 Act set a similar example, and in any case the future of independent primary schools will be powerfully affected by the Public Schools Commission, the body to whose Chairmanship Sir John Newsom has moved since acting as Lady Plowden's deputy. It is rather more surprising to see a somewhat meagre ration of space devoted to rural schools, which can surely claim some social distinctiveness (EPE II, pp. 81–5), though here the Council has more justification than its predecessor the Consultative Committee of the Board of Education under Sir Henry Hadow which, having been specifically asked to consider primary education 'with special reference to the needs of children in rural areas' did not even give them one chapter of their own. I also find it disappointing that the internal social processes of the schools are treated in a rather formal and limited way, when (I, p. 2) the Council itself declares that the section on 'The Children in the Schools' is 'the heart of the Report'.

By contrast with these possible sociological shortcomings, the prominence given to the special needs of 'educational priority areas', and the sensitivity with which the ensuing problems are handled, could scarcely be bettered, while the financial and administrative implications of the Report are faced with a realism that outstrips that of any of its predecessors. This no doubt reflects the expertise of some of the Council's members, though it is also a blunt reminder of our long-term economic situation.

Throughout the present book and its companion volume, I have felt obliged to stress the need for more social research in the field of primary education in England. In this respect there can be no doubt that the studies commissioned by the Council and embodied in Volume II of the Report, as well as the mammoth classification of all the English primary schools by Her Majesty's Inspectors (I, p. 101), have added very decisively and substantially to the available data, while one chapter (I, 30) reiterates the call for more of it. Collectively, it is by far the most important single contribution yet made to research on English primary education. Even so, it is necessary to remember that the big majority of the research projects used or specifically commissioned by the Council exemplified two particular types of large-scale investigation, one based on question-naires and the other dependent on structured interviews: the latter includes the 1964 National Survey among Parents of Primary School Children, from which a considerable part of the statistical data in the Report were drawn. However subtle the statistical analysis of such information may be—and in the Plowden Report a high level of sophistication is maintained—the raw data inevitably lack the richness that can arise from the use of a number of techniques within a fairly restricted research situation such as a particular school. Material collated in this way may also prejudge rather closely the nature of the available responses. For example, it would be rather an exaggeration to call the National Survey a genuine study of parental attitudes. The advantages of a more diverse pattern of research are seen in particular in two of the Appendices in Volume II, namely the Manchester study of ten-year-olds conducted by Professor Wiseman (II, 9) and the N.F.E.R. 'streaming' research, an interim report on which is included (II, 11).

Surprisingly, it appears that no attempt was actually made to study and follow up the social processes in any specific school, except perhaps incidentally to the observation of the effects of bold innova-tion in school building at the Evelyn Lowe School at Rolls Road (I, 28) (EPE I, pp. 15–16 and 46) and elsewhere. For information about what actually goes on in schools, the members depended on reports from H.M.I. and on personal and vicarious experience, including an extensive programme of visits which must have been a stimulus and a pleasure to the Council but which cannot have afforded a great deal in the way of continuity.

To the average citizen, and indeed to the average student of education, the most important considerations in Volume I of the Report are those which point the way to positive action. Mention should first be made of their general tenor, before closer attention is given to those of specifically sociological interest. Perhaps inevitably, they are a heterogeneous collection, ranging from the boldly radical (social priorities) to the gently progressive (curriculum), and from the speculative (aims of primary education) to the rigorously scientific (prediction of costs). In sum, they give the impression of being distinctly though not uncritically on the Left of the socio-political spectrum, not hesitating to put the needs of society before anyone's inherited habits, even those of teachers, but declining to assume that this can be achieved through simple administrative procedures. No doubt the Report will be regarded, in the respectively appropriate quarters, as both a revolutionary and a reactionary document: that would place it firmly in the tradition of our major reports on education.

A Comment on Plowden

Main Proposals of Sociological Interest

These will be considered in turn: the order of social priorities, then the proposals for nursery education, for the age-distribution of primary education, for aspects of social structure and social process, for teachers and their preparation, for other adults, and finally for the status and government of primary schools.

(a) *The order of social priorities.* It is in itself significant that the Report's priorities are couched in social terms. Following on the Council's previous suggestions made in *Half our Future*[5] (when Sir John Newsom and Lady Plowden were respectively Chairman and Vice-Chairman before changing places to study primary education), the main effort is to be concentrated in educational priority areas (I, 5) whose definition is not conclusively enjoined by the Council either on Local Education Authorities or on the Secretary of State, but on whose behalf 'positive discrimination' is called for. Though everyone knows in broad terms what are the characteristics of such areas, the Report spells them out in detail. This is a courageous and realistic proposal, all the more so since it is coupled with the use of such areas as pilot projects for some of the Council's other proposals. It does, however, seem likely that there will be problems arising from the actual demarcation of these areas, one of which the Report itself foresees (I, p. 61)i n discussing the distribution of teachers. As soon as an area is designated (whoever does it), its slightly less adversely affected neighbour in a twilight zone may slip down to take its place; perhaps this is inevitable unless major social reconstruction is carried out. One other difficulty is that the provision of local housing for teachers, advocated as part of a specific programme of social aid, may be liable to the limitations which I have already indicated (EPE II, pp. 103–4), though for young unmarried teachers these will carry less weight provided that the prospects of promotion through service in priority areas are perceived as real.

The order of the other main priorities (I, 31) is based more evidently on administrative considerations. Each of them—teachers' aides, improvement of buildings, extension of nursery education, revision of age-span, in that order—will be mentioned subsequently. Taken together they constitute a realistic series, provided that the time-tabling, spread as it is over more than a decade, does not prove too optimistic. If it does, then it is hard to see that much can be achieved without some actual reduction of standards in the lusher places, despite the smooth words (I, p. 65):

> For it would be unreasonable and self-defeating—economically, professionally and politically—to try to do justice by the most deprived children by using only resources that can be diverted from more fortunate areas.

If they do have to be diverted, then it is hard to see how that can be

190

fully reconciled with another principle that is upheld; that of parental choice (I, p. 44). For it will be surprising if parents in the more favoured districts do not then intensify their efforts to secure for their own children entry into those schools whose quality has been least conspicuously lowered—the pecking order would soon be known—or alternatively, if zoning is enforced, they are more likely to seek places in independent schools, thus impeding the progress of social integration. No solution can be perfect without the magic wand of increasing real wealth.

(b) *Nursery education* (I, 9). It is particularly welcome to find emphasis laid on the desirability of extending nursery-school provision, mainly on a part-time basis. The arguments here are both social and individual, and the actual suggestions humanely considered. The proposed extension includes, incidentally, some possibility (I, p. 122) of the establishment of nursery groups and centres covering the provision now made in nursery schools and classes and even in day nurseries, all firmly under local education authorities and not local health authorities; and this seems to be a sensible improvement in organisation.

It is interesting to see that, in one of the 'Notes of Reservation' at the end of Volume I, the suggestion is made that parents might contribute towards the cost of nursery education. If this procedure were to be adopted, the objection might be raised that those who could afford it were purchasing a still greater advantage at the most impressionable age. To this the authors of the Note give an adequate, though not incontrovertible, reply, claiming that it would be legitimate to make a small charge for education outside the statutory age-range if thereby it became possible to do something that would otherwise remain undone. Since it would provide facilities which could also be used for other children for whom fees would be remitted (that is, outside the educational priority areas where there would be no charges in any case), the relatively needy might indirectly gain. That, after all, is what happened in many parts of the English educational world in the past.[6]

Meanwhile it is worth remembering that the substantial expansion of nursery education could have other social consequences. One might be the extent of parental and other opposition based on non-economic grounds, that is, for example, on preference for the extension of pre-school play groups more closely associated with homes, the consideration which led one member of the Council to make a Note of Reservation of her own (I, p. 486). Another might be that the eventual regular inclusion of the age-range 3–5 within the normal period of school attendance would, especially if combined with an upward extension of primary education and a redistribution of the 'ages and stages', result in a disruption of the comparative unity of the 'Midlands of childhood' as described in this book, and the substitution of a sequence of culture-periods more akin to those traversed by children in the U.S.A.

(c) *The proposed amendment of the 'ages and stages'* (I, 10). On this theme there is in fact a series of proposals. The first of these is for the eventual establishment of a single date of entry to infant schools, and for an interim transition period the use of two dates, rather on the same basis as the interim procedure for leaving dates from secondary schools. This is unexceptionable, and will go far towards eliminating the irregularities in opportunity resulting from differences in birth date. The second is intended to mitigate the rigidity of the school-entry procedure for individual children by allowing part-time attendance at first (EPE I, 3 and II, p. 120). This, too, is in line with current opinion on child development, and is to be unequivocally welcomed.

The third proposal is consequent on the suggested single entry date and involves the substitution of eight for seven as the normal termination of infant-school life. The arguments (I, pp. 140–1) are mainly based on the homogeneity and purpose of infant schools and are on balance wise, provided that they are not too much influenced by the proposals made for the subsequent stages.

The next suggestion, for raising the age of leaving from junior schools, seems to me more doubtfully argued. Now that the Education Act, 1964, has allowed for some modification in the age of transfer, there remains no legal obstacle, and indeed there is a logical case for upward extension of primary education if and when the preceding reforms are implemented, and if and when the statutory leaving-age is raised to sixteen. This case is not invalidated because, while the average age for leaving secondary schools goes up, the average age for entry into the teenage culture goes down. But the question remains, whether the age should be raised to twelve or to thirteen. The Council discussed the issues fully (I, pp. 144–6) and concluded that:

> The danger of the extension of the middle[7] school course for one year only would be that the change might not provide sufficient challenge to the schools to think afresh about what they provide for older pupils. The danger of a two year extension would be that the middle school might forget that it was still a primary school. There is a risk either way; on the whole we think that transfer at 12 is more likely to give us the middle school we want to see.
>
> The arguments in favour of 12 and 13 as the age of transfer are fairly evenly balanced, and there is . . . no one age which is right for every child. But on nearly every count it seems to us that the balance of advantage is just with 12 year old transfer. . . .

My own view is that the balance of advantage falls the other way. I think that a secondary school starting at thirteen would (after the school-leaving age is raised) acquire a greater sense of momentum

192

and social purpose than one commencing at twelve, since it would be less likely to 'sag' in the middle, while an upper primary school stretching from 8 to 13 could, especially in view of recent curricular trends, create a separate identity in which, indeed, it might be something of an advantage to 'forget that it was still a primary school'. It is true that some children would lose by staying too long in the 8–13 school but here, as in the case of infant-school entry or infant–junior transfer, the Council's recommendations about flexibility in individual cases should be taken into account.

Of course, a change of this kind would also affect the social characteristics of the various age-levels, a point which the Council considered when writing on secondary schools (I, p. 143) but oddly enough not when treating of primary schools. At the upper end, there would be scope for a more developed formal and informal structure, with a wider range of status-positions and a greater opportunity for children to organise their own work and to take collective responsibility for their own behaviour. Again, 'conspicuous competitive co-operation' might become more elaborate, especially in those suburban and commuter-belt schools which could well be regarded as the 'A' stream of primary education in general. Possibly, too, the prolongation of the primary stage, with its accompanying tendency to concentrate high status-ascription for girls and boys alike at the age of twelve or thirteen, might strengthen the good-pupil outlook in early adolescence for both sexes at the cost of allowing some growth of irresponsibility in midstream among the ten-year-olds, especially the boys, and with perhaps an increasing divergence between the main and alternative value-systems of the schools. On the other hand, the inclusion of substantial numbers of pubescent girls within these schools might have the effect of reducing the girls' predominance in the good-pupil role. It is difficult to forecast which social outcome would actually result in any particular case. As for the continuing influence of primary schools within secondary schools, there might be considerable changes if the transfer were postponed until after the age at which within-sex solidarity and between-sex cleavage are usually at their maximum.

At the lower end of the primary age-range there might be other, less conspicuous changes. In what ways, for example, would vertical grouping develop in the 5–8 schools, and what roles would the oldest boys be able to play at an age when they normally at present draw aside both from girls and from younger boys? Incidentally, how far would the deployment of staff permit boys of eight to find male identification models among their teachers?

Of course, if the age-span of primary education were extended to twelve or thirteen, this would also have still wider consequences. It is one thing to permit the nominal end of childhood to fall at this age for a minority who are accustomed to continue formal education considerably longer, and quite another to raise the transfer age for the majority within whose culture secondary education itself is sometimes precariously established. Several times, in the preceding chapters, it was indicated that the effective boundaries of the 'Midlands of childhood' are themselves partly determined by the legal limits of primary education. If these limits are altered, and especially if the upward limit is raised, the social characteristics of schools may be considerably affected, particularly since the frontiers of puberty and of the teenage culture (EPE II, 5, pp. 127–30) are encroaching on the Midlands years anyhow. The Council has shown its awareness of the physiological, if not so explicitly of the social, trends involved. For upper primary schools might come to resemble in some ways American junior high schools, with the first 'dating belt' lying within their confines. This might have its advantages; it would certainly involve some reconsideration of the normal cultural expectations of schools, especially since the older primary pupils might also be more likely to develop individual and group criticism of the values officially promulgated by their schools. All of these developments may come to be accepted, and welcomed, but it is important that they should not come upon us unawares.

The Council's final suggestion in respect of age-structure is for a new nomenclature: nursery schools (or groups, or centres) up to 5, first schools 5–8, and middle schools 8–12. The introduction of new names is useful, for they can symbolise genuine changes in significance, but these particular choices are rather unfortunate. It seems to me strange to call schools 'first schools' if they are to be preceded by nursery education, or to use the term 'middle schools' when this has already come to be associated with very different institutions in other countries, including the Chinese People's Republic.

(d) *Social structure* (I, 20) *and social process* (I, 17–19). The treatment in the Report of social structure and social process, the principal subject-matter of the present book, is somewhat uneven. There is an important accretion of information about streaming (on which attention was already focused) through the interim report of the National Foundation for Educational Research, in the light of which the Council is confirmed in its general preference for non-streaming, though it emphasises the importance of intelligent planning for any organisation which is to replace it. There is also (I, 6) a timely chapter on immigrants, whose children are becoming increasingly important as an element within the social structure of primary schools in many places, but the Council remains pragmatically noncommittal on the question whether the children of immigrants should be dispersed over various schools or concentrated in a few, leaving it to local education authorities to strike the wisest balance of policy in each particular case. These two chapters are likely to be scrutinised with increasing interest, since both are concerned with topics likely to remain controversial, and both are, largely for that reason, the subject of extensive ongoing research.

A more strictly 'educational' issue which is explicitly examined is the degree of rigidity according to which children should be divided into separate, age-graded classes irrespective of streaming. As partial specialisation among teachers (not the same thing as specialist teaching) becomes more familiar in primary schools, and as buildings of a more flexible pattern are developed, it will become more necessary to think of a Staff as a team of mutually supportive experts who sometimes teach individual classes, sometimes combine them into larger groups as for music and some aspects of physical education where numbers can be a positive asset, and sometimes divide them into smaller units for remedial work or special interests or the use of mechanical aids. Meanwhile, with the growth of vertical grouping, the reign of age-grading may be coming to an end in junior as well as in infant schools. The Report welcomes these developments but wisely suggests that there should still be a class-unit of some sort, akin to a 'home room' in an American school, for the younger children, and progressive modification of this pattern as they grow older. As for the overall teacher/pupil ratio, there is a call for its reduction and for the termination of the differential between primary and secondary class size; scarcely a novel suggestion, but advanced in this case with cautious optimism and linked interestingly with proposals for action-research into optimum class sizes at different age-levels. There is also a practical, though rather inconclusive, discussion (I, 13) about the optimum size of whole schools, and some unusual and interesting suggestions for modifying the length of the school day and the arrangement of the school year.

Finally in respect of structure, recent exciting developments in primary-school architecture, already mentioned as a prerequisite of greater flexibility in the social organisation, are themselves discussed (I, 28) and useful indications are given of ways in which building methods could be used to give a face-lift to older schools.

There is, in the main, little novelty about the references to social processes in schools. As regards instruction, recent developments in the curriculum are discussed with infectious enthusiasm, tempered by caution. There is, incidentally, no specific support for the case advanced in this book for a curriculum emphasising the arts as a basis for an autonomous culture, within which role-playing can be developed without the restrictions of social class, the veto of social custom or the barrier of stereotype. For when individual children, and teachers, have developed an awareness of the loyalties and satisfactions which arise within an autonomous primary-school community, they can evolve a 'security of creativity' akin to Dewey's 'security of procedure', which can enable them to encounter change without going on the defensive. It seems to me that, in an age of rapid social change, an autonomous culture which expresses the best (I use the adjective without apology) within each school's capacity is more necessary than ever, especially since primary education may have the special responsibility of nourishing children's creative imagination when social pressures in general are in many ways inimical to it. This, combined with the fostering of critical awareness during secondary education, may be essential for developing the outlook needful in an adult citizen of a mature but changing democratic society (EPE II, 5, pp. 127–30). But the Council does not appear to have forged this link between instruction and autonomy, or indeed to have been very concerned about specifically cultural issues at all. There was, as it happens, no Hoggart among its members.

This has not caused much concern among the general public, or indeed among educators. Where instruction is concerned, attention has been focused on the proposals about religious education, and in particular on the fourth and fifth Notes of Reservation (I, pp. 489–93). This concern is probably a result of the history of English primary education, and indeed of English society itself. The Council as a whole sponsored changes that would have raised eyebrows in 1944, but some of its members also called for root-and-branch abolition of compulsion and asked (I, p. 491):

> that opting in should be substituted for the present system of opting out

This may well be what many people, by no means all of them Humanists, would advocate if they allowed themselves to think through the present situation, but it is worth adding that it might involve in conspicuous isolation no longer the children of unbelievers, but those of the adherents of particular denominations and faiths; and this could give rise to group pressures of an equally cogent nature, none the less invidious because they happen to be more fashionable. However, the resulting stimulus to Churches and Sunday Schools (EPE II, pp. 67–70 and 113–18) is something to which they should be eager to respond, and it should not be impossible to devise a solution to the in-school problem along lines characterised by the wisdom and charity to which all concerned lay claim and which, incidentally, is admirably exemplified in the final statements of the Council itself.

The classificatory role also receives some attention, in a chapter (I, 11) giving a brief obituary on selection for secondary education and another (I, 22) which gives sympathetic though tentative consideration to the question, ultimately much more important, of the special needs of highly gifted children. It is gratifying to note that, in calling for further research on this question, the Council showed some awareness that it has sociological dimensions and that, even in a democratic society, one need not be ashamed to mention them. It may also be noticed, though the Report does not specifically say so, that the raising of the age of transfer from primary to secondary education would considerably broaden the scope of the classificatory role of primary schools and would lay upon them a greater responsibility for the diagnosis and fostering of talents and interests than has hitherto been usual. This is what the Norwood Report[8] proposed for lower secondary schools, and it has also been practised in the French 'cycle d'observation'.

As for the other roles outlined in this book, welfare figures prominently in the Report, and has a chapter (I, 7) to itself. Socialisation in the wider sense is implicit in the whole document, though the more limited patterns of socialisation within the classroom are given little attention.

The chapter (I, 19) on 'the child in the school community' is in fact disappointing. With all the richness of community interaction to consider, the Council devoted almost one-half of this brief summary to the question of punishment, the most negative aspect of social cohesion and control. The rest, too, is largely an apologia for modern primary education apparently drawn up in order to assuage some anonymous critic of contemporary methods. To make room for this, all discussion of the relations between child and child and of the formation of personality is omitted, or at best dispersed elsewhere in the Report. This imbalance is more the fault of English society than of the Council, who obviously felt under some obligation to give priority to the single recommendation that corporal punishment should be administratively and legally abolished. Even so, its members indicated (I, p. 271) that:

Our recommendations are likely to meet with some opposition;

and they have. First, they provoked yet another Note of Reservation from one of the teacher-members of the Council (I, p. 493) and subsequently there has been a succession of protests from elsewhere. Perhaps it was impolitic, on the Council's part, to leave the impression that 'the cane' should be abolished before basic improvements in primary education such as the reduction of class size were achieved, though (I, p. 271) it is pointed out that the use of corporal punishment as a police measure is connected, as it almost always has been, with the stark consequences of oversize and undermotivated classes. Be that as it may, the call for prohibition is a wise and a courageous move, marred only by the disproportionate emphasis given to it.

Finally, in respect of social change, it should be pointed out that the Report itself exemplifies and advocates change, and indicates in some detail and with some sensitivity how it can be conducted on both of the levels that matter: that of the school, and that of society.

(e) *Teachers and Teacher Education* (I, 23–25). The Report gives full consideration both to the roles of teachers in primary schools and to the question of teacher supply which, as has been justifiably pointed out,[9] more explicit attention should have been given in the present book. In general, the Council's suggestions are sensible and forward-looking. The particular discussion (I, pp. 332–5) of the role of the Head Teacher in relation to the rest of the Staff embodies some excellent ideas, though it does not draw upon role-theory in the sense in which this is familiar to sociologists.

The comments on the training of primary-school teachers are sensible and balanced for the most part, and the emphasis laid on in-service and higher training is particularly apposite. It is reassuring to know that the Council deplored the present legal position whereby untrained graduates can be qualified as primary-school teachers. However, it is not so clear why (I, p. 339):

> This is the time when there should be a full study of the whole subject of the training of teachers. Undertaken now, it could help to influence the ways in which expansion takes place instead of being an inquest on what has been done. . . .

which would be true enough, if the Colleges of Education were not still running to keep up with change and thereby disinclined at present to go through the procedure of yet another external enquiry. Neither is it clear how one could justify the rather improvised 'realism' of the minority who suggest, in the final Note of Reservation (I, pp. 493–5) the postponement, for some students, of the final year of the normal three-year course. This avowedly amateur suggestion by a few members is not calculated to endear to Colleges the major investigation proposed by the Council as a whole.

In accord with the emphasis laid in the earlier parts of the Report on the sociological aspects of primary education, there is a call (I, pp. 347–8) for the inclusion of specifically sociological material in the training of all primary teachers, and for the use of sociologically appropriate methods of College learning too. However, this is specified mainly in connection with home-school relations and in practice it is also important that it should involve a general introduction to the study of schools as social institutions and to the more delicate question of teachers' roles. I would also suggest the inclusion of some consideration of cultural issues and of an opportunity for all students to develop skills and experiences in one of the arts, so as to be able to contribute to an autonomous culture in school; but, as I have already pointed out, the Council was not particularly concerned with cultural questions.

(f) *Other Adults* (I, 24, 26). Although only a few of the 'other adults' mentioned in EPE I, 7, are discussed in the Report, the Council suggested adding to the list a new one, the trained *teacher's*

198

aide, a proposal which has caused more furore than any other of their recommendations. Nobody doubts the value to teachers of some kind of ancillary help, and everyone is agreed that this would also assist in building up the status of teaching as an occupation. But the suspicion has taken root, and remains, that the Council has for economic or other reasons deliberately sought to blur the distinction between the role of the teacher and that of the aide. This impression apparently depends on two sentences which, taken out of context, read (I, p. 331):

> On no account should children be in charge of untrained helpers without supervision by a qualified teacher. It is preferable that, when circumstances make some arrangement of this kind necessary, children should be looked after by a trained aide and their class linked with a qualified teacher.

Professional opinion has seized on this second sentence and has vehemently expressed its determination that 'circumstances' should never 'make some arrangement of this kind necessary'. It would be a thousand pities if the scheme for trained ancillary help were to founder on these suspicions; but perhaps a little more sociological finesse on the part of the Council, a clearer emphasis on the limits envisaged for the functions of aides, and a frank recognition of the delicate role-problems inevitably associated with an innovation of this character, might have managed to avoid the verbal provocation that this passage appears to have given. Since the Council were obviously aware of the delicacy of the issue, it is unfortunate that this dispute has arisen, and doubly unfortunate that it has attracted such disproportionate attention. For in the long run the role of the primary-school teacher will be rendered less diffuse and more congenial if ancillary help is encouraged on the analogy, which the Council rightly and cogently draws (I, 26) with nursery assistants (EPE I, pp. 177–8). The provision for aides of reasonable career prospects, including further quite extensive training for a few to become teachers (I, p. 374) is a wise proposal; but perhaps the forecasts of potential recruitment of aides (I, 26 and 31) is over-optimistic in view of the other claims that the economy may make on the female labour force.

(g) *The Status and Government of Primary Education* (I, 31). This is a part of the Report that must be welcomed unreservedly. It epitomises the principle implicit in the document as a whole, namely that no legal or administrative obstacles should be allowed to impede primary schools from winning an appropriate status in public esteem. The position of teachers in relation to Head Teachers, to educational administration, and to society as a whole is examined sympathetically, and facilities for their active participation in the government of education are advocated. The role of managers is also scrutinised, in the hope that they can become more influential, and in some cases where there is scope for it, more humane too in their relations with the schools. In general, the hope is expressed that primary schools can be made to appear less like minor departments of the local government service, as some do; though to be sure they do not actually indicate how this can be achieved.

After Plowden

Whatever the actual outcome of the Plowden Report may be, it has certainly raised the general level of thinking about English primary education. This thinking must now be maintained and developed, with an eye to political and social action. Here is an inescapable issue, on which we all have to make up our minds. Personally, I believe that the implementation of the Report's highest priorities must claim precedence even over the reorganisation of secondary education and the raising of the limits of compulsory education to sixteen, to both of which we are already committed. This is not because I regard either of these as in themselves undesirable or impracticable objectives, but because without prior reforms in primary education, I believe that they will both be seriously impaired.[10]

Any views on this weighty issue, including my own, are liable to contamination by dogmatic assertion until we have a great deal more of relatively objective information. For that reason it will be more necessary than ever to bear in mind another of the Report's major lessons (I, 30; II) and to extend and develop serious study and research in the field of primary education. Social research, with due consideration of the significance of social change, will be particularly important. In this way current and future needs for policy and decision-making will reinforce the regular development of research, which should in any case be the prerogative and the academic hall-mark of any branch of educational studies.

In the present, then, and still more in the future, there is a demand for social research and sociological understanding to permeate English education at the primary level no less than elsewhere. For here, the rising generation is undergoing social experience and forming social concepts before our very eyes. They are already laying the basis for their adolescent roles and values. If we wait until they erupt as teenagers before noticing what is happening or caring to do anything about it, the pattern will be set before we act. It is in the Midlands years that the children's world (EPE II, 3) first acquires autonomy, and it is then also that children turn willingly to school and place themselves for a while under the collective wing of society. If we do not follow the lead of the Plowden Report and concern ourselves with what takes place during those years, then we neglect the seed-bed of English society itself. It is encouraging to realise that

English primary education, which has often received so little, has already achieved so much; but (I, 32) this must not render us in the least degree complacent. The determination with which we now seek to improve primary education in all its aspects, and to reform it radically if necessary, is a key to the future of English society and a measure of our concern for the development of the nation and for the self-fulfilment of the individuals who comprise it.

If the argument developed in this book is valid, we should promote, by all institutional means at our disposal, an autonomous culture within each school from the primary stage onwards. Such a policy constitutes the necessary means, within the limits of the sociologically possible, of fostering what I, and many of us, regard as in principle desirable alike for children and for society: the integration of the individual and social aims of education in a modern liberal democracy.

This takes us, inevitably, beyond sociology, for sociology cannot in itself determine the aims of education. What it can do is to provide a conceptual framework and a repertoire of techniques of investigation which can enable us to interpret what does happen, to predict in some small measure what may happen, and to deduce how far what we regard as desirable may also be possible. This is a valuable possession, one that was denied to Plato. It should be built right into our thinking about the future of English primary education.

References

INTRODUCTION

[1] Notably the writings of Susan Isaacs, Charlotte Bühler, Piaget and his associates, Gesell and his collaborators, and J. M. Tanner, as listed in the bibliography.

[2] Which despite its title actually confined its attention to children from seven to eleven.

[3] However, junior departments of direct-grant grammar schools are separately classified in Ministry of Education statistics (e.g. *Statistics of Education in 1962*, Part I, Table 8) i.e. they do not figure as independent schools there.

I. AN ANALYSIS OF PRIMARY SCHOOLS AS SOCIAL INSTITUTIONS

[1] In the American sense of the term, i.e. the first six grades or their equivalent.

II. NURSERY AND INFANT SCHOOLS

[1] These conditions were slightly relaxed on 28th February 1963, when the then Minister of Education announced in the House of Commons that a slight expansion of nursery classes might be permitted where accommodation was already available and where this would release a substantial number of qualified married women to teach in maintained primary and secondary schools. A report in the *Guardian* for 27th December 1963, indicated that local education authorities had not responded very vigorously to this limited relaxation.

[2] By kind permission of the Secretary, Miss D. E. Warren, 89 Stamford Street, London, S.E.1.

[3] i.e. the L.C.C. area, not the G.L.C.

[4] Annual Report of the Ministry of Health: *The Health and Welfare Services*. Cmnd. 2062. London, H.M.S.O., 1963. Tables E and F, p. 193.

[5] 45 Russell Square, London, W.C.1.

[6] *Statistics of Education in 1962*, Part I, Table 14, p. 45.

[7] It is an odd historical anomaly that 'infant' comes later than 'nursery' in the terminology of English education.

[8] This situation has been cited in proposals to amend the age of entry to compulsory full-time education. However, it is not widespread, as may be seen from the percentages quoted in the following paragraph. If there was extensive deferment of entry to infant schools, the percentage of five-year-olds in maintained primary schools should be markedly lower than that of six- or seven-year-olds: in fact it is almost identical.

[9] I am indebted to my colleague Dr. J. B. Coltham for pointing out that in 1962 Ceylon raised its school-entry age to six.

[10] For a eulogy of vertical grouping, see E. Margaret Lawson, 'Growing up with the class', *Guardian*, 16th July 1963, or M. R. Killon, 'The mixture as before', *Bulletin* of the National Froebel Foundation, No. 133. December 1961.

[11] Mellor (1950, Part II, Ch. 4) gives a particularly good analysis of social development within infant schools.

[12] Education Act, 1944, Section 48.

[13] I once had occasion to pay several visits to an infant class in which one small girl, who had been deeply disturbed psychologically, screamed throughout my stays until a slightly older girl was given the task of removing her protégée whenever I appeared. This she did with great aplomb, discharging her protective role admirably, and treating me to a knowing smile as she did so.

[14] The assembly itself need not be at the start of the day. Sometimes it is most effective at the end of the afternoon.

III. THE SOCIAL STRUCTURE OF JUNIOR SCHOOLS

[1] Some of the seven-year-olds (59,726 girls and 63,369 boys) were in separate *infant* schools; hence the proportion of children in separate junior schools was slightly greater than these figures suggest.

[2] See *Periods of Stress in the Primary School*. National Association for Mental Health. 1955. p. 17.

[3] The latest official advice about new primary-school building is given in *Primary School Plans: a second selection*. Ministry of Education Building Bulletin 23. London, H.M.S.O., 1964. See also Plowden Report Vol. I, Part VIII.

[4] A balanced survey of the whole question of streaming in junior schools was published in the *Times Educational Supplement* for 1st March 1963.

[5] A brief reference to sociometry was made in Chapter I above. Here it will be more fully discussed, but space forbids an actual outline of the techniques, which can be assimilated easily from the books listed here and also (less easily) from the writings of the founder of sociometry, J. L. Moreno (1953).

[6] Detailed evidence is presented in my unpublished thesis. (Blyth, 1961).

IV. SOCIAL PROCESSES IN JUNIOR SCHOOLS

[1] Middle-class values often appear to reign, with general approval, in junior schools in entirely working-class districts. Of course there are exceptions. Sometimes, indeed, parents at various social levels may have cause to regret that the standards promoted by some schools are *lower* than those expected in some homes.

[2] Much the same tendency can survive into adult life, as is evident for example in the allocation of popular roles in a club.

[3] In 1962, according to *Criminal Statistics for England and Wales*, Table XIV, for that year, 4,283 boys and 321 girls under twelve were placed on probation owing to their own infringement of the law.

[4] It is advisable to avoid imitating ancient grammar schools, Urban District Councils, and other heraldic prototypes, but to aim at something more satisfying than a solitary cowslip. (These things do happen.)

[5] Commenting on their survey of teachers' opinions around 1950, Highfield and Pinsent state that:

> These results point quite clearly to a tendency to resort to physical punishment in the face of misdemeanours which offend standards embodied in traditional English culture. These misdemeanours are liable to arouse strong emotional reactions in a professional group which has been selected to a great extent on the basis of qualities of character and conscience which would render them more than usually prone to make moral judgments in questions of this kind (pp. 271–2).

It is unlikely that the position is substantially different today.

[6] This point needs to be considered when streaming is abolished or vertical grouping introduced.

[7] This opinion is based on the generalised outcome of my own researches. (Blyth, 1961.)

[8] It requires little imagination, for example, to see what social forces were employed by the girls whose secret society, so one of them told me, was called a Put-them-right club 'because if anybody does anything wrong we put them right' (Blyth, 1961, p. 235, note). Actually these girls were in their first secondary-school year, but their behaviour in this respect is quite characteristic of older juniors too.

[9] See for example Cartwright and Zander. (1960). Ch. 28.

[10] An important investigation of intentional change in junior schools is planned as part of a large-scale N.F.E.R. study. (*New Society*, 26th March 1964).

V. A NOTE ON MINORITY SCHOOLS

[1] The cohort five–ten is chosen for discussion both because it is a usual sub-division in vital statistics for England and Wales and thus facilitates comparison with other years and other data, and also because the exclusion of eleven-year-olds eliminates the statistical difficulties involved in including an age-group divided between primary and secondary education. If eleven-year-olds had been included, this would not have involved any material modification in the conclusions drawn in this chapter.

[2] Report of the Ministry of Health for the year ended 31st December 1962. *The Health and Welfare Services*. Cmnd. 2062. London, H.M.S.O., 1963. Table A, Part 2, p. 187: Subnormal or Severely Subnormal Persons receiving or awaiting Training provided by Local Health Authorities.

[3] *Statistics Relating to Approved Schools, Remand Homes and Attendance Centres in England and Wales for the year 1961*. Cmnd. 2051. London, H.M.S.O., 1963. Table 6, p. 4.

Approved Schools include so few pupils in the Midlands years (and will include still fewer now that the age of criminal responsibility is raised) that they are not separately considered in this chapter. Even if eleven-year-olds are added (268 boys, 8 girls in 1961) the total (404) remains statistically negligible, although the figures do indicate the great preponderance of boys and the beginnings of the steep increase in numbers which reaches a peak for boys at fourteen (1,615) and for girls at sixteen (335).

Partly for this reason, the sexes are separately catered for. There is for boys a category of Junior Approved Schools covering the age-range up to thirteen. In 1961 (ibid, p. 1) there were 27 of these, of which 4 were limited to boys up to ten-and-a-half and a further 9 included some boys below that age. The few primary-age girls were accommodated in 7 Junior Approved schools which in their case have generally an upper age-limit of fifteen (in one case, sixteen). These schools are thus generally more aligned with the world of adolescence than with the children's world. However administratively necessary this may be, it raises the question whether assignment to an Approved School may involve conferring on children just the sort of status among their peers which might encourage them to repeat their misdemeanours and just the opportunities for behaviour contagion which might reinforce their proclivities, even where the régime of the schools is wise and progressive. This and other sociological issues might be investigated now that criminologists are turning towards Approved Schools some of the attention already bestowed on Borstals and Remand Homes. (See *British Journal of Criminology*, IV, 2, 1963–4, and Rose (1967) in supplementary bibliography).

[4] 1,235 pupils below the age of eleven were in secondary schools.

[5] (Pupils beyond their fifth birthday.)

[6] Including rounding error for table as a whole.

[7] Education Act, 1944. Sections 8(2)(a) and 61.

[8] For comparable data for children under five, see Chapter II, p. 29.

205

References (*pages 112–150*)

[9] In Table 8 of the 1962 *Statistics*, the 'lower' and 'upper' figures by age-groups appear to have been inadvertently transposed in the case of girls. The error is corrected here.

[10] Actually the term 'special school' is given a broader connotation here than in the statistics issued by the Ministry of Education.

[11] *The Handicapped Pupils and Special Schools Regulations, 1959*, (S.I. 1959, No. 365) require that the (nominal) maximum for classes of deaf, partially-hearing or speech-defect children should be 10, for blind, partially-sighted or maladjusted children, 15, for E.S N. epileptic or physically-handicapped children, 20, and for delicate children, 30. The corresponding nominal maximum for primary classes in maintained schools is 40. (*Schools Regulations 1959*, S.I. 1959, No. 364, Section 6(c).)

[12] In fact, they are often prepared for this and tend instead to look beyond to the time when they will resume authority. This, and the corresponding situation in maintained secondary schools, will receive further comment in Chapter VI.

[13] This is too extensive to quote. However it is interesting to observe that the N.U.T. Report (N.U.T. 1963) found no maintained infant schools in 'entirely middle class' areas (Table 4, p. 32), the assumption being that independent schools were used instead.

[14] These results show some similarity to those of Croft and Grygier in their study of truants and juvenile delinquents in a secondary modern school. See *Human Relations*, IX, 4, 1956, pp. 439–66. But the boarding-school context will have modified the actual behaviour pattern.

[15] This appears unlikely at present. See *Times Educational Supplement*, 10th April 1964, p. 891.

[16] As in the sociometric study by Murray (1953) already mentioned.

[17] Kellmer Pringle's article actually compares residential schools for the maladjusted with other boarding schools, but comparisons are not given here since these other schools were rather unrepresentative.

VI. FROM PRIMARY SCHOOLS TO SECONDARY SCHOOLS

[1] This is a part of the terms of reference of the Plowden Committee.

[2] The word *allocation* will be used when possible, since it does not necessarily imply selection.

[3] In his researches Mays (1962) found (see Vol. II, Chapter IV) that working-class children in part of central Liverpool aimed at grammar-school places even when their teachers regarded them as technical-school material. Douglas (1964, p. 17) stresses the general popularity of grammar-school places, even perhaps where their significance and demands are not understood.

[4] See Adam Curle on 'Education and the future in rural areas', in Judges (1955), p. 166, and also Highfield and Pinsent (1952), p. 136.

[5] Future advances in embryology may render fashionable a still earlier date.

[6] The instance from Shropshire cited on p. 139 is one of the rare exceptions.

[7] According to *Statistics of Education in 1962*, Part I, Table 7 (pp. 30–1) there were in January 1962, 775 all-age schools in England and Wales, catering for a total of 170,465 pupils.

[8] Details may be consulted in the original thesis in the University of Manchester library (Blyth, 1961, pp. 267–79 and 303–12).

VII. ADULTS IN PRIMARY SCHOOLS

[1] It has already been pointed out (Chapter II, p. 28 above) that in the official statistics nursery schools are not fully reckoned as primary schools.

[2] In the case of direct-grant schools, these teachers were working in junior departments which are themselves ineligible for direct grant.

[3] The very small number of teachers in Approved Schools for younger children, or in institutions, are omitted from this crude summation.

[4] The N.U.T. Report (N.U.T., 1963, p. 9) gives an average class size of 30·0 in primary schools, with part-time equivalents of full-time teachers taken into account. The nearest data for nursery schools and classes are shown in the subsequent nursery-school report (N.U.T., 1964, pp. 9, 18).

[5] This coincides very closely with the statement in the N.U.T. Report (N.U.T., 1963, p. 9) that 75 per cent of primary-school staffs other than nursery teachers were women.

[6] Percentage of men teachers somewhat inflated through inclusion of 'primary and secondary' schools.

[7] Each of these Reports was published at H.M.S.O., London, as a Command Paper in the following year, until 1961 when the present system of publishing statistics was introduced (Ministry of Education, 1962).

[8] Including 27,249 uncertificated or supplementary teachers.

[9] Including nursery, all-age, visiting and relief teachers.

[10] Last two columns of the original table combined.

[11] Urban by location of school.

[12] The social issues involved in the closure of small rural schools are discussed in Vol. II, Chapter IV.

[13] The slight discrepancies from the figures on p. 152 arise because these totals apply to 31st March, the others to 1st January 1962.

[14] The percentage of graduates in primary schools had remained very stable since 1953 (*Statistics of Education in 1962*, Part I, Table 37, p. 83).

[15] Data are not given for direct-grant nursery schools, nor separately for lower schools of direct-grant grammar schools.

[16] Some evidence of the relative stability of graduate strength in modern schools is given in *15 to 18* (Crowther Report) Vol. I, p. 96 (London, H.M.S.O., 1959).

[17] *Higher Education*. Cmnd. 2154. London, H.M.S.O., 1963, Chapter IX.

[18] According to Schools Regulations, 1959 (S.I. 1959, No. 364, Section 16(1)) every nursery school must have a superintendent teacher, and every other school or department a head teacher 'who shall take part in the teaching'.

[19] More accurately, perhaps, those whose P.E. days are finished.

[20] See *Primary Education*, London, H.M.S.O., 1959, p. 97.

[21] Some Local Education Authorities are beginning to improve the position in primary schools. For a brief and outspoken statement of primary schools' disadvantages in the recent past, see England, J., 'The neglect of the primary school', *Forum*, Autumn 1960, pp. 9–10.

[22] Except in nursery classes where the nominal maximum is thirty. See *Schools Regulations, 1959*. S.I., 1959, No. 364, Section 6.

[23] A different situation obtains in nursery schools and classes. See p. 178 below.

[24] London, Duckworth, 1960.

[25] Some comments on teachers' roles in the U.S.A. may be found in Havighurst and Neugarten (1957), Part IV.

[26] *Allgemeine Pädagogik*, tr. Felkin, 1904, pp. 94–5. The original was published in 1806.

[27] The results of the Lippitt-White experiments have often been too readily generalised from the boys' club to the classroom context, but this role-aspect seems approximately true for teachers as well as club-leaders.

[28] *Macbeth*, IV, 3.

[29] Some examples of these are:

Have your classroom ready before they come in: Make use of the children's immediate experiences: Make your own apparatus to suit your own class: Don't shout: Keep them guessing: Don't ask questions of the whole class: Don't talk too long: Use their fondness for rhythm and routine: Be a

References (pages 175–194)

bit of an actor: Never punish the whole class: If you must punish, deprive them of something they like doing: Never get really annoyed.

The principles underlying such directives are that the procedure of social control in the classroom should be comprehensible, secure and effective.

[30] A further list of possible roles, at the junior level, is given in the N.U.T. report on junior-school curriculum (N.U.T., 1958, pp. 36–7).

[31] *Schools Regulations, 1959.* S.I., 1959. No. 364, Section 16(3)(c); also Circular 8/60, Ministry of Education, 1960, Sections 16–18.

[32] A 59 per cent sample of nursery schools, and a lower but indeterminate percentage of nursery classes (N.U.T., 1964, p. 5).

[33] Many small schools still have no clerical assistance: 32 per cent in 1962 (N.U.T., 1963, p. 10).

[34] They are rather neatly epitomised in verse in the passage quoted by Blackie (1963, pp. 23–4). Although this quotation from Charles Graves refers to a Public School matron, it could apply with equal felicity to her colleague in a prep. school.

[35] H.M.I., and also the local inspectorate.

PLOWDEN COMMENT

[1] *Children and their primary schools.* A report of the Central Advisory Council for Education (England). 2 vols., London, H.M.S.O., 1967.

[2] My personal views are indicated in a rather more committed manner in an article entitled 'Plowden: what do we do next?', in the *Bulletin* of the Liberal Education Association, No. 10, Summer 1967.

[3] A close reading of the Report will reveal a number of parallels with the present book, an advance copy of which was submitted to the Council.

[4] Although many commentators have referred to 'the Plowden Committee', I have in the present chapter used the more accurate term 'Council', since the Report was prepared by the Central Advisory Council for Education (England), which had been reconstituted for this purpose. However, the more usual terminology has been retained in earlier chapters, e.g. p. 16 above.

[5] *Half our future.* A report of the Central Advisory Council for Education (England). (Newsom Report). London, H.M.S.O., 1963.

[6] There is also a possibility that a place could be found for the adaptation of this procedure for supplementary financing of some features within the statutory age-range, as is sometimes done in the U.S.A. If the social distance between primary schools were not too great, and if the more affluent parents came increasingly to use primary schools within the national system, this collective munificence might afford a means of enabling them to benefit particular schools on behalf of their own children and others, instead of paying fees for their own children alone. See the article mentioned under note (2), above.

[7] For the Council's proposals for nomenclature, see below.

[8] *Curriculum and examinations in secondary schools.* Report of a committee of the Secondary Schools Examination Council, 1943, pp. 17–18.

[9] Review by John Vaizey in *New Society*, 30 September 1965, p. 29.

[10] See note (2), above.

Bibliography

I WISH to thank the Registrar of the University of Manchester for giving me permission to refer to unpublished theses in the University Library; to the authors of the specified theses, for allowing me to do so; and to those research students in the University of Manchester who have agreed to my mentioning their current investigations in the course of the book.

I am also indebted to The Free Press of Glencoe, 60, Fifth Avenue, New York, 11, for permission to quote the passage by Talcott Parsons reproduced on p. 18.

ALEXANDER, W. P. (1961): *Teachers' salaries*. London: Councils and Education Press.

ATKINSON, MARY. (1949): *Junior school community*. London: Longmans.

BAKER, JOY. (1964): *Children in chancery*. London: Hutchinson.

BANKS, OLIVE. (1955): *Parity and prestige in English secondary education*. London: Routledge and Kegan Paul.

BARKER, R. G. and WRIGHT, H. F. (1954): *Midwest and its children: the psychological ecology of an American town*. Evanston, Ill.: Row, Peterson.

BERGER, M. (1959): *Les maternelles*. Paris: Centre National de la Recherche Scientifique.

BERNSTEIN, B. (1958): 'Some sociological determinants of perception.' *Brit. J. Sociol.*, IX, 2, pp. 159–74.

BLACKIE, JOHN. (1963): *Good enough for the children*. London: Faber.

BLAIR, A. W. and BURTON, W. H. (1951): *Growth and development of the pre-adolescent*. New York: Appleton-Century-Crofts.

BLYTH, W. A. L. (1958): 'Sociometry, prefects and peaceful co-existence in a junior school.' *Sociol. Rev.* (New Series), VI, 1, pp. 5–24.

BLYTH, W. A. L. (1959): 'School groups and neighbourhood groups: a study in predictive sociometry.' Paper read to the Education section of the Fourth World Congress of Sociology. Stresa.

BLYTH, W. A. L. (1960): 'The sociometric study of children's groups in English schools.' *Brit. J. Educ. Studies*, VIII, 2, pp. 127–47.

BLYTH, W. A. L. (1961): *Children's groups and their social background. A study based on sociometric analysis in schools in different parts of Manchester*. Thesis for degree of Ph.D., Manchester.

BOARD OF EDUCATION. Annual reports: *Education in 1938*, etc. London: H.M.S.O.

BOARD OF EDUCATION. (1943): *Educational reconstruction*. Cmd. 6458. London: H.M.S.O.

BOWYER, R. (1961): 'Individual differences in stress at the eleven-plus examination.' *Brit. J. Educ. Psychol.*, XXXI, 3, pp. 268–80.

209

Bibliography

BRADBURN, ELIZABETH. (1960): 'Friendliness in schools.' *Educ. Rev.*, XII, 2, pp. 112–24.

BROOKOVER, W. B. (1955a): *A sociology of education.* New York: American Book Co.

BROOKOVER, W. B. (1955b): 'Research on teacher and administrator roles in the educative process.' *J. Educ. Sociol.*, XXIX, 1, pp. 2–13.

BRUNT, H. N. (1963): *Some aspects of the relationship between social status, educational achievement and interests among children in a voluntary primary school.* Thesis for degree of M.Ed., Manchester.

BÜHLER, CHARLOTTE. (1937): *From birth to maturity.* London: Kegan Paul, Trench and Trubner.

BUTCHER, H. J. (1959): *The opinions of teachers and student teachers about education.* Thesis for degree of Ph:D., Manchester.

CAMPBELL, F. C. (1956): *Eleven plus and all that.* London: Watts.

CARTWRIGHT, A. W. and ZANDER, A. (1960): *Group dynamics: research and theory.* 2nd edition. London: Tavistock Publications.

CASTLE, MARGARET. (1954): 'Institution and non-institution children at school.' *Human Relations*, VII, 3, pp. 349–66.

CATHOLIC EDUCATION COUNCIL FOR ENGLAND AND WALES. (1960): *Catholic education: a handbook, 1960–61.* London: C.E.C.E.W.

CATHOLIC EDUCATION COUNCIL FOR ENGLAND AND WALES. (1962): *Catholic education: a handbook, 1962–63.* London: C.E.C.E.W.

CENTRAL ADVISORY COUNCIL FOR EDUCATION (ENGLAND). (1959): *15 to 18.* (Crowther Report), London: H.M.S.O., 2 vols.

CENTRAL ADVISORY COUNCIL FOR EDUCATION (ENGLAND). (1963): *Half our future.* (Newsom Report). London: H.M.S.O.

CHAZAN, M. (1962): 'School phobia.' *Brit. J. Educ. Psychol.*, XXXII, 3, pp. 209–17.

COLEMAN, J. S. (1961): *The adolescent society.* Glencoe, Ill.: Free Press.

COMMITTEE ON HIGHER EDUCATION. (1963): *Higher education.* (Robbins Report). Cmnd. 2154. London: H.M.S.O.

CONNOR, D. V. (1960): 'Behaviour in class groups of contrasting climate.' *Brit. J. Educ. Psychol.*, XXX, 3, pp. 244–9.

CONSULTATIVE COMMITTEE OF THE BOARD OF EDUCATION. (1931): *The Primary School.* London: H.M.S.O.

CONSULTATIVE COMMITTEE OF THE BOARD OF EDUCATION. (1933): *Infant and Nursery Schools.* London: H.M.S.O.

CURLE, A. (1947–8): 'Transitional communities and social reconnection.' *Human Relations*, I, 1, pp. 42–68 and (with TRIST, E. L.) 2, pp. 240–88.

DAHLKE, H. O. (1958): *Values in culture and classroom.* New York: Harper.

DANIELS, J. C. (1961a): 'The effects of streaming in the primary school. I—What teachers believe.' *Brit. J. Educ. Psychol.* XXXI, 1, pp. 69–78.

DANIELS, J. C. (1961b): 'The effects of streaming in the primary school. II—A Comparison of streamed and unstreamed schools.' *Brit. J. Educ. Psychol.*, XXXI, 2, pp. 119–27.

DENT, H. C. (1944): *Education in transition.* London: Routledge and Kegan Paul.

DENT, H. C. (1954): *Growth in English education.* London: Routledge and Kegan Paul.

DENT, H. C. (1955): *The Education Act, 1944.* London: University of London Press.

Bibliography

DENT, H. C. (1961): *The educational system of England and Wales.* London: University of London Press.

DOBINSON, C. H. (1963): *Schooling 1963–1970.* London: Harrap.

DOTTRENS, E. (1962): *The primary school curriculum.* Paris: U.N.E.S.C.O. (London: H.M.S.O.)

DOUGLAS, J. W. B. (1964): *The home and the school.* London: Macgibbon and Kee.

EVANS, K. M. (1962): *Sociometry and education.* London: Routledge and Kegan Paul.

EVANS, K. M. (1963–4): '*Sociometry in School.* I—Sociometric techniques. II—Applications.' *Educ. Research,* VI, 1–2, pp. 50–8 and 121–8.

FLEMING, C. M. (ed.) (1951): *Studies in the social psychology of adolescence.* London: Routledge and Kegan Paul.

FLOUD, J. E., HALSEY, A. H. and MARTIN, F. M. (1957): *Social class and educational opportunity.* London: Heinemann.

FLOUD, J. E. and HALSEY, A. H. (1957): 'Intelligence tests, and selection for secondary schools.' *Brit. J. Sociol.,* VIII, 1, pp. 33–9.

FLOUD, J. E. (1962): 'Teaching in the affluent society.' *Brit. J. Sociol.,* XIII, 4, pp. 299–308.

FOSHAY, A. W., WANN, K. D. *et al.* (1954): *Children's social values.* New York: Bureau of Publications, Teachers College, Columbia University.

GARDNER, D. E. M. (1942): *Testing results in the infant school.* London: Methuen.

GARDNER, D. E. M. (1964): 'Threat to the foundation of British education.' *Forum,* VI, 2, pp. 59–61.

GESELL, A. and ILG, F. (1943): *Infant and child in the culture of to-day.* London: Hamish Hamilton.

GESELL, A. and ILG, F., with AMES, L. B. (1946): *The child from five to ten.* London: Hamish Hamilton.

GINSBERG, M. (1944): 'The present position of sociology' in *Sociology and education: addresses given at the winter school of sociology and civics . . . January, 1943,* ed. Dymes, D. M. E. Malvern: Le Play House.

GITTINS, JOHN. (1952): *Approved school boys.* London: H.M.S.O.

GLASS, D. V. (ed.) (1954): *Social mobility in Britain.* London: Routledge and Kegan Paul.

GOODACRE, E. J. (1961): 'Teachers and the socio-economic factor.' *Educ. Research,* IV, 1, pp. 56–61.

GORDON, C. WAYNE. (1956): *The social system of the high school.* Glencoe, Ill.: Free Press.

GRAMBS, JEAN. (1952): 'The sociology of the "born teacher".' *J. Educ. Sociol.,* XXV, 9, pp. 532–41.

GRAY, K. R. (1955): 'Social welfare and the teacher.' *Social Welfare,* IX, 5, pp. 104–10. Published by the Manchester and Salford Council of Social Service (Incorporated).

GRONLUND, N. (1959): *Sociometry in the classroom.* New York: Harper.

GROSS, N. *et al.* (1958): *Explorations in role analysis.* New York: John Wiley.

HALLWORTH, H. J. (1953): 'Group relations among grammar school boys and girls between the ages of eleven and sixteen years.' *Sociometry,* XVI, 1, pp. 39–70.

HALSEY, A. H., FLOUD, J. E., and ANDERSON, C. A. (eds.) (1961): *Education, economy and society.* Glencoe, Ill., Free Press.

211

Bibliography

HARWOOD, A. C. (1958): *The recovery of man in childhood: a study of the educational work of Rudolf Steiner*. London: Hodder and Stoughton.

HEBB, D. O. (1949): *The organisation of behaviour*. London: Chapman and Hall.

HENRY, JULES. (1955): 'Docility, or giving Teacher what she wants.' *J. Social Issues*, XI, pp. 33–41.

HETZER, H. and MORGENSTERN, G. (1952): *Kind und Jugendlicher auf dem Lande*. Lindau: Piorkowski.

HIGHFIELD, M. E. and PINSENT, A. (1952): *A survey of rewards and punishments*. London: Newnes, for National Foundation for Educational Research.

HIMMELWEIT, H. T., HALSEY, A. H. and OPPENHEIM, A. N. (1952): 'The views of adolescents on some aspects of the social class structure.' *Brit. J. Sociol.*, III, 2, pp. 148–72.

HOLLAMBY, LILIAN. (1962): *Young children living and learning*. London: Longmans.

HOLLINGSHEAD, A. B. (1949): *Elmtown's youth*. New York: John Wiley.

HOMANS, G. C. (1950): *The human group*. London: Routledge and Kegan Paul.

HOPKINS, K. (1939): 'Punishment in schools.' *Brit. J. Educ. Psychol.*, IX, 1, pp. 8–28.

ISAACS, S. (1933): *Social development in young children: a study of beginnings*. London: Routledge.

JACKSON, B. (1961): 'Teachers' views on primary school streaming. *Educ. Research*, IV, 1, pp. 44–52.

JACKSON, B. and MARSDEN, D. (1962): *Education and the working class*. London: Routledge and Kegan Paul.

JUDGES, A. V. (ed.) (1955): *Looking forward in education*. London: Faber.

KELLMER PRINGLE, M. L. (1957): 'Differences between schools for the maladjusted and ordinary boarding schools.' *Brit. J. Educ. Psychol.*, XXVII, 1, pp. 29–36.

KENDON, GLADYS. (1954): *Children of the new estate*. London: Methuen.

KILPATRICK, W. H. and VAN TIL, F. (1947): *Intercultural attitudes in the making*. New York: Harper.

KLEIN, J. (1956): *The study of groups*. London: Routledge and Kegan Paul.

LEE, T. (1957): 'On the relation between the school journey and social and emotional adjustment in rural infant children.' *Brit. J. Educ. Psychol.*, XXVII, 2, pp. 101–14.

MACAULAY, EVE, and WATKINS, S. (1926): 'An investigation into the moral conceptions of children.' *Forum of Education*, IV, 1, pp. 13–33, and 2, pp. 92–108.

MANNHEIM, K. and STEWART, W. A. C. (1962): *Introduction to the sociology of education*. London: Routledge and Kegan Paul.

MARSHALL, SYBIL. (1963): *An experiment in education*. Cambridge: Cambridge University Press.

MAY, D. (1963): *Children in the nursery school*. University of Bristol Institute of Education Publication No. 13. London: University of London Press.

MAYS, J. B. (1962): *Education and the urban child*. Liverpool: University of Liverpool.

Bibliography

MELLOR, EDNA. (1950): *Education through experience in the infant school years*. Oxford: Blackwell.

MEREI, F. (1949): 'Group leadership and institutionalization.' *Human Relations*, II, 1, pp. 23–40.

MERTON, R. K. (1957a): *Social theory and social structure*. (Revised and enlarged edition.) Glencoe, Ill. Free Press.

MERTON, R. K. (1957b): 'The role-set: problems in sociological theory.' *Brit. J. Sociol.*, VIII, 2, pp. 106–20.

MINISTRY OF EDUCATION. Annual reports: *Education in 1947*, etc. London: H.M.S.O.

MINISTRY OF EDUCATION. (1945): *The nation's schools: their plan and purpose*. Pamphlet No. 1. London: H.M.S.O.

MINISTRY OF EDUCATION. (1962a): *Statistics of education in 1961*. Part I. London: H.M.S.O.

MINISTRY OF EDUCATION. (1962b): *The health of the school child 1960–1*. London: H.M.S.O.

MINISTRY OF EDUCATION. (1963): *Statistics of education in 1962*. Part I. London: H.M.S.O.

MONTESSORI, M. tr. GEORGE, A. E. *The Montessori method*. London: Heinemann.

MORENO, J. L. (1953): *Who shall survive?* 3rd edition. Beacon, New York. Beacon House.

MORETON, C. A. and BUTCHER, H. J. (1963): 'Are rural children handicapped by the use of speeded tests in selection procedures?' *Brit. J. Educ. Psychol.*, XXXIII, 1, pp. 22–30.

MORRIS, J. M. (1959): *Reading in the primary school*. London: Newnes, for National Foundation for Educational Research.

MURRAY, H. A. (1953): 'The sociometric stability of personal relations among retarded children.' *Sociometry*, XVI, 2, pp. 113–41.

MUSGROVE, F. (1961): 'Parents' expectations of the junior school.' *Sociol. Rev.* (New Series), IX, 2, pp. 167–80.

NATIONAL ASSOCIATION FOR MENTAL HEALTH. (1955): *Periods of stress in the primary school*. London: N.A.M.H.

NATIONAL UNION OF TEACHERS. (1958): *The curriculum of the junior school*. London: N.U.T.

NATIONAL UNION OF TEACHERS. (1963): *The state of our schools*. Report of the national survey of school conditions. Parts 1 and 2. London: N.U.T.

NATIONAL UNION OF TEACHERS. (1964): *The state of nursery education*. London: N.U.T.

NEDELSKY, RUTH. (1951–2): 'The teacher's role in the peer group during middle childhood.' *Elementary School Journal*, LII, pp. 325–34.

NORTHWAY, M. L. and WELD, L. (1957): *Sociometric testing*. Toronto: University of Toronto Press.

OPIE, I. and OPIE, P. (1959): *The lore and language of school-children*. Oxford: Oxford University Press.

OTTAWAY, A. K. C. (1953): *Education and society*. London: Routledge and Kegan Paul.

PARSONS, TALCOTT. (1952): *The social system*. London: Tavistock Publications.

PEEL, E. A. (1960): *The pupil's thinking*. London: Oldbourne.

213

Bibliography

PIAGET, J. et al. (1932): *The moral judgment of the child*. London: Kegan Paul, Trench and Trubner.

PIAGET, JEAN. (1959): *The language and thought of the child*. (Revised and enlarged edition.) London: Routledge and Kegan Paul.

RADKE, M. et al. (1949): 'Social perceptions and attitudes of children.' *Genet. Psychol. Monographs*, XL, 2, pp. 327–447.

ROSS, A. M. (1960): *The education of childhood*. London: Harrap.

ROUSSEAU, J. J. tr. FOXLEY, B. (1911): *Emile*. London: Dent. (Everyman Series.)

RUDD, W. G. A. and WISEMAN, S. (1962): 'Sources of dissatisfaction among a group of teachers.' *Brit. J. Educ. Psychol.* XXXII, 3, pp. 275–91.

SARNOFF, I. et al. (1959): 'Test anxiety and the "eleven plus" examination.' *Brit. J. Educ. Psychol.* XXIX, 1, pp. 9–16.

SECONDARY SCHOOLS EXAMINATION COUNCIL. (1943): *Curriculum and examinations in secondary schools*. (Norwood Report.) London: H.M.S.O.

SHAW, H. (1954): 'A study of popular and unpopular children.' *Educ. Rev.*, VI, 3, pp. 208–20.

SILBERMAN, L. and SPICE, BETTY. (1950): *Colour and class in six Liverpool schools*. Liverpool: University Press of Liverpool.

SIMON, B. (ed.) (1957): *New trends in English education*. London: Macgibbon and Kee.

STAINES, J. W. (1958): 'The self-picture as a factor in the classroom.' *Brit. J. Educ. Psychol.* XXVIII, 2, pp. 97–111.

STEELE, P. M. (1958): *Changes in attitude amongst training college students towards education in junior schools*. Thesis for degree of M.Ed., Manchester.

STENDLER, C. B. (1949): *Children of Brasstown*. Urbana, Ill.: Bureau of Research and Service to the College of Education, University of Illinois.

STONE, A. L. (1949): *Story of a school*. Ministry of Education Pamphlet No. 14. London: H.M.S.O.

SWIFT, D. F. (1964): 'Who passes the eleven-plus?' *New Society*, 5th March, pp. 6–9.

TABA, HILDA. (1955): *School culture*. Washington, D.C.: American Council on Education.

TANNER, J. M. (1961): *Education and physical growth*. London: University of London Press.

TARGET, G. W. (1960): *The Teachers*. London: Duckworth.

TAYLOR, W. (1963): *The secondary modern school*. London: Faber.

THORPE, R. (1955): 'An investigation into some correlates of sociometric status within school classes.' *Sociometry*, XVIII, 1, pp. 49–61.

TYERMAN, M. (1958): 'A research into truancy.' *Brit. J. Educ. Psychol.* XXVIII, 3, pp. 217–25.

VACHELL, H. A. (1909): *The Hill*. London: John Murray.

VAIZEY, J. (1962): *Education for to-morrow*. (*Britain in the Sixties* series). Harmondsworth: Penguin Books.

VERNON, P. E. (ed.) (1957): *Secondary school selection*. London: Methuen.

WADMORE, M. E. (1921–2): 'An inquiry into children's ideas on social and industrial questions.' *J. Exper. Pedagogy*, VI, 5–6, pp. 303–17.

WALLER, WILLARD. (1932): *The sociology of teaching*. New York: John Wiley.

Bibliography

WARR, E. B. (1951): *Social experience in the junior school.* London: Methuen.

WATSON, W. (1952): 'Society and children's play.' *Scottish Educational Journal,* XXXV, 8–9, 22nd and 29th February, pp. 113–14 and 130.

WAYNE GORDON, C. (1956): *The social system of the high school.* Glencoe, Ill.: Free Press.

WILKIE, J. S. (1955): *A study of some effects of free choice of certain activities and companions for group work of junior school children.* Thesis for degree of M.A. (Education), London. Referred to in EVANS, K. M. *Sociometry and Education.* 1962. London: Routledge and Kegan Paul. Chapter 6.

WILKINSON, R. (1962): 'Political leadership and the late Victorian public school.' *Brit. J. Sociol.,* XIII, 4, pp. 320–30. (See also the same author's *The prefects: British leadership and the public school tradition.* Oxford: Oxford University Press, 1964.)

WILLIG, C. J. (1963): 'Social implications of streaming in the junior school.' *Educ. Research,* V, 2, pp. 151–4.

WILSON, BRYAN. (1962): 'The teacher's role—a sociological analysis.' *Brit. J. Sociol.* XIII, 1, pp. 15–32.

YATES, A. and PIDGEON, D. A. (1957): *Admission to grammar schools.* Third interim report on the allocation of primary school leavers to courses of secondary education. London: Newnes, for National Foundation for Educational Research.

215

Supplementary Bibliography

THIS includes a few references of particular importance which have been published since the first printing of this book. They are classified by chapter. In each case, reference is made first to the relevant sections of the Plowden Report itself. (*Children and their primary schools*. A report of the Central Advisory Council for Education (England). London, H.M.S.O., 2 vols., 1967). These references will be simply listed as *Plowden*, with Roman numerals to indicate the volume, and Arabic to indicate the chapter.

INTRODUCTION

On 'Midlands of childhood': *Plowden* I, 2 and I, 8, pp. 97–100.

On legal basis: *Plowden* I, 29 and II, Appendices 13 and 14.

I. AN ANALYSIS OF PRIMARY SCHOOLS AS SOCIAL INSTITUTIONS

Plowden I, *passim*, especially I, 28 on buildings.

MANNING, PETER (1967): *The primary school: an environment for education.* Pilkington Research Unit, Department of Building Science, University of Liverpool.

On social change within schools and elsewhere:
YOUNG, M. *Innovation and research in education.* London, Routledge and Kegan Paul, 1965.

II. NURSERY AND INFANT SCHOOLS

Plowden I, 9–10, 12, 13 and Part V *passim*; also Notes of Reservation, I, pp. 486–9.

HOWE, ELSPETH. (1966): *Under '5.* London, Conservative Political Centre.
JINKS, P. C. (1964): 'An investigation into the effect of date of birth on subsequent school performance.' *Educational Research*, VI, 3, pp. 220–5.
PIDGEON, D. A. (1965): 'Date of birth and scholastic performance.' *Educational Research*, VIII, 1, pp. 3–7.
RIDGWAY, LORNA (1965): *Family grouping in the infants' school.* London, Ward Lock.
WILLSHER, BETTY (1959): *School before five.* London, Faber and Faber.

217

Supplementary Bibliography

III. THE SOCIAL STRUCTURE OF JUNIOR SCHOOLS

Plowden I, esp. 10, 13, 20.

GOLDMAN, R. J. and TAYLOR, FRANCINE M. (1966): 'Coloured immigrant children: a survey of research, studies and literature on their educational problems and potential—in Britain.' *Educational Research*, VIII, 3, pp. 163–83 (and references given).

LYONS, GEOFFREY. (1966): 'Primary school.' *New Society*, 15 September, pp. 395–401 (on a 'downtown' school).

SWIFT, D. F. (1965): 'Meritocratic and social class selection at age eleven.' *Educational Research*, VIII, 1, pp. 65–73.

YATES, A. (ed.). (1966): *Grouping in education*. London, John Wiley.

IV. SOCIAL PROCESSES IN JUNIOR SCHOOLS

Plowden I, part V *passim*, but especially 16, 17, 19, and Notes of Reservation, pp. 489–93.

DOUGLAS, J. W. B. and ROSS, J. M. (1965): 'The effects of absence on primary school performance.' *British Journal of Educational Psychology*, XXXV, 1, pp. 28–40.

GARDNER, D. E. M. (1966): *Experiment and tradition in primary schools*. London, Methuen.

GOOCH, S. and KELLMER PRINGLE, M. L. (1966): *Four years on*. London, Longmans.

PICKARD, P. M. (1965): *The activity of children*. London, Longmans.

'PRIMARY SCHOOL HEADMASTER' (1965): 'Parents and the primary school: a survey of parental opinion.' *Educational Research*, VII, 3, pp. 229–35.

SWIFT, D. F.—as cited under Chapter III, above.

V. A NOTE ON MINORITY SCHOOLS

Plowden I, Part VII. (Note: special schools were not considered in the Report.)

JACKSON, S. (1966): *Special education in England and Wales*. London, Oxford University Press.

MASTERS, P. L. (1966): *Preparatory schools to-day: some facts and inferences*. London, A. and C. Black.

Although the age-range of approved schools now begins at ten, an upward extension of the limits of primary education may again bring about a considerable overlap and therefore it is relevant also to mention:

ROSE, GORDON (1967): *Schools for young offenders*. London, Tavistock.

VI. FROM PRIMARY SCHOOLS TO SECONDARY SCHOOLS

Plowden I, 11–12.

NISBET, J. D. and ENTWISTLE, N. J. (1966): *The age of transfer to secondary education*. London, University of London Press.

SWIFT, D. F.—as cited under Chapter III, above.

218

Supplementary Bibliography

VII. ADULTS IN PRIMARY SCHOOLS

Plowden I, Part VI *passim*, and Note of Reservation, I, pp. 493–5; II, Appendix I (on teachers' attitudes).

GARDNER, D. E. M. and CASS, J. (1965): *The role of the teacher in the infant and nursery school.* Oxford, Pergamon Press.

NOTE: Henceforth, summaries of articles on topics relevant to the sociology of education and published in reputable journals may be found in *Sociology of Education Abstracts*, published under the sponsorship of the University of Liverpool School of Education.

Index

OF PRINCIPAL REFERENCES

IN VOLUME I

226

For Product Safety Concerns and Information please contact our EU
representative GPSR@taylorandfrancis.com
Taylor & Francis Verlag GmbH, Kaufingerstraße 24, 80331 München, Germany